TELLING LIES FOR FUN & PROFIT

BY LAWRENCE BLOCK

A Manual for Fiction Writers

Telling Lies FOR FUN & PROFIT

by Lawrence Block

Introduction by Brian Garfield

ARBOR HOUSE

NEW YORK

For HAL DRESNER

COLLEAGUE, COMPANION,
AND CORSICAN BROTHER

CONTENTS

How to discover your options as a writer. Using your reading prefer-ences as a selection mechanism. Deciding what to write via identifi-cation with another writer.

The mechanics of market analysis. Reading with a purpose. Defining a category through plot summaries. How to write stories that are the-same-only-different.

The question of slanting for an editor's taste. How to maintain in-tegrity as a writer without making things hard for yourself. The Stepmother—*a case study in decision-making.*

The disadvantages of short fiction. Why not write a novel? Plots and outlines. The first novel as a learning experience.

9

PART TWO **NOSE TO THE GRINDSTONE, SHOULDER TO THE WHEEL:** *Fiction as a Discipline* **81**

13. WRITER'S HOURS 83

Do writers work all the time? Writing, research and the guilt trap. Knowing when enough is enough. Starting early. Working regularly. Postponing routine work.

14. THE CARROT AND THE STICK 87

The art of self-discipline. Giving writing top priority. Setting goals for yourself. Staying in the now. Getting the job done. "Listen, it's only a book."

15. CREATIVE PROCRASTINATION 91

Coming to terms with the thief of time. Developing fictional ideas through procrastination. Creative use of the back burner. "And Miles to Go Before I Sleep"—a case study in Creative Procrastination.

16. TIME OUT 95

Writer's block and creative sloth. Coping with indolence. What to do when the words won't come. Learning to regard stretches of inactivity as part of the creative process.

17. DO IT ANYWAY 99

What to do when the words have to come. Giving yourself permission to write badly. Learning to override your own critical instincts. Getting through bad patches.

18. F U CN RD THS 104

Writing faster without sacrificing quality. Fast writers vs. slow writers. How to find your own natural speed.

19. WASHING GARBAGE 108

The pleasures and pains of rewriting. How revision can drain a story of its freshness. How to minimize the need for extensive revision. Rewriting as you go along. Doing mental first drafts.

The importance of sharing your work with others. Making use of readers' reactions. Why fellow writers make the best audience. Ways to avoid disappointment.

How to keep having something to write about. The relationship of input and output. Remaining open to new experience. Four ways to stay out of ruts.

When stealing is legitimate—and when it isn't. Improving on what you read. Working variations on a theme. "The Ehrengraf Defense"—a case study in Creative Plagiarism.

How to generate fictional ideas. Putting bits of fact together. Getting ideas from writers and publishers. The hazards of other people's ideas. Harnessing the creative power of your own frustrations.

The importance of strong openings. Getting the story moving. Setting the tone. Establishing the problem. How to get your story off to a good start.

The trick of not beginning at the beginning. Switching Chapters 1 and 2. When not to use this approach. Case studies.

Skipping around in time. Taking a stitch in time in transitions. The art of starting in the middle. Mini-flashbacks.

How to avoid getting bogged down in detail. The perils of over-explaining. Fast cuts—the difference between film and prose.

44. NAME CALLING   226

How to pick apt and memorable names for your characters. Avoiding confusion. Keeping a notebook. Watching out for cuteness. Shortcuts in research.

45. REPEAT PERFORMANCES AND RETURN ENGAGE-MENTS   231

Special problems in creating and developing a series character. Writing a series one book at a time. How to keep from going stale. Letting a character grow and evolve.

46. WE CAN ALWAYS CHANGE THE TITLE   239

What makes a good title? Coming up with memorable titles. Titles that fit their stories. Using your imagination. How titles get changed.

PART FIVE   **ISN'T THAT THE TRUTH:** *Fiction as a*
Spiritual Exercise   **245**

47. A WRITER'S PRAYER   247

INDEX   252

PREFACE

IN THE summer of '75 I hit the road. I gave up my New York apartment, sold or gave away most of the possessions of a lifetime, packed the remainder into the back of a diseased station wagon, and set out for Los Angeles.

It took me about eight months to get there. I followed the coast down to Florida, then drifted west. I would linger in a spot for a couple of days or weeks, then pull up stakes on a whim. Once I checked out of a motel and drove five miles down the road because the television set at the first place wouldn't pick up a football game I wanted to watch.

During this time I continued writing. I had, after all, done virtually nothing else since college. I wrote the first draft of a novel which ultimately became *Ariel.* I wrote several books that withered and died after fifty or sixty pages; when I think of them now I imagine them as mummified fruit on a tainted tree.

I wrote short stories, too, something I hadn't done in years. And I wrote an article which I called "Where Do You Get Your Ideas?" I did a mental first draft in the car heading west from Wilmington, North Carolina, typed it the following morning in a motel room, and mailed it the next afternoon from a branch post office in Greenville, South Carolina.

And had not the slightest idea what I was getting into.

Half a year later I was living at the Magic Hotel in Hollywood. One day I remembered that article I'd sent to *Writer's Digest.* I'd never heard from them. I wrote, asking *wha hoppen,* and got a phone call in reply from *WD*'s editor John Brady. He'd been attempting to buy the piece for months but some secretary had garbled my address and the correspondence had gone

awry. We discussed a couple of changes he wanted me to make. I mentioned I'd be driving east sometime in August, and he invited me to say hello if I got within hailing distance of Cincinnati.

By August I decided *Writer's Digest* needed a fiction column. I made a point of stopping in Cincinnati on my way back to New York, and after a hearty lunch continued east with an assignment to write a column every other month on the techniques of fiction. After I'd done five or six columns there was some editorial reshuffling and my column went monthly. I've been at it ever since.

Looking back, I found myself wondering what ever prompted me to write that piece on the genesis of fictional ideas in the first place. I can think of a couple of factors. I'd been deprived entirely of the company of other writers for a few months at that point, and I guess I was feeling the isolation; it must have concentrated my mind upon the nature of my work and its underlying processes. For another thing, I was writing short stories again after a long layoff, and my mind was serving up plot ideas one after the other. I found the process interesting enough to write about.

I certainly never suspected that a few pages on the development of ideas would eventually transform me into someone who spent a significant amount of his time writing about writing. But that is what has happened, and it has had interesting effects above and beyond my monthly check and the ego gratification of a regular column.

It's a commonplace in the profession that writers work twenty-four hours a day. (See Chapter 13, "Writer's Hours.") I don't know about that, but I do know that my column keeps me working far more than the time I devote to its actual composition. Everything I read is potentially grist for this particular mill. Does a particular author foreshadow a coming plot development in an interesting way? Hmmm. Should I consider a column on foreshadowing as a literary device? What other examples come to mind? Examples, say, of ineffective foreshadowing as well?

Similarly, I've become more interested than ever in what other writers have to say about writing, whether they're discussing their writing methods, offering tips, or commenting upon the nature of the profession. I'm forever clipping things—and, more often than not, losing the clips.

Once or twice a year *WD*'s capable Rose Adkins writes me a plaintive note asking for a list of my prospective column topics for the next however many months. Once or twice a year I try to make her understand that I could more easily supply maps of the far side of the moon. More often than not, I complete each column convinced I'll have to give up the job, that I'll never again be able to come up with a viable theme for a column. Somehow

within the next thirty days a topic suggests itself and I find a way to approach it. I've learned to take it on faith that this will happen.

Even more than writing in general a monthly column is a two-way street. From the column's inception I have received letters in a steady stream—letters offering suggestions, letters seeking advice, letters thanking me or calling me to task for something I did or didn't say. Both the volume and the fervor of this correspondence continually impress me with just how important all of this business of stringing words together is to all of us who do it. Whatever our degree of commercial or artistic success, whether we be fresh as paint or older than rust, writing appears to be an imperative.

Letters from readers often furnish me with ideas for future columns. Equally important, the feedback they constitute keeps me in touch with my audience and with my material. I read every letter I get, and I reply to most of them. I almost always reply to those accompanied by a stamped self-addressed envelope. A word to the wise . . .

This present volume had its origin in correspondence. Any number of readers have written suggesting that my columns might be collected and published in book form. While I have to admit that the very same idea did occur to me all by itself, the letters helped assure me that a market for such a book existed.

It has been an interesting experience editing four years' worth of columns for book publication. I have done relatively little editing, largely confining myself to changing "column" to "chapter" now and then, and deleting occasional duplications from one column to the next. I have, too, been able to correct mistakes, both grammatical and factual, although I don't doubt for a moment that I have unwittingly left numerous examples of both sort uncorrected.

Sometimes, rereading this material, I've been struck by a tendency to say the same thing over and over. At other times it seems to me that I give conflicting advice from one month to the next. Ultimately I've decided not to apologize for either the redundancy or the contradictions. They strike me as inescapable in material written at various times and from various perspectives.

Several persons deserve my thanks in this venture. The good people at *Writer's Digest,* especially John Brady, Rose Adkins, Bill Brohaugh, and publisher Dick Rosenthal, have been unfailingly helpful and supportive since the column's inception. Book publication might not have happened but for the encouragement and enthusiasm of Don Fine of Arbor House; I know no one in the industry who cares more about fiction, or publishes it with greater conviction and respect.

Jared Kieling, my editor at Arbor House, is responsible for the book's scheme of organization. It was he who was able to see that the columns grouped themselves naturally into four general areas—fiction as a profession, as a discipline, as a structure, and as a craft. I embraced this plan wholeheartedly, finding it potentially more useful to the reader than the two organizational modes which had occurred to me—viz., chronologically and alphabetically.

When I write a column, it's impossible for me to know if anyone will find it useful. The nuts-and-bolts columns of Part Four seem to me to offer the most real help to a writer, and yet it is almost invariably the more general inspirational columns which draw the heaviest reader mail. Of course what's helpful and what prompts one to respond may not be the same thing.

In any event, it's similarly impossible for me to know how valuable readers will find this book. I know that it's been enormously valuable to me to write it, column by column, and I have all of you who read it to thank for the opportunity.

New York City
March 9, 1981

INTRODUCTION

LAWRENCE BLOCK is a writer's writer. From his early crime fiction (*The Girl With the Long Green Heart*) to his gritty Paul Kavanagh suspense thrillers (*The Triumph of Evil, Such Men Are Dangerous*) to his comedy-crime novels featuring the cheerful but sometimes hapless Bernie Rhodenbarr (*Burglars Can't Be Choosers,* etc.) his stories consistently have displayed that illusion of polished seamless effortlessness which characterizes the best craftsmen in the writing game.

That Larry Block is a good writer is not surprising; he started with plenty of talent and he has had plenty of practice. Like many of us he served an underpaid but invaluable apprenticeship in pseudonymous paperbacks— the kind of apprenticeship the lack of which is sorely evident in the work of many younger writers, mostly through no fault of their own; that paperback market no longer exists. It makes me worry about the next generation of popular writers: where will they get their on-the-job training?

I don't know the answer to that one; but I do know that they can be helped along by a book like this one. Larry is not only a good writer; he's also an analytical one. He understands and can describe what he's doing and why he's doing it. He understands not only that there are rules for good writing but that there are reasons for the existence of those rules; and he understands the reasons as well. In this book I think he does a better job of articulating the principles and methods of creative writing than I've seen in any how-to book since Lajos Egri's *The Art of Dramatic Writing* (a book to which Block's should make a useful companion, since they cover quite different ground and do not overlap very much).

I'm pleased in this Introduction to have the chance to acknowledge both a friendship of nearly two decades' duration and my continuing admiration for Larry Block's talent and skill, both as a writer and as an explicator of writing.

Many artists make lousy teachers; Larry Block is one of the exceptions—he likes to teach and he does it well. At the same time he is an invaluable guide for the beginning writer (or even the established one—reading this book I've come across ideas that were new to me, and most useful) because he is that relatively rare writer, the pro who is not a hack. Writing, to him, isn't merely an occupation; it's a craft, an art and a pleasure. He has often written genre books (detective stories, spy thrillers) but none of them is routine or formulaic, and his richly varied body of work also includes such "mainstream" novels as *A Week As Andrea Benstock,* such comedies as *Ronald Rabbit Is a Dirty Old Man* and such unusual anti-genre yarns as *Ariel,* in which Block's ingenious imagination turns some of the occult-horror-fantasy genre's most cherished cliches inside out. He points out that when he writes a book he is trying to write a book that he would want to read if someone else had written it. That isn't the objective of a hack; that's the objective of a pro.

One of the values of this book is its having been written in installments as monthly columns. Reading the book, one becomes aware that one is following the writer through developmental changes in his own working life. Each column attacks a target that has sprung up just that very moment in his current work-in-progress. This immediacy creates a freshness and spontaneity; in attacking each target-of-the-month Block is dealing with a current problem of immediate importance to him and I think this makes it possible for him to bring his best aim to bear on it, since he has an immediate stake in it. The book virtually lets us watch over the writer's shoulder as he performs the tasks of his craft.

It is probably true that talent can't be learned. But if it exists in its raw state it can be developed; it can be polished; it can be helped along a great deal by the guidance of a good teacher who has been there and paid his dues and knows not only his craft but how to articulate the methodology of that craft.

Lawrence Block is such a teacher. I commend this book to you.

—Brian Garfield

PART ONE

The Liar's Trade:
Fiction as a Profession

CHAPTER **1**

Setting Your Sights

A COUPLE of months ago I returned to Antioch College to teach an intensive week-long seminar on fictional technique. One of the first things I remembered as I crossed the campus was a cartoon which had been displayed on the English Department bulletin board during my first year as an Antioch student. The cartoon showed a sullen eight-year-old boy facing an earnest principal. "It's not enough to be a genius, Arnold," the man was saying. "You have to be a genius *at* something."

I recall identifying very strongly with Arnold. I had known early on that I wanted to be a writer. But it seemed that it wasn't enough merely to *be* a writer.

You had to sit down and write something.

Some people receive the whole package as a gift. Not only are they endowed with writing talent but they seem to have been born knowing what they are destined to write about. Equipped at the onset with stories to tell and the skills required to tell them, they have only to get on with the task. Some people, in short, have it easy.

Some of us don't. We know *that* we want to write without knowing *what* we want to write.

How are we to decide what to write?

By chance, I suspect, more often than not. Yet there seem to be some steps one can take in order to find oneself as a writer. Let's have a look at them.

1. DISCOVERING THE OPTIONS. When I was fifteen or sixteen years old and secure in the knowledge that I'd been born to be a writer, it didn't even occur to me to wonder what sort of thing I would write. I was at the time

furiously busy reading my way through Great Twentieth Century Novels, Steinbeck and Hemingway and Wolfe and Dos Passos and Fitzgerald and all their friends and relations, and it was ever so clear to me that I would in due course produce a Great Novel of my own.

I'd go to college first, naturally, where I might get a somewhat clearer idea of what constituted a Great Novel. Then I'd emerge from college into the Real World. There I would Live. (I wasn't quite sure what Capital-L Living entailed, but I figured there would be a touch of squalor in there somewhere, along with generous dollops of booze and sex.) All of this Living would ultimately constitute the Meaningful Experiences which I would eventually distill into any number of great books.

Now there's nothing necessarily wrong with this approach. Any number of important novels are produced in this approximate fashion, and the method has the added advantage that, should you write nothing at all, you'll at least have treated yourself to plenty of booze and sex along the way.

In my own case, my self-image as a writer was stronger than my self-image as a potential great novelist. I began reading books about writers and their work. I became a sporadic student of *Writer's Digest*. I loved the success stories and identified with their subjects. And, reading the market reports, I became aware that there was a whole world of professional writing that lay outside the more exclusive world of significant literature. I came to realize that, whatever my ultimate goals, my immediate aim was to write something—anything!—and get paid for it and see it in print.

I began reading a great many different kinds of books and magazines, trying to find something I figured I could write. I didn't care whether it was significant or artistic or even interesting. I just wanted to find something I could *do*.

2. YOU HAVE TO BE ABLE TO READ IT. When I was starting out, confession magazines were generally acknowledged to constitute the best and most receptive market for new writers. They paid fairly well, too.

I think I understood what a confession story was, the basic structure of its plot, and what made one story good and another unacceptable. During the year I spent working for a literary agent, the two confessions I pulled out of the slush pile both sold on their first submission, and the author of one of them came to be a leader in the field.

On several occasions, I bought or borrowed confession magazines and decided to read my way through them. I never made it. I could not read one of the damned things all the way through without skimming. I couldn't concentrate on what I was reading. And I couldn't shake the conviction that the entire magazine, from front to back, was nothing but mind-rotting garbage.

Nor, consequently, could I produce a confession story. The ideas my mind came up with were either numbingly trite or at odds with the requirements of the market. I never did turn any of these ideas into stories, never wrote a confession until one bizarre weekend when I wrote three of them to order for a publisher with a couple of holes to fill and a deadline fast approaching. Those stories were awful. I wrote them because I'd taken the assignment, and the publisher printed them because he had to, and that was the hardest money I ever made.

I know other writers with similar experience in other fields. The moral is simple enough. If you can't stand to read a particular type of story, you're wasting your time trying to write it.

3. IDENTIFYING WITH THE WRITER. As a lifelong compulsive reader, I had little trouble finding categories of stories I could read with enjoyment. What I learned then, and have confirmed on many occasions since, is that just because I can read a particular story doesn't perforce mean I can write it.

For example, there was a time when I read a great deal of science fiction. I liked most S-F stories, and I liked the good ones a lot. Furthermore, I used to hang out with several established science-fiction writers. I found them a congenial lot, and I liked the way they grabbed hold of ideas and turned them into stories.

But I couldn't write science fiction. No matter how much of the stuff I read, my mind did not produce workable S-F ideas. I could read those stories with a fan's enjoyment, but I could not get the sort of handle on those stories that left me thinking, "I could have written that. I could have come up with that idea, and I could have developed it the way he did. I could have been the writer of that story."

One of the things that makes a story work is that you identify with the characters. Well, one of the things that makes a story writable, if you will, is when you read it and identify not only with the characters but with the writer.

I remember the first time that happened. It was the summer after my freshman year at Antioch. I picked up a paperback anthology of short stories entitled *The Jungle Kids.* The author was Evan Hunter, who had recently made a name for himself with *The Blackboard Jungle.* I read the dozen or so stories in the book, all of them dealing with juvenile delinquents, virtually all of them originally published in *Manhunt,* and I experienced a shock of recognition. I identified, not so much with the characters in the stories, but with Evan Hunter himself.

I can still remember how excited I was when I got to the end of the book.

Here was someone writing and publishing well-written stories that I could respect and enjoy—and I could see myself doing what he had done. I felt it was something I could do and I saw it as eminently worth doing.

Had I known then what I know now, I would have immediately gone to a back-magazine store and purchased every available copy of *Manhunt*. This never occurred to me. I did check one newsstand, and when they proved to be out of the magazine I forgot all about it. I went on to write a couple of stories about juvenile delinquents, but they were lousy and I didn't try submitting them anywhere.

Some months later, I wrote a story about a young criminal. It had nothing in common with the Hunter stories, and I had indeed forgotten about them when I wrote it. A couple of months after that, I read the listing for *Manhunt* in a copy of *Writer's Digest,* remembered the magazine as having published Hunter's stories, and sent them mine. It came back with a note from the editor criticizing the ending. At that point I finally took the trouble to locate a copy of *Manhunt*, read it from cover to cover, and rewrote my story with a new ending. It was not, however, a very good ending, and it came back by return mail.

I kept reading *Manhunt,* however, and a month later I saw how to make the story work, and rewrote it once again, and they bought it, and I decided crime fiction was my metier. I can't say I've never regretted the decision, but I do seem to have stuck with it over the years. Now, as then, I'm sustained by the hope that, if I just keep at it long enough, sooner or later I'll get it right.

That shock of recognition, that identification with the writer, is difficult to describe but impossible to ignore. A similar epiphany preceded the writing of my first novel.

At that point I'd been writing and publishing crime stories for a year and felt it was time to write a detective novel. I'd read hundreds of them, liked them very much, and had made a couple of attempts at writing one of my own. For one reason or another, however, I couldn't get a handle on a novel.

During this time I had read perhaps a dozen lesbian novels. The sensitive novel of female homosexuality was a popular category in the fifties and I suspect I read the books more for information and titillation than anything else. I didn't know any lesbians then, and all I knew about the subject was what I read in these dumb books. But I did find the books compulsively readable, and one day I finished one and realized that I could have written it. Or one quite like it. Possibly, by Georgia, one a shade *better* than what I'd read.

In the name of research, I promptly read every other lesbian novel I could lay my hands on. Then one morning the plot came to me, and I outlined it, and a few weeks later I sat down and wrote the thing start to finish in two weeks flat, finishing four days before my twentieth birthday. (This seemed highly significant at the time. I've no idea why.) It sold to Fawcett, the first publisher to see it, and I was a published novelist just like that.

Deciding what you're going to write is a major step on the road to discovering yourself as a writer. Once you've found your particular field of endeavor, there are some more steps you can take that will make it a little simpler for you to get into that chosen field.

We'll get to them in the next chapter.

CHAPTER **2**

Studying the Market

IN THE preceding chapter we had a look at the process of determining what kind of story to write, what area of the market to aim at. Let's assume now that you've zeroed in on a category of fiction that seems suited to you. You enjoy reading it; moreover, you can visualize yourself writing it. For one reason or another you've decided you want to become a writer of confessions, or science fiction, or gothic novels, or mystery stories.

Now what?

The next step, it might appear, is to sit down to the typewriter and get on with it—and it's possible that you're ready to go ahead and do just that. Perhaps, now that you've chosen a fiction category, your unconscious has obligingly coughed up enough fully developed story ideas to keep your typewriter humming for months. If so, more power to you—and why aren't you busy writing instead of reading this book?

For many of us, however, there's an interim step between deciding what sort of thing to write and setting out to write it. It consists of subjecting one's chosen field to a detailed analysis. The analytical process is such that the writer winds up with both an ingrained gut-level understanding of what constitutes a successful story in the field and a mind trained to produce and develop the ideas for such successful stories.

I can't think of a better name for this process than *market analysis,* yet something in me recoils at the term. It's too clinical, for one thing, and it seems to imply that writing can be approached scientifically, that the problem of selling to *Mind-Boggler Science-Fiction Stories* lends itself to a case study a la Harvard Business School.

Besides, the process I'm talking about constitutes less a study of the markets than of the individual stories themselves. Our object is to learn what makes a story work, not what makes a particular editor buy it.

Okay—whatever you call it, I want to do it. What do I do first?

Good question.

What you do is you read.

Last chapter we established that the category of story you elect to write had better be one you enjoy reading. Now that you've picked a category, you're going to have to do some really intensive reading.

In my own case, I pretty much backed into writing for the crime-fiction magazines. But once I had made that first sale to *Manhunt,* I proceeded to study that magazine and all the others in the field more intently than I ever studied anything before or since. I bought *Manhunt* and *Hitchcock* and *Ellery Queen* and *Trapped* and *Guilty* and a few other magazines whenever they appeared on the stands. In addition, I made regular visits to back-magazine shops, where I picked up every back issue of those publications that I could find. I carried lists in my wallet to avoid buying the same issue twice. And I carted them all home and arranged them in orderly fashion on my shelves, and then I read every last one of them from cover to cover.

I still remember quite a few of those stories that I read twenty years or so ago. Some of them were very good. Others were not very good at all. But by reading hundreds and hundreds of those stories over the months, the good and the bad and the indifferent, I learned what constituted a successful crime story in a way I could not have learned otherwise.

Understand, please, that I did not learn any formulae. I don't know that such a thing exists. What I did learn, in a manner I cannot entirely explain, is a sense of the possible variations that could be worked upon the crime story, a sense of what worked and what didn't.

Of course I didn't just read and read and read for months on end.

Throughout this period I occasionally came up with an idea and took the time to hammer out a story. Nor did this habit of reading voraciously in my chosen field come to a halt once I was regularly turning out and selling stories of my own. I still read a great deal of suspense fiction, short stories and novels. I do so because I enjoy much of what I read, but I also do so because I regard it as part of my work as a writer.

That's it, then, this market-analysis business? You just read a lot?

Sometimes it's enough. But there's something else you can do that may increase the effectivness of your reading.

It's simple enough. You outline what you've read.

I don't mean that you take apart a story as if it were an exercise in literary criticism. You can do so, of course, and you might or might not find the process rewarding. But this method of outlining has nothing to do with criticism, with how you feel about the story, with whether the story works or doesn't work. Having read the story, you simply write down a summary of the plot, relating in a few sentences just what happens in the story.

For example:

Two brothers are on their way to commit a big-time robbery when they run low on gas in the middle of nowhere. The service-station operator keeps telling them their car needs additional work and they sense they're being conned, yet they don't want to take chances. They let the man make more repairs than they have cash to pay for, finally robbing the station at the end because there's no other way out.

Or:

Narrator and his wife come home from vacation to find their house torn inside-out by burglars. Narrator goes off to work with his partner, complaining about what happened, the damage the burglars had done, the mess they made, etc. Turns out the two men are professional burglars on their way to knock off a warehouse themselves.

This method of outlining, of writing out plot summaries of what you have read, serves to pare away the writer's facility with prose and dialogue and characterization and reduce each story to its basic plot. In this fashion you can see after the fact just what it was that you've read. I don't know that there's any specific value in studying these plot summaries after you've written them, as a paleontologist studies dinosaur bones, but I do think that the simple act of stripping the stories to the bones will give you an intuitive understanding of what holds them together that you could not readily obtain just by reading them.

Outlines are an even more effective tool in learning how longer fiction works. When you take an outline you have read and reduce it to a chapter-by-chapter summary of its plot, you are in effect reversing the process the author followed in writing the book in the first place. Although they're often easier to write, novels are generally more difficult to *grasp* than short stories. So much more happens in them that it's harder to see their structure. Stripped down to outline form, the novel is like a forest in winter; with their branches bare, the individual trees become visible where once the eyes saw only a mass of green leaves.

If you plan to prepare an outline for a novel of your own some day, there's yet another advantage in outlining. Quite simply, you learn in this fashion what outlines look like. In order to feel comfortable in any form of writing, I have to know what it looks like on paper. Before I could write a screenplay, for example, it was not enough for me to go to the movies and see how films worked on the screen. I had to get a sense of how they worked *on the page*—because I was going to be writing a screenplay, not a film. When an outline, too, becomes something you can look at in typescript instead of merely sensing it as the invisible skeleton of a bound book, it becomes a good deal easier to outline your own as-yet unwritten novel.

Question—with all this reading and analyzing and outlining, all this mechanical crap, aren't we stifling creativity? I have a feeling I'll be trying to duplicate what's been written rather than writing my own stories.

That's not how it works. If anything, a bone-deep knowledge of your field helps you avoid unwittingly writing those stories that have been written already.

What every editor wants—and every reader, for that matter—can be summed up in four paradoxical words: *the same only different.* Your story must be the same as innumerable other stories so that it may provide a similar kind of satisfaction to the reader. Yet it must simultaneously differ sufficiently from all of those other stories so that the reader will not feel it's something he's read over and over in the past.

We achieve this same-only-different quality not by borrowing bits and pieces from a variety of other stories, not by synthesizing and amalgamating what we've read, but by so imbuing ourselves in our chosen field that the requirements of the field soak into our subconsious minds.

I don't believe anyone knows enough about the mind to say just how story ideas are produced. It may not be necessary to know this, any more than you have to understand electricity to turn the light on. I do know that a basic understanding of how a particular kind of story works, acquired by the process described above, seems to make things a good deal easier for the mind.

I don't know about you, but my mind needs all the help it can get.

CHAPTER **3**

Decisions, Decisions

COUPLE OF months ago I was chatting with a fellow at some sort of symposium on suspense fiction. He was writing his first novel, or getting ready to write his first novel, or thinking about getting ready, or whatever, and he had a lot of questions. And, since he'd artfully positioned himself between me and the cheese and crackers, I had little choice but to answer him.

Did editors, he wanted to know, prefer novels in the first or third person? Did editors prefer books where a murder occurs right away? Did editors prefer books with an urban or a rural setting? Did editors prefer multiple viewpoint or single viewpoint? Did editors prefer—

"Look," I said, "that's not how I write. I don't try to imagine just what sort of book some editor is going to fall in love with and then set out to produce it. For one thing, editors are individuals. They don't share a single set of preferences. For another, what any editor prefers most is a book that turns him on, and that he has reason to believe people will buy, and his judgment ultimately hasn't got too much to do with questions of first or third person, single or multiple viewpoint, or urban or rural setting.

"Anyway," I went on, "I myself am pretty much of an intuitive writer. I try to write the sort of book I would want to read if I hadn't happened to have written it myself. The more I write to please myself, the more likelihood there is that I'll please other people in the process. But when I deliberately set out to please other readers, I usually turn out an inferior book. So I'd advise you to write the book your own way. Give it your best shot and then when you've finished worry about finding somebody who likes it enough to publish it."

I wheeled about and made my way to the refreshment table at this point lest I find myself in the middle of Polonius's little spiel to Laertes, advising the poor man neither to borrow nor to lend. I hadn't actually *said* "To thine own self be true," but that was certainly the thrust of my comments.

Afterward, through the medium of what one might call sober reflection, I wondered if I hadn't overstated the case. I hadn't said anything I didn't believe, but perhaps I had glossed over the fact that writing for certain markets demands a familiarity with the requirements of those markets.

This is especially true for the neophyte writer who is aiming at one of the more accessible markets—gothics, let us say, or light romances, or confession stories. I devoted considerable space in *Writing the Novel: From Plot to Print* to a discussion of how to analyze the requirements of a particular fictional genre and how to write one's own story within such a framework. Wasn't I being inconsistent, saying this in print and then loftily advising this chap to go follow his own star?

Years ago, when I worked for a literary agent, I had dealings with a would-be writer who was possessed of enormous energy, a serviceable way with prose and dialogue, and the survival instincts of a lemming. All he ostensibly wanted was to see his work in print, yet all he did was sabotage himself at every turn. Advised that confessions constituted a particularly receptive market for newcomers, he produced several, but insisted upon writing them from a male viewpoint. At the time, a confession magazine might publish one male-viewpoint story an issue, if they happened to run across one they really liked. By writing his confessions from a male point of view, the man was deliberately making things harder for himself.

I had occasion to remember all of this just a few days ago when I began work on a new novel. The basic plot notion was one that had suggested itself to me some months ago—a girl's mother dies, her father remarries, and the girl becomes convinced that her stepmother is trying to kill her. I hadn't given the idea any conscious thought in months, but evidently my subconscious had been playing with it while I was at work on something else, and I found bits and pieces of the plot coming to me rapidly.

I also found myself with decisions to make. Did I want an urban or a rural setting? Would I write the book in the first or the third person? Single or multiple viewpoint?

I don't always have to make decisions of this sort. Quite a few of the novels I've written over the years have recounted the continuing adventures of series characters, and in such a case a lot of these questions are predetermined. When I write a mystery about burglar Bernie Rhodenbarr, for example, I know I'm going to use the first person. I know, too, who the character is and how he operates, where he lives, who his friends are, and so on. A series involves turning out books that are "the same only different," and while that requirement presents problems of its own, it does eliminate certain decisions.

A year ago I spent a week in Savannah, where I scouted locations with the intention of using the city in a novel sooner or later. When I first got the idea for *The Stepmother,* I felt it would fit quite neatly into that charming Georgia seaport.

Two factors changed my mind. First off, I recognized that there were already elements of plot and character in *The Stepmother* that were evocative of *Ariel,* a recent novel of mine. *Ariel* was set in an old house in Charleston, and while Charleston and Savannah are by no means indistinguishable one from the other, they do have points of similarity. This might not have kept me from setting the book in Savannah if I had been convinced it would work best there, but it did predispose me to look for another setting.

As I thought further about the book, a second reason for getting away from Savannah came to mind. I decided I wanted to make the girl a New Yorker out of her element. I saw her as a child who has grown up in Greenwich Village, not so much precocious as sophisticated. Suppose the family moved to the country? Someplace fairly isolated, say. Delaware County, Schoharie County, one of those forgotten areas of upstate New York a few hours from the city and hence out of commuting range.

With the choice of location, more of the plot immediately began to take form. Why would the family move from the Village out into the middle of nowhere? Maybe the father's a writer who just made a lot of money and wants to play landed gentleman for a change. I began to get a sense of the house and grounds. I decided there would be an old overgrown cemetery on the property, and I saw a few ways this would fit into the plot.

At this point I wrote out a few hundred words of notes, talking to myself at the typewriter, and a couple of days later I started actually writing the book. I wrote half a dozen pages and stopped, because I had another decision to make.

First person or third person? I had automatically begun the book in the third person, writing the opening scene, in which the family first visits the country house, from Naomi's point of view. (I had by this time selected a name for her.)

But was that the best choice?

I stayed away from the typewriter for several days weighing the pros and cons. First-person narration comes very naturally to me, and I found the prospect seductive in this instance. I'm much better able to get inside the skin of my lead character when I write in the first person. It has always seemed to me the most natural voice for fiction, and I thought it might be particularly useful in *The Stepmother* for a couple of reasons.

For one, I had a very good sense of Naomi and felt she would be a terrific character. The more effectively and compellingly I could present her to the reader, the more gripping and engaging the book would be. For another, I felt it might be difficult to get inside Naomi as well in the third person.

Ariel was written in the third person, but there were two elements present which facilitated my getting inside the character and making her come alive. I used lengthy extracts from a diary she was keeping, which in effect constituted first-person sections within a third-person narrative. I also had quite a few scenes in which she conversed intimately with Erskine, a classmate of hers, and the relationship between the two kids was one of the more interesting elements of the book.

I didn't want to have Naomi keep a diary, partly because I didn't want to write *Ariel* all over again, partly because I did not envision her as a diarist. Nor did I expect her to develop a close relationship with a classmate at the new school in the country; on the contrary, I saw her as essentially isolated, contemptuous of her new schoolmates and rejected by them in turn.

So why not switch to first person? Well, that presented problems of another sort. For openers, I'd be limited to scenes in which Naomi was present. The reader couldn't be privy to any information that she didn't know. It seemed to me that the sort of suspense novel I was writing worked best if the reader occasionally knew things the lead character did not know.

It also seemed to me that the book would be more effective if the reader was never entirely certain whether the peril Naomi fancied herself to be in was real or imaginary. The use of first-person narration didn't automatically rule out this ambivalence, but it made it more difficult to bring it off.

One other thing. Suspense would be further heightened, I felt, if the reader didn't know everything that Naomi knew, and if he wasn't aware of everything she did. Perhaps there might be a point where suspicion was raised about Naomi's having been responsible for her own mother's death, say. While it's possible for a narrator to withhold certain information from the reader—I've done that sort of thing in detective stories, certainly—I didn't think it would work well here.

So I decided to go with my original impulse and write the book in the third person. And, in the course of making the decision, I thought up bits of plot business that would enable Naomi to reveal herself to the reader through interaction with other characters. I decided there could be an old man who walks along that particular road every day, a rustic who's a source of information on the area, and he and Naomi could develop some sort of friendship. I had already thought she might run off to New York and be brought back by a private detective, and I now saw how she could have further dealings with the detective. An occasional letter to her best friend in New York might serve a function similar to that of Ariel's diary.

And, in considering and rejecting the first person, I became increasingly aware of the need for writing the book from multiple viewpoint, and got a sense of some of the scenes that would have to be written, and of some of the characters from whose points of view they would be shown.

One consideration, I must admit, was that novels of the sort I was writing are most commonly written in the third person. But I did not regard this fact as evidence of a requirement, or elect to go along with the majority out of a desire to make my publisher happy. Instead, I learned in the course of making my decision *why* third-person narration predominates, and found that it does so for very sound reasons.

I thought it might be interesting to share the factors involved in making this sort of literary decision, and to show how the decision-making process itself sparks the invention of plot and character elements. I still think Polonius was quite right, and that "To thine own self be true" ought to be every writer's first principle, but any number of decisions nevertheless need to be made in order to be true to one's own vision, whether they are arrived at intuitively or through the sort of processes I've described.

You'll excuse me, won't you? Now that I've made all these decisions, I've got to sit down and write the damned thing.

CHAPTER **4**

Novel Approaches

WHEN I first got started in this ridiculous profession, I wrote nothing but short stories. For a year after my first sale I hammered out crime fiction, a couple of thousand words at a clip. I peddled some of it for a cent a word, some for a cent and a half a word, and watched much of it go unsold.

After a year of this, I finally got courageous enough to write a novel. It took me two or three weeks to write it, sold to the first publisher who saw it, and brought me a vast sense of accomplishment and an advance of two thousand dollars. It did not make me rich and famous, but I was a youth of nineteen summers at the time and as callow as they come, and fame and fortune would have spoiled me for sure.

I've recounted all this because I think my initial approach was typical for most beginning writers. We start out writing short stories because it certainly looks like the easiest way to break in. The short story is a compact and controllable form. One can grasp it all at once. It's short—that's how it got its name—and it won't take a year and a day to write. A person can do a few dozen of them, learning as he goes along, in less time than it might take him to write a novel.

These arguments sound logical enough, but they overlook some basic facts. Foremost of these is that the short story is infinitely more difficult to sell than the novel. The market for short fiction was minuscule when I was starting out twenty years ago. Since then it has consistently shrunk to the point of invisibility. Every year there are fewer magazines buying short stories and still more hopeful writers submitting manuscripts to them.

The economics of the short-story business are discouraging at best. *Hitchcock* and *Queen,* my markets for short fiction, pay the same nickel a word they doled out twenty years ago. The confession mags pay a shade *less* than they did then, and are less eager to buy than they used to be. And each year it seems as though a few more of the top magazines have (a) gone out of business, (b) discontinued fiction, or (c) stopped reading unsolicited manuscripts.

I don't mean to talk anyone out of writing short stories. I wouldn't go on writing them myself if I didn't find them a great source of satisfaction. It's more my intention to suggest that the novel is a much better place for the beginner to get started.

But wait a moment. My vaunted writer's imagination sees a lot of you waving your hands in the air. Ask your questions, then, and perhaps I can answer them.

Isn't it harder to write a novel than a short story?

No. Novels aren't harder. What they are is longer.

That may be a very obvious answer, but that doesn't make it any less true. It's the sheer length of a novel that the beginning writer is apt to find intimidating. Matter of fact, you don't have to be a beginner to be intimidated in this fashion. I'm writing this chapter during a momentary respite from a World War II novel which will ultimately run to five or six hundred pages. My suspense novels generally stop at two hundred pages or thereabouts, and I had a lot of trouble starting this book because its vastness scared the adverbs out of me.

What's required, I think, is a change in attitude. To write a novel you have to resign yourself to the fact that you simply can't prime yourself and knock it all out in a single session at the typewriter. The process of writing the book is going to occupy you for weeks or months—perhaps years. But each day's stint at the typewriter is simply that—one day's work. That's true whether you're writing short stories or an epic trilogy. If you're writing three or six or ten pages a day, you'll get a certain amount of work accomplished in a certain span of time—whatever it is you're working on.

I'd love to write a novel. But I don't know how to begin.

Page one's as good a place as any.

I'll tell you a secret—*nobody* knows how to start a novel. There are no rules, because each novel is a case unto itself.

Sometimes an outline helps. I've used outlines frequently and have mixed feelings about them. It's comforting, certainly, to know where a book is going, and an outline spells all of that out for you in advance and saves you worrying that you'll plot yourself into a corner.

On the other hand, an outline can keep a novel from developing organically. There's no way an outline can include absolutely everything, and the little elements of characterization and incident that crop up while you're writing can change the shape and direction of your novel. If you're tied to an outline, the book can't grow as it wants to; its final form is as predetermined as a paint-by-number canvas. Of course you can always modify the outline as you feel the need, but that's sometimes easier said than done.

Even if you don't use an outline, isn't it necessary to know where the book is going?

Not really. I know several writers who have written quite a few books by rolling a sheet of paper into the typewriter just to see what happens.

My friend Don Westlake's a good example. Some years ago he showed me a first chapter in which a surly guy named Parker stalks across the George Washington Bridge, snarling at a motorist who offers him a ride. When Don wrote that chapter, he knew no more about the character or his story than the chapter itself contained. But the book took shape and the character came to life, and Don's since written sixteen books about Parker under his pen name of Richard Stark.

The advantage of this particular novel approach, the Narrative Push method, is that you're by no means locked into a formula. I think it was Theodore Sturgeon who argued that if the writer has no idea what's going to happen next, the reader certainly won't know what's going to happen next.

For my own part, I've come to prefer to know a little bit more about a book than how I'm going to open it. I've written too many books in recent years that ground to a halt somewhere around page seventy because I couldn't think of anything to have happen on page seventy-one. But I don't have to know everything. I like to know where the book's going and what direction it'll take to get there, but I don't need to have the whole route mapped out for me.

Suppose I spend a year writing a novel and it proves unsalable. I can't risk that much time—wouldn't it be safer to stick to short stories?

Would it? Let's assume that you could write twelve or twenty short stories in the time it would take you to write a novel. What makes you think you'd have a better chance of selling them? And why would a batch of unsalable short stories feel less like a waste of time than an unsalable novel?

I think what keeps a lot of us from attempting a novel is simple fear. Fear that we'll give up and leave the book uncompleted, or the greater fear that we'll complete it and have produced something unpublishable. I don't think these fears are justified even when they prove true.

So what if a first novel's unsalable? For heaven's sake, the great majority of them are, and why on earth should they be otherwise? In every other trade I've ever heard of it's taken for granted that one will put in a lot of work before attaining the level of professionalism. Why should we expect our writing to be instantly publishable?

Writing a novel is an extraordinary learning experience. You have room in a novel, room to try things out, to make mistakes, to find your way. The writing of an unpublishable first novel is not a failure. It is an investment.

A few years ago I read Justin Scott's first novel in manuscript. It was embarrassingly bad in almost every respect, and hopelessly unpublishable. But it did him some good to write it, and his second novel—also unpublishable, as it happened—was a vast improvement. As I write this, his novel *The Turning* is Dell's leader for the month, and his forthcoming book *The Shipkiller* is shaping up as a strong candidate for bestsellerdom. Do you suppose Justin regrets the time he "wasted" on that first novel?

I'd like to write a novel—but I don't have a good enough idea for one.

If you're having trouble coming up with ideas, you're better off with a novel than short stories.

Does that seem odd? You might think that a novel, covering so much more ground and so many more pages, would require more in the way of ideas. But it doesn't usually work that way.

Short stories absolutely demand either new ideas or new slants on old ones. Often a short story is little more than an idea polished into a piece of fiction.

I like to write short stories—I get more sheer enjoyment out of writing them than novels, if less remuneration. But each one requires a reasonably strong idea, and the idea's used up in a couple of thousand words. I've written whole novels out of ideas with no more depth to them than short-story ideas, and I've written other novels without having had a strong story idea to begin with. They had plot and characters, to be sure, but those developed as the book went along.

Ed Hoch makes a living writing nothing but short stories—he may be the only writer of whom that's true—and he manages because he seems to be a never-ending fount of ideas. Getting ideas and turning them into fiction is what gives him satisfaction as a writer. I sometimes envy him, but I know I couldn't possibly come up with half a dozen viable short-story ideas every month the way he does. So I take the easy way out and write novels.

Hmmm. Time's up, and I see a lot of you have your hands raised. Take a deep breath and go on to the next chapter.

CHAPTER 5

Nothing Short of Novel

IN THE foregoing chapter we had a look at the advantages of writing a novel rather than limiting oneself to short stories. We noted that novels are easier to sell, more profitable for their authors, and constitute a considerable learning experience for the novice writer. Now let's deal with a few more questions some of you have on the subject.

I'm afraid to write a novel because I'm not that smooth a stylist. Don't you have to be a better craftsman to make a novel come off?

I don't think so. Sometimes it's just the reverse—a novelist can get away with stylistic crudity that would ruin a shorter piece of fiction.

Remember, what a novel gives you more than anything else is room, room for your characters and storyline to carry the day. While a way with words never hurts, it's of less overwhelming importance to the novelist than the ability to grab ahold of the reader and make him care what happens next.

The bestseller list abounds with the work of writers whom no one would call polished stylists. I don't want to name names, but I can think offhand of half a dozen writers whose first chapters are very hard going for me. I'm overly conscious of their style—writing does change one's perceptions as a reader—and I find their dialogue mechanical, their transitions awkward, their descriptions vague. But twenty or thirty pages into their books, I'll stop seeing the trees and begin to perceive the forest—i.e., the story grips me and I no longer notice what's wrong with their writing.

In shorter fiction, the storyline wouldn't have a chance to take over.

So perhaps you have to be a better craftsman for short stories and a better storyteller for novels, but both are equally important aspects of the writer's art. Obviously, the finest novels are skillfully shaped, just as the finest short stories catch up the reader in their narrative spell. But I certainly wouldn't avoid writing a novel out of lack of confidence in writing skills.

All right, next question. Are you trying to raise your hand back there? You keep putting it up and taking it down.

That's because I'm uncertain. I have a good idea for a novel but I just can't seem to get started on it. Somehow it seems pointless to begin something that's going to take forever to finish.

I know the feeling. I remember the first time I wrote a really long book. When I sat down to begin it I knew I was starting something that had to run at least five hundred pages in manuscript. I put in a good day's work and wound up knocking out fourteen pages. I got up from the typewriter and said, "Well, just four hundred and eighty-six pages to go"—and went directly into nervous prostration at the very thought.

The thing to remember is that a novel's not going to take forever. All the old clichés actually apply—a journey of a thousand miles begins with a single step, and slow and steady honestly does win the race.

Consider this: if you write one page a day, you will produce a substantial novel in a year. Now writers who turn out a book a year, year in and year out, are considered to be quite prolific. And don't you figure you could produce one measly little page, even on a bad day? Even on a *rotten* day?

Maybe it's not the length, exactly. But when I write a short story I can hold the whole thing in my head when I sit down at the typewriter. I know exactly where I'm going and it's just a matter of writing it down. I don't have that kind of grasp on a novel.

Of course not. Nobody does.

There are a few approaches you might consider. One involves writing progressively more detailed versions of your outline until you have essentially fleshed it out into a book, having outlined each scene in each chapter before beginning the actual writing. Writers who use this approach say it makes the writing a breeze. I would think it would transform what's supposed to be a creative act into a fundamentally mechanical process, but that doesn't mean it might not work like a charm for you.

As an alternative, you might come to realize that the control you seem to have over short stories is largely illusory. What you have is confidence—because you *think* you know everything about the story by the time you set out to write it.

But, if you're like me, you keep surprising yourself at the typewriter.

Characters take on a life of their own and insist upon supplying their own dialogue. Scenes that looked necessary at the onset turn out to be superfluous, while other scenes take a form other than what you'd originally intended. As often as not, midway through the story you'll think of a way to improve the basic plot itself.

This happens even more markedly in novels, and that's fine. A work of fiction ought to be an organic entity. It's alive, and it grows as it goes.

Maybe it would help you if I said something about the novel I'm working on at present, an extremely complicated thriller set during World War II. I'm about halfway through the book as I write this, and I've been able to get this far solely by taking it One Day at a Time.

Whenever I project, whenever I start envisioning the novel as a whole, I'm paralyzed with terror. I'm convinced the whole thing is impossible and can't conceivably work out. But as long as I can get up each morning and concentrate exclusively on what's going to happen during that particular day's stint at the typewriter, I seem to be doing all right—and the book is taking form nicely.

One day at a time—that seems to work for me. And if you realize that you can only affect what you do now, things become a good deal more manageable.

Maybe I haven't started a novel because I'm afraid I wouldn't finish it.

Possibly so. And maybe you wouldn't finish it. There's no law that says you have to.

Please understand that I'm not advocating abandoning a novel halfway through. I've done that far too often myself, and it's not something I've ever managed to feel good about. But you do have every right in the world to give up on a book if it's just not working, or if you simply discover that writing novels is not for you. As much as we'd all prefer to pretend our calling is a noble one, it's salutary to bear in mind that the last thing this poor old planet needs is another book. The only reason to write anything is because it's something you want to do, and if that ceases to be the case you're entirely free to do something else instead.

You know, it strikes me that we may all of us be too caught up in the desire to finish our work. That has to be our aim, obviously, but it's easy to overemphasize that aspect of writing.

I do this myself. I became a writer because I thought I'd enjoy the process of literary creation, and in no time at all this urge transformed itself into an obsession with getting manuscripts finished and seeing them in print.

I suspect the business of writing a novel becomes less a source of anxiety and more a source of pleasure if we learn to concern ourselves more with the writing process and less with the presumptive end product. The writer who does each day's work as it comes along, enjoying it as activity and not merely enduring it as a means to an end, is going to have a better time of things. I suspect, too, he'll wind up producing a better piece of writing for his efforts; his work won't suffer for having been rushed, whipped like a poor horse to the finish line.

All that's required here is an attitudinal change. And if you manage it, I hope you'll tell me how—I have a lot of trouble in this area, yearning less to write than to have written.

You've got me convinced. I'm going to sit down and write a novel. After all, short stuff isn't really significant, is it?

It isn't, huh? Who says?

I'll grant that commercial significance singles out the novel, and that long novels are automatically considered to be of more importance than short novels, and sell better. And I won't deny that your neighbors will take you more seriously if you tell them you've written a novel. (Of course if that's the main concern, just go and tell them. You don't have to write anything. Just lie a little. Don't worry—they won't beg to read the manuscript.)

But as far as intrinsic merit is concerned, length is hardly a factor. You've probably heard of the writer who apologized for having written a long letter, explaining that he didn't have the time to make it shorter. And you may have read Faulkner's comment that every short-story writer is a failed poet, and every novelist a failed short-story writer.

Well, now you've got me confused again. Maybe I'll write a novel, maybe I'll stick to short stories. One thing I know, though, and that's that I'm not going to accomplish anything sitting on my duff. I'm going straight to the typewriter. No more putting things off.

Congratulations. But I hope you'll take time to read Chapter 15. The title's "Creative Procrastination."

CHAPTER 6

Sunday Writers

A COUPLE of weeks ago a friend of mine was nice enough to compliment me on something he'd read in a recent column. While I was basking in the glow, he said, "It must bother you, huh? Sort of like taking money under false pretenses."

I asked what he meant.

"Well, here you are writing this column," he said, "and you know full well that the vast majority of your readers are never going to write anything publishable, and you're in there every month telling them how to improve their technique. Hell, you're just encouraging 'em in their folly."

I was really annoyed with him, not least because he was calling my attention to doubts I'd had myself. I once turned down an opportunity to teach writing in an adult education program for reasons along the lines of what he'd said. But after my friend and I had gone our separate ways, I gave some further thought to the whole question—and I wound up grateful to him for raising the point.

For one thing, he made me realize the extent to which we're all hung up on publishing what we write. Now that may look painfully obvious at first glance, but when you look at the other forms of creative endeavor you can see the difference.

Every writer I've ever known has written with the hope of eventual publication. Contrast that with all the Sunday painters daubing oil on canvas for their private enjoyment, all the actors whose ambitions have never strayed beyond amateur theatrical presentations, all the folks taking piano lessons without the vaguest dream of a debut at Carnegie Hall. Millions of people snap pictures without hoping to see them published. Millions more make jewelry and throw pots and knit shawls, free altogether from the craving to profit from their craft.

I've known quite a few Sunday painters, including several in my own family. They're quite accomplished and they get enormous satisfaction from what they do. Some exhibit in local shows, occasionally winning a little recognition. But they don't sell paintings, they've never tried to sell paintings, and they don't consider themselves failures.

These painters are very fortunate—they don't need to prove themselves in the marketplace in order to get a sense of accomplishment from their work. They can produce a painting and either give it to a friend or hang it on a blank wall. Their artistic struggles may be rewarding or frustrating according to whether they do or do not achieve what they aimed at artistically. But, once a painting's finished, they don't succeed or fail if it does or does not sell.

Why aren't there more Sunday writers? Why don't those of us who write as a hobby find our work satisfying in and of itself?

I think there are some good reasons. Foremost, I suppose, is that communication is absolutely implicit in writing. If a story is not to be read, why write it down in the first place? An unpublished piece of fiction is an incompleted act, like a play staged in an empty theater.

We can't effectively hang our manuscripts on the wall. Some of us do give them to friends—by having our work privately published. But that's expensive, and in addition there's a certain stigma that often attaches to it. If it's really good, we and our friends wonder, why should we have to pay to have it published? And if it's not of professional caliber, why don't we keep it in the attic?

Poets have an edge here. The prospect of making a living from poetry is so remote as to be nonexistent, and that's very liberating. Since every poet's a financial failure, no odium attaches to such failure. Only a minuscule proportion of skilled poets ever have their works published in book form, and they make no more than a pittance from such publication. So the poet who circulates his verses privately, or pays to have them printed, is less likely to feel qualms about it than the fiction writer who does the same thing. When all poets are essentially amateurs, one's not ashamed to be less than professional. One's friends and neighbors probably don't know the names or work of many widely published poets. They're not forever reading in the gossip columns of staggering sums paid for film rights to a sonnet sequence. Poetry, like virtue, is its own reward.

Where's the reward in unpublished fiction?

As far as I've been able to determine, it does not lie in the sheer joy of the act of writing.

Because writing's not much fun.

I really wonder why that is. Again, comparison with other art forms is instructive. It's been my observation that painters, both professional and amateur, love to paint. They get genuine enjoyment out of the physical act of smearing paint on canvas. Sometimes they're blocked, sometimes they're frustrated, but when they're painting the very process of creation is a joy to them.

Same thing certainly holds true for musicians. They only seem to feel alive when they're performing. The jazz musicians I've known spend their afternoons practicing scales and such, work all night performing, then jam for free at an after-hours joint until dawn, just for the sheer pleasure of it.

In sharp contrast, almost every writer I know will go to great lengths to avoid being in the same room with his typewriter. Those of us who are driven to produce great quantities of manuscript don't necessarily get any real pleasure out of the act; it's just that we feel worse when we *don't* write. It's not the carrot but the stick that gets most of us moving.

I don't mean to suggest that there's no positive pleasure connected with writing. I enjoy getting ideas, for example—both the initial plot germs and the ideas that develop in the course of extended work on a novel. And I very much enjoy having written; the satisfaction of having completed a taxing piece of work can be monumental.

This latter pleasure, come to think of it, is a negative one, isn't it? When I'm delirious with joy over having finished something, my joy stems in large part from the fact that I do not have to work on it any more, that the dratted thing is over and done with.

So it's nice being about to write, and it's nice to have written. But is there no way to enjoy writing while it's going on?

One thing that impedes enjoyment, I would think, is that writing's hard work. Painters and musicians work hard, too, but there's a difference. You can't really relax and go with the flow while you're writing—at least I can't, and if anyone can show me how, I'll be delighted to learn. Writing demands all of my attention and focuses me entirely in the present. I can't let my mind wander, and if my mind wanders in spite of itself I find I can't write, and when I want to write and can't write I find myself possessed of murderous rage.

When a painting doesn't go well the artist can keep on painting and cover it up. When a musician's not at his best, the notes he plays float off on the air and he can forget about them.

When I'm off my form, the garbage I've written just sits there on the page and thumbs its nose at me. And when it gets into print that way, it's there for all the world to see, forever.

There are some writers who enjoy writing. Isaac Asimov, for one, seems to enjoy every minute of it, and there may be others similarly blessed. And everybody enjoys it now and then, when the words flow effortlessly and you feel plugged into the Universal Mind and the stuff on the page is worlds better than what you had in mind when you sat down. That doesn't happen very often, but I'll tell you it's a kick when it does.

Sometimes I think the Sunday writer enjoys a great advantage over those of us who have to do this stuff to put bread on the table. What constantly mitigates his enjoyment is his desire to give up his amateur standing and turn professional. I don't know that every foot soldier carries in his knapsack the baton of a marshal of France. I do know that, when it comes to writing, everybody wants to get into the act, and every Sunday writer thinks his typewriter ought to be able to turn out a bestseller.

Maybe it just has to be that way. Maybe we can't put up with the hard work of writing in the first place unless we're goaded by the urge to publish.

I would certainly hope, though, that Sunday writers can avoid equating failure to publish with failure as a writer. If you are gaining satisfaction from writing, if you are exercising and improving your talent, if you are committing to paper your special feelings and perceptions, then you can damn well call yourself a success. Whether you wind up in print, whether you ever see money for your efforts, is and ought to be incidental.

No, I don't feel guilty for writing my column each month. It may well be that many of my readers will never publish anything, but so what? Perhaps some of you will write a little better for having read one of my efforts.

"You're just encouraging them in their folly."

Am I indeed? That presupposes that writing stories which will not ultimately be published is folly, and that's an assumption I'm unwilling to grant. And the very word *folly* calls to mind a line of William Blake's—"If the fool would persist in his folly he would become wise."

I don't know that persistence on the part of the Sunday writer leads to wisdom. I don't even know that it will lead to publication. But it can definitely lead to satisfaction, and I'd regard that as no small reward.

CHAPTER 7

"Dear Joy"

Dear Joy,

By now I suppose you're pretty well settled in at college. When I talked to your dad recently he did some pardonable boasting about your scholarship, and I'd like to offer my congratulations.

He also said you were thinking about becoming a writer. On that score I don't know whether congratulations or condolences are in order. As an alternative, let me furnish you with a little unsolicited advice.

The first point that comes to mind is the question of what a future writer ought to study in college. When I went to school I automatically majored in English Literature; since I intended to write the stuff, it seemed fitting and proper to find out first what other people had done in that area.

I don't suppose this did me any discernible harm, but neither am I sure it did me much good. I don't think there's any question that writers ought to be readers, and I've never known a professional writer who wasn't a virtually compulsive reader, but studying literature and reading are not the same thing. As in most academic disciplines, the student of literature undergoes a course of study which most prepares him to become a teacher of literature. This is not a bad thing to be, nor are teaching and writing mutually exclusive; a lot of writers who don't make the grade, or are emotionally unsuited to life as a free-lancer, find teaching a comfortable occupation.

The only reason *not* to major in English is that it might keep you from studying something else that you're more interested in. The most important single thing you can do at college is pursue your own interests, whatever they might turn out to be and however remotely they might appear to relate to a career in writing. I don't honestly think it makes a bit of difference what you study—just so long as it's what you *want* to study. Humanities or hard sciences, history or botany or philosophy or calculus, whatever excites you intellectually at the time is the most useful thing for you as a student and, ultimately, as a writer.

As a corollary to the principle of following your own interests, you would do well to find out who the most provocative professors are at your school. Then contrive to take at least one course from each of them, whatever the hell they're teaching. The specific facts learned in a classroom, the content of the required reading, rarely lingers in the mind too long after graduation. But the stimulation of intellectual interchange with an exciting and exceptional mind is something which will be with you forever.

Nobody can teach you to write, not on a college campus or anywhere else. But this doesn't mean that writing courses are a waste of time.

On the contrary, they're a *source* of time—and this may very well be their most important function. They provide you with time and academic credit for your own experimentation at the typewriter. You might be doing this writing anyway, stealing the time from other courses. When you take a writing course you're expected to devote a certain amount of time to writing, and that's often useful, just as the need to produce assignments on demand is an inordinately valuable discipline.

Most writing courses involve the submission of manuscripts which are read aloud to the class, by the instructor or the individual authors, after which they are subjected to group criticism. I hope someone improves on this format soon. Prose is not written to be read aloud, and the effect of a short story so presented has little to do with its effect in print. Even with these limitations, writing courses can be very valuable for you, less for the criticism you'll receive from others than for the opportunity you'll have to observe what doesn't work in other people's writing.

This is an important point. The best and easiest way to learn writing by reading consists of exposing yourself to large doses of inferior amateur work. It's easier to spot a flaw than comprehend the reasons an unblemished piece is flawless. Nothing helped my own writing like a few months of work reading unsolicited manuscripts at a literary agency. Every day I worked my way through mountains of swill; at night I sat at home writing, and I knew what mistakes to avoid in my own work.

Try to read your classmates' efforts in manuscript. Seeing beats hearing when it comes to teaching yourself how prose and dialogue work on the page. And take criticisms of your own work, from fellow students or instructors, with a generous splash of soy sauce. Shrugging off their sass will prepare you for the task of ignoring the carping of editors and publishers in years to come.

Whether you take many writing courses or not, I hope you'll do as much writing as possible during your college years. As far as what you ought to write, well, that depends on you.

Prospective writers, in and out of school, approach the profession from different circumstances and with different goals. Some have a particular perspective which they want to be able to render in fiction. Others want first and foremost to establish themselves as writers; just what they wind up writing is a secondary consideration.

If you're of the first sort, the best advice I can give you is to avoid listening to any advice, mine included. You already know, on some intuitive level, what it is that you want to do. Go ahead and do it, at your own pace and in your own way. Take all the time you need for your writing and let its form and content be whatever proves most suitable and natural to you.

As far as commercial considerations are concerned, don't be concerned with them. It is exceedingly rare that anything produced by a college writer has any objective value, either commercially or artistically. While you may prove a happy exception, it's not terribly likely that anything you turn out in the next four years will make you rich and famous. This is a very good thing for you. It means you ought to consider yourself completely free from commercial requirements, at least for the time being.

But maybe your main interest lies in satisfying commercial requirements. Maybe you want chiefly to become a writer, a professional wordsmith. This needn't mean that what you write will be of less artistic value. It's more a question of where you're coming from as a writer.

When I was your age—and you can't imagine how I hate the sound of that phrase—all I wanted to do was get published. I wanted to see my name in print and on checks. I already knew that a writer was the only thing worth being and I was impatient to go ahead and officially become one.

If you find yourself similarly obsessed, perhaps some advice might not be amiss. First of all, write as much as possible. The more active you are the quicker you'll get into the habit of developing ideas and encouraging them to hatch into stories.

Study the markets. I think it's possible to become market-oriented without cheapening yourself as a writer. I don't think you should try to teach yourself to write confessions or juveniles or whatever because you know there's a market for them. Instead, read a lot of different kinds of magazines until you find some that contain the kind of stories that you think you might enjoy producing, and might be proud of at the same time. You'll never do good work in a field you can't enjoy as a reader and respect as a writer.

Act like a pro. Learn the proper format for your manuscripts and use it when you type them. Submit things. Send out the pieces you write, send them out over and over again. I literally papered a wall with rejection slips my first two years in college, and if nothing else it established my own self-image as a writer, albeit not a terribly successful one. I suppose it also helped me get used to rejection. And then one wonderful day an editor asked me to revise a story, and he subsequently bought it, and all that acting *as if* paid off. All of a sudden I was a professional writer.

Most campuses offer a variety of literary and journalistic activities—the college newspaper, the literary magazine, that sort of thing. Students with an interest in writing commonly get involved in these areas. They can be very rewarding, but only if you're interested in them for their own sake. I'd recommend that you choose your extracurricular activities the same way you choose your courses, for their intrinsic interest to you.

The time I put in editing the college paper was valuable to me in several ways. It helped me learn to write to space requirements, taught me to work against the pressure of a deadline, and assured me that I did not want to spend my life on a newspaper. But the most important extracurricular activity for me was hanging out. The college I attended, like the one you've chosen, was a small innovative liberal-arts college with a bizarre assortment of students and a comfortingly eccentric faculty. The personal growth and expansion I achieved through contact with all of these madmen and crazy ladies was far more useful to me over the years than anything I ever acquired in a classroom. And that's been the experience of every writer I've known—and most non-writers too, as far as that goes.

It may occur to you that, while writing is certainly what you want to do eventually, it would be nice to be able to make a living after you graduate. You may think, and may be advised, that you ought to make specific preparations for a career so that you can support yourself while you're getting established as a writer.

Don't waste your time. You may indeed wind up holding any number of jobs after college, but they'll take care of themselves when the time comes. Planning now for a non-writing career when you actually want to become a writer is no more than preparing for failure. Spend the present growing, and learning, and writing, and enjoying yourself. And let tomorrow take care of tomorrow.

Have fun, Joy. I don't expect you to believe this, but there will come a time when these four years will be the good old days. Meanwhile, enjoy yourself—and thanks for providing me with this month's column.

Love,

Larry

CHAPTER 8

How to Read Like a Writer

WHILE LEADING a writing seminar at Antioch College, I had a chance to renew my friendship with Nolan Miller, in whose writing workshop I made some of my first attempts at fiction right around the time Teddy Roosevelt led the lads up San Juan Hill.

We talked of students, then and now. "They all want to be told whether they have *talent*," Nolan said. "Talent's no guarantee of success, of course. The most talented writer in the world won't get anyplace if he lacks the discipline to exploit his talent. But they always want to know if they have it or not, and I never tell a student he *lacks* talent."

"Why's that?" I wondered.

"Because I simply can't tell. I may be able to detect talent on occasion but I can never be certain of its absence. I can't know that a man or woman lacks the capacity to grow, to develop, to improve. Besides," he added, "I don't think it does them any harm to try their hand at writing. If nothing else, it makes them much better *readers*."

Years ago I heard the perhaps apocryphal story of the great violinist. I've recounted his approach in Chapter 12, "It Takes More Than Talent." Nolan's is gentler, and I very much prefer it.

But do we actually become better readers by virtue of our efforts at writing? That would certainly seem to be a logical assumption. Personal knowledge of how a thing is done ought to give one a finer appreciation of that same thing when it is done by someone else. I am well aware, certainly, that my musician friend hears music very differently than I do, that my mother has a fuller experience in an art gallery as a result of the years she's spent painting.

This principle applies outside of the arts as well. There's a reason beyond their celebrity value for employing retired athletes as sports announcers. Having played the game, they know it better than you or I.

When it comes to reading, I'd have to say that most of us are pretty good at it to begin with. The one common denominator I've observed among writers of my acquaintance is a longstanding appetite for the printed word. Most of us have been well-nigh compulsive readers all our lives. Don Westlake once admitted that if there's nothing else in the house, he'll go read the ingredients label on the bottle of Worcestershire sauce. Over the years I've met a couple of writers who are not like this, but their number's so few as to qualify them for the endangered species list.

While I've always read voraciously, the nature of my reading has changed considerably over the years. In my college years I went through books like bluefish through a school of menhaden, chewing up and bolting down everything that came within my reach. In a sense, I read a great many books with the determination of a smoker breaking in a new pipe, as if each book I read would somehow season and improve me. When I didn't like a book I simply lowered my head and bulled my way through it anyway, as if setting it aside half-finished would be somehow immoral.

Alas, no more. I don't finish half the books I start nowadays, and a good many get hurled across the room after a couple of chapters. Part of this, I'm sure, stems from the self-confidence of middle age. The narrator of Toby Stein's *All the Time There Is* confides that she vowed on turning thirty-five never to finish a book merely because she had started it, and I submit that that's a good vow to make and a reasonable time in life to make it.

I think, though, that an increasing ability to discriminate between good and bad writing has had at least as much to do with my changed attitude toward what I read. The writing I do, day in and day out (whatever that means), has served to make me perhaps excessively aware of the technique of other writers. When I read the work of someone lacking in craft, I know it. This knowledge, this acute awareness, interferes with the voluntary suspension of disbelief upon which fiction depends for its effectiveness.

If my writer's ear tells me the dialogue I am reading is unnatural and clumsy, how am I to make myself believe in the existence of the characters who are speaking it? If my writer's perceptions force me to notice that I am reading lumpish prose, how can I lose myself in the story?

As a result, any number of bestsellers with considerable popular appeal leave me colder than an editor's smile. They may tell a good story, but if I can't get past the writing I can't enjoy that story.

I don't mean to imply that people who do enjoy such books are to be condemned for their enjoyment. More often than not, I envy them. They're having a good time, while I, a lifelong reader, am having an increasingly difficult time finding something to read.

There are compensations, however.

Because when I do find something good, I can enjoy it on several levels at once. On the most basic level, I can get caught up in the story as inextricably as the rankest soap-opera addict. I can laugh when it's funny and cry when it's sad. That, after all, is what fiction is for, and if anything, my professional involvement with the stuff has intensified my ability to respond to it—when it's good.

At the same time, I always have my writer's eye open when I read something well-written. However involved I may be in the fate of the characters, I allow myself to notice what the writer is doing. When something works, I try to figure out what makes it work so well. When one paragraph in an otherwise smooth novel seems a little rough, I take a moment to try to figure out what off-note soured the chord.

Sometimes, when I'm reading, I find myself doing a little mental rewriting. Does this one particular conversation go on too long? Suppose a couple of responses were eliminated—would that speed things up? Is this transition too abrupt? Or would things move more effectively if we had a fast cut here?

You might think that reading like this would be like sleeping with one eye open, that the writer's awareness would inhibit the reader's involvement. Curiously enough, it doesn't seem to work that way. I've seen musicians at concerts sitting in the audience and following the score as they listen to the music, and I've been given to understand that this can heighten their enjoyment of what they're hearing. In a similar fashion, my involvement in what I read can be intensified by my awareness of just what the writer is doing.

The flip side of the whole process is at least as important. One never stops learning the tricks of our particular trade, and I've found that my continuing education takes place in two classrooms, my office and my library. I learn by writing and I learn by reading. If the years I've spent writing have raised my consciousness as a reader, so do the books and stories I read continue to sharpen my skills as a writer.

The extent to which I've changed as a reader is never more apparent than when I reread something I haven't looked at in years. Sometimes this can be a very disappointing experience. There are writers I treasured in adolescence whose books I find quite impenetrable today, not because they've deteriorated but because I look on them with altogether different eyes now. I was less critical then, less capable of reading as a writer, and when I turn their pages now I want to weep for my own lost innocence.

These disappointments are more than made up for by the great delight of rediscovering an old favorite and finding I like it more than I ever did—because now I'm far better equipped to appreciate the author's excellences. It seems to me that every time I return to John O'Hara and Somerset Maugham I discover new evidence of their enormous craft. Years ago I read their novels and short stories for several reasons—for sheer story value, to make the acquaintance of their characters, and for what light their auctorial intelligence could shed upon such matters as Life and Truth and Beauty.

I still read them for these reasons, and get more out of them than I ever did. But at the same time I am more aware now of the manner in which they achieve particular effects. I observe, while caught up in the story of *The Moon and Sixpence,* say, how Maugham wields the perspective of his narrator like a conductor's baton. Reading *Ten North Frederick* for the fifth or sixth time, I am no less caught up in the inexorable decline of Joe Chapin for my noticing how O'Hara uses the viewpoints of various characters to reveal facets of his protagonist.

I've slowed down in my reading. I used to dash through books like a self-taught speedreader. Now I take more time, savoring what I read, chewing each mouthful thoroughly before swallowing. Writing has indeed made me a better reader, just as reading continues to make me a better writer.

How to read like a writer? I'm afraid I can't think of many specific tips toward that end. One thing I've observed is that I'm more critical and detached when I read a manuscript than when I read galleys, more so too with galleys than with a bound book. The closer I am to what came out of the writer's typewriter, the more conscious I am that I'm reading a person's work rather than something that came down from the mountaintop carved in stone tablets. By the same token, it's easier for me to get caught up in a bound book than a manuscript.

But that's by the way. I don't know that you have to make a particular effort to learn to read like a writer. If you keep writing—and keep reading—it just happens.

Enjoy it.

CHAPTER 9

Rolling With the Punches

A COUPLE of months ago a writing student of mine was discussing a story he'd written a year or two previously. It had come within a hair's breadth of being accepted by a prestigious literary quarterly. The author then submitted it to *Harper's* and got it back with a personal letter from Lewis Lapham.

"Well?" I said. "Where'd you send it next?"

"I didn't."

"Beg pardon?"

"I put it in a drawer," he said, shrugging. "I figured it got rejected twice so there must be something wrong with it, so why should I waste my time sending it out again?"

Extraordinary, don't you think? Any story that came that close to acceptance at these two markets is almost certainly publishable somewhere. But this particular story will almost certainly *not* be published—because the author isn't sufficiently determined to give it every possible chance of publication.

When novice writers ask my advice about getting published, one point I can't emphasize too strongly is the importance of being absolutely relentless about submissions. Once you've got a story to the point where you think it's worth submitting, you must submit it and submit it and submit it until someone somewhere breaks down and buys it. Before this happens, you will very likely accumulate rejection slips sufficient to insulate an attic. Your collection may not represent any near misses, may not include any personal notes from eminent editors. You may not even experience the wee thrill of seeing *Sorry* hand-scrawled across the bottom of a printed slip.

Tough. If you really want to be in this silly business, you cannot let this sort of thing bother you. You paste the rejection slip on the wall or toss it in the wastebasket. You take the story out of the envelope it came back in and tuck it into a fresh one. You consult your records, see where it's been, then flip through *Writer's Market* and pick out a place where it hasn't been. And then you put it in the mail, and you repeat this process *ad infinitum* until the damn thing sells.

Over and over. Again and again. Relentlessly.

What do you suppose it means when your manuscript comes back to you like a well-hurled boomerang? It doesn't mean you're a brain-damaged churl who couldn't write your name in the dirt with a stick. It doesn't mean your story stinks on ice. It doesn't mean you should forget about writing and pay more attention to those ads promising high profits raising chinchillas in your bathtub.

All it means is that a particular editor didn't want to buy a particular story on a particular day.

Maybe he didn't even read it. Editors are as apt to be overworked as the rest of it, and sometimes the prospect of wading through slush is uninviting, and who's to say that no one ever had a bad day and just rejected everything unread? This doesn't happen often, but even an editor with the best will in the world can have a headache or a hangover and simply not like anything he reads under those conditions.

Suppose the editor does read your story, and reads it on a good day. He can still despise it—but that doesn't mean it's despicable. When all is said and done, editorial reactions to all material, and most especially to fiction, are ultimately subjective. The fact that one person dislikes something does not mean it is bad.

Furthermore, a rejection doesn't have to mean the editor dislikes the story. Maybe it simply means he doesn't like it enough to buy it. Maybe he's over-inventoried on fiction at the moment, and you'd have to knock him out of his chair in order to sell him, and he just doesn't like your story all *that* much. Maybe he just bought a story very much like yours. Maybe your story's about eggs and he got a bad one at breakfast. Maybe—

Well, you get the idea. Bad stories get rejected, but so do most good stories most of the time.

It's important to recognize—and then dismiss—the enormous odds we all face every time we put a story in the mail. I was talking recently to the editor of one of the little literary magazines. He buys three or four stories an issue and publishes four issues a year. So he's in the market for twelve or fifteen stories annually, and how many fiction submissions per year do you suppose he receives?

Four thousand.

The odds would seem overwhelming. On due reflection, the inference you might draw might be that anyone would have to have his head examined to buck those odds. On the other hand, twelve or fifteen people every year do get a story accepted by this publication, and those twelve or fifteen stories have one thing in common.

They all came out of the pile of four thousand.

The more you submit, the more you reduce the odds against eventual publication. But nobody ever sold a story by leaving it in a desk drawer.

Yes? Did you have a question out there?

I agree with what you say, but when one of my stories keeps coming back I get discouraged. I figure they're right and I'm wrong. It's only natural, isn't it?

Of course. Even a seasoned pro finds rejection disheartening, and for a beginner it's that much more of a blow. What you have to do is work on your attitudes so that rejection doesn't lead inevitably to dejection.

The best way I know to manage this is to make your resubmission policy as automatic as you possibly can. Establish a hard and fast rule to get a manuscript back in the mail within twenty-four hours of its receipt. Better yet, send it out immediately—make it the first order of business to get that script off your desk and back in the mail.

One reason not to keep it around is you might read it, and that's a bad idea. You've already read it enough. The addition of a rejection slip isn't going to heighten your enthusiasm. So don't read it. Don't even keep it around long enough to tempt yourself.

Just submit the damn thing forever?

Well, forever's a long time. You can work out your own system, but I'd recommend keeping it constantly at market for a minimum of a year. Then, if you want, read it. Maybe you'll see something you want to change. Maybe you'll decide you hate it altogether. After a year, you can give yourself permission to withdraw it from market—or you can confirm your original judgment and resubmit for another year.

Isn't it a mistake to submit a story to an editor who's already rejected a different story of mine?

No, and why should it be? Remember, you weren't rejected. Your story was rejected. It's not the same thing.

It costs a lot to keep a story in the mail. Don't you reach a point of diminishing returns?

Admittedly, the whole process was less of a wrench when first-class mail cost four cents an ounce. Even so, the high cost of submission isn't all that high. If you ultimately sell the story, you'll come out ahead. If the story proves ultimately unsalable, you'll have spent a few dollars establishing its unsalability. Depending on your current status, you may regard the expense of stamps and envelopes as part of the cost of doing business, an aspect of one's apprenticeship, or the price of a relatively inexpensive hobby.

I don't believe it when someone tells me he stopped submitting a story because of the expense. I think he's simply rationalizing an unwillingness to face further rejection.

You mentioned the long odds we all face. Isn't part of the problem the amount of amateurish tripe every editor has to wade through? It seems to me that people who submit inferior work make it harder for the rest of us. Why don't you say something to discourage them from wasting editors' time?

I received a letter from a Florida writer who made essentially this point. What she failed to realize is that a writer's own perception of a story's salability is no index of anything.

Unquestionably, a great many would-be writers submit inferior work. But I don't think they do so knowing it to be inferior.

Nor is this glut of inferior work a problem for the rest of us. If my story doesn't sell, it's not the inferior stories that have kept it from selling. Quite the opposite. It's the stories that were better than mine that got in my way.

If I were going to be self-seeking, then, I'd try to discourage *good* writers from submitting their work for publication. Of course nothing I might say would be likely to influence their behavior—any more than it would influence those people sending in amateurish efforts.

Back up a few steps. You dismissed the pain of rejection very blithely a few mintues ago. Believe me, it's real pain!

No kidding. Do you think I enjoy it myself?

There are some things you can do, however, to minimize the pain. First of all, you can keep involved in the constant production of new work. By focusing your concentration upon the work itself and making the marketing process as mechanical as possible, you can shrug off rejection more easily.

This leads to the second method of reducing pain. Keep as many things in the mail as possible. That way when a story comes back it's not your entire output that's been rejected but only a very small fraction thereof. By the same token, you'll have so many swallows up in the air that one will be returning to Capistrano every day or so. Oddly, this makes things easier. When rejection becomes a routine fact of life, a virtual daily occurrence, you get used to it.

Ultimately, you may reach the point where you see rejection not as a negation of your worth as a writer, not even as condemnation of a particular story, but as what it is—an inescapable part of the process which ultimately results in acceptance. Don't be too upset, though, if it takes time before you acquire this philosophical detachment in full measure. Until then, just sum up the editor's ancestry and personal habits in a few terse sentences—and get your manuscript back in the mail.

CHAPTER **10**

Bic, Scripto, Parker and Cross

"So you're a writer," they say, time and time again. "That must be very interesting."

Must it? My work, such as it is, consists of sitting alone at a typewriter and tapping fitfully at its keys. It has occurred to me that the only distinction between what I do and what a stenographer does lies in my having to invent what I type.

If I say as much, it's generally assumed that I'm joshing, whereupon my questioner will very likely chuckle. Should another question seem called for, he'll ask where I get my ideas, or if I've had anything published.

Or he may ask what name I write under.

I've written under any number of things in my life. Low ceilings. Hanging plants. Threats of exposure. Duress. I have also written under a whole host of aliases at one time or another. In recent years, however, I have written solely under my own name, but if I say as much to my interlocutor I'm going to put him off-stride; he'll feel he's committed a *faux pas,* having assumed I use a pen name since he's so clearly unfamiliar with my own. And I'll only make things worse by obligingly trotting out some pen name I used in the past, for it surely will be equally unfamiliar to him.

"Norman Mailer," I'll say. Or Erica Jong. Or both of them, if the mood strikes me. It may be my doing that any number of people are walking around today, secure in the knowledge that Norman Mailer is a pen name of Erica Jong's, and for all I know they may be right. Did you ever see those two at the same time?

But let's shift gears before all of this cuteness gets irretrievably out of control. Pen names, to judge from my mail, are a subject of at least passing concern to many of my readers. I had a letter just the other day from a woman intent upon keeping her true identity a secret not only from her readers but from her prospective publisher as well, and wanting to know how she could do all this without getting into a tangle with the tax authorities. I assume she has her reasons.

But just what *are* the reasons for writing under a name other than one's own? Surely the ego gratification of seeing one's name in print is a powerful motivator for most of us. Why should we pass up that satisfaction for the dubious pleasure of seeing our words attributed to Helena Troy or Justin Thyme or some other appropriately altered ego?

At the present time, I'm a fairly strong believer in writing under one's own name. It has taken me over twenty years and the occasional use of at least that many pseudonyms to arrive at that conclusion. Before I explain my position, perhaps we can examine some of the reasons why a pen name can be useful.

1. THE AUTHOR'S OWN NAME IS UNSUITABLE. A writer's name can be a liability for any of several reasons. It may be too similar to that of an established writer. Journalist Tom Wolfe is evidently willing to chance confusion with the late novelist Thomas Wolfe, and there are several John Gardners and Charles Williamses who write for a living, but why tempt fate?

A pen name may be indicated if one's own name is unpronounceable or somehow ridiculous. Remember, though, that nomenclatural absurdity is largely subjective; consider the pop singer who rose to fame after changing his own inoffensive name to Engelbert Humperdinck.

Sometimes a lackluster name clamors to be changed. Martin Smith published several mysteries under his own name, and while the books were excellent nobody could remember who he was. (The situation was compounded by the fact that his friends all call him Bill.) In the course of time, Smith's agent dubbed him Martin Cruz Smith, interposing the author's mother's maiden name, and his first book under that name, *Nightwing,* soared on to bestsellerdom. Perhaps it would have done so regardless, but the added Cruz certainly didn't hurt.

2. THE AUTHOR HAS A SPECIFIC REASON TO AVOID RECOGNITION. I know at least one writer who uses a pen name solely to shield his identity from his ex-wife. If she knew he was publishing novels, she'd almost certainly peti-

tion for an increase in alimony, and she'd very likely get it. By using a pen name, this author gets to keep his literary earnings.

Of course he still pays taxes on them, and lists them on his tax return. To do otherwise would be to risk a jail term for tax evasion.

3.   THE AUTHOR IS WRITING DIFFERENT TYPES OF BOOKS. This is a standard argument for employing a pen name. Suppose you're writing juveniles for one publisher, shoot-'em-up thrillers for another. Won't your readers be upset to learn that the same person's writing gory stuff on one typewriter and sweet verses about bunny rabbits on the other? Won't you be better off doing the juveniles as Hillary Everbright, the rough stuff as Studd Bludgeon?

I'm not sure it matters. Most readers won't even notice what you're doing in fields they themselves don't read, and won't hold it against you if they do. But this maintenance of different literary identities for different kinds of writing is a time-honored principle.

4.   THE AUTHOR IS TOO PROLIFIC. Some writers use several names because they publish several books a year. They feel that neither the bookselling industry nor the reading public will take them seriously if all these books are identifiable as the produce of a single writer.

I don't know how valid this is. On the one hand, I've seen reviewers take a shot at "this latest potboiler cranked out in nothing flat by Writer X." On the other, over the long run your books help each other. Fans want to read everything you've written, and have an easier time of it if they know what to look for. I don't think Isaac Asimov is hurt by having published so many books of so many different sorts, all under his own name. Yet I could name other writers who have lost credibility with critics in this fashion.

5.   THE AUTHOR WANTS TO LOOK LIKE AN EXPERT. Years ago, I wrote a series of books that purported to be case histories of various anonymous souls. The subjects of these case histories were indeed rather more than anonymous. They were fictional, made up out of the whole cloth, with their sexual histories displayed for the reader's education and/or titillation. I used a pen name on these books—you bet your bippy I used a pen name—and the pen name had an M.D. (In this particular instance, the publisher knew the name was a phony but thought the author was a legitimate physician operating under an alias. Ah, what a tangled web . . .)

It is quite lawful, I was told, to use a doctor's pen name so long as one does not usurp the prerogatives of a doctor. Since I neither diagnosed nor prescribed, I was presumably within my rights. As far as the ethics of all of this may have been concerned, I'm not sure there's any good sense in imposing questions of ethics upon a profession which has muddled along for centuries without any.

More recently, I used a female pen name on a novel written from a woman's point of view, thinking that the book would be better received for my doing so. I don't think I would take this particular position now.

6. THE AUTHOR IS NOT PROUD OF WHAT HE HAS WRITTEN. Here, finally, is the strongest single reason for using a false name. When one is well aware that one is publishing trash, one can salvage at least a modicum of self-respect by refraining from publishing it under one's own name.

An objection comes quickly to mind. If it's tripe, why publish it at all? Why not limit oneself to the publication of work one is proud to see printed under one's own name?

This is a good argument, logically unassailable, but I don't know that it is too closely grounded in reality. This is no easy business for the neophyte, and to publish anything, trash or treasure, is very much an accomplishment. The beginning writer must make it his first priority simply to write and get paid for it. In the greater majority of cases, he cannot expect to be doing so at the top of his form. Someday he may write first-rate work for first-rate markets, but that may take a while.

In the meantime, he may write and publish a lot of lesser work. He may not be actively ashamed of this work, may indeed take a professional's pride in it, but may still recognize it as unworthy. Why shouldn't he reserve his own name for work of which he is altogether unashamed?

There's a thin line here. A person's reach does exceed his grasp, after all, and if you wait for perfection you'll wait forever, publishing your entire life's work under one pseudonym or another. Similarly, there are books I liked well enough when I wrote them but regard as inferior work now; ought I to regret having published them under my own name? I do not regret having done so, any more than I regret being a better writer now than I was twenty years ago.

As I started to say earlier, I've come grudgingly to the position that a pen name ought not to be used unless it seems necessary. I am able to see now that I used pen names as a way to avoid taking responsibility for my own work, not in the eyes of others as much as in my own.

By the same token, I got a kick out of the element of deception that is inherent in pseudonymous writing. Pen names provided me with a vehicle for escaping the prison of self. The lure of a false identity always appealed to me, and there was a time when I traveled around the country under a pen name, acting out in a rather bizarre fashion. I had two of my pen names carrying on an affair, dedicating books to one another. It was all a touch schizoid, now that I think back on it.

I don't know that I would go so far as to say I regret it. Pen names hurt me professionally in two ways that I can think of. They diluted my efforts and thus kept me from building a following as quickly as I might have, and they allowed me to spend more time writing recognizably inferior work than I might otherwise have done. All the same, the freedom of a pen name may have constituted a liberating influence at the time; perhaps, knowing I intended to publish everything under my own name, I'd have tightened up and written nothing at all.

Should *you* use a pen name? I wouldn't presume to advise you. Your own circumstances, like everyone else's, are special. The choice must be entirely your own.

CHAPTER **11**

Writing With Two Heads

COLLABORATION ALWAYS *seems* like such a good idea. Two heads, after all, are purported to be superior to one, especially if they're attached to two different bodies. Why shouldn't a piece of writing go faster and more smoothly if two minds conceive it and two pairs of hands commit it to paper? Nobody's perfect, and if one combines one's talents with another writer, perhaps the match will be complementary, with each making up for the other's deficiencies. With luck, the union may even prove synergistic, with the collaborative persona of two writers yoked in harness greater than the sum of their separate abilities. Where, after all, would Beaumont be without Fletcher? Gilbert without Sullivan? Abbott without Costello? Jekyll without Hyde? Leopold without Loeb?

Ahem. By collaboration I mean those joint ventures wherein two writers work together. This might well seem obvious, but for the fact that the opportunity for collaboration most frequently presented to us is something rather different. Typically, we are offered this sort of chance by a bore at a cocktail party.

"You know, we ought to get together," a chap will say upon learning my occupation. "I got some stories you wouldn't believe. My problem is I have tons of ideas but I'm not a writer; I can't put them on paper. So what we'll do is I'll give you the ideas and you'll do the writing and we'll split the money. How's that?"

"Suppose we switch roles?" I'm apt to say, particularly in the party's later stages. "Suppose I give you *my* ideas, and *you* do the writing. And *then* we'll split the money."

Whoever's ideas we use, I'm not inclined to call this sort of literary partnership collaboration. It's a good deal closer to what the non-fictioneer calls ghostwriting. And on occasion it's exactly that.

I know of one instance, for example, in which it was decided that what this country most needed was a novel of political intrigue by a muckraking Washington columnist, since deceased. Unfortunately the man in question was either unequipped or disinclined to write such a novel. He was, however, quite willing to see his name below the title, so a competent novelist was quickly found to handle the actual chore of hatching a plot, dreaming up characters, and tapping out a few hundred pages of unexceptional prose and dialogue. The columnist's contribution, in addition to the use of his name, consisted presumably in his sharing some inside poop with the writer and reading the final manuscript to make sure its reflection of the Washington scene contained no obvious clinkers.

In this case the book sold reasonably well, so none of the parties concerned had reason to complain of the financial result. Still, the process was substantially less collaborative than the ghosting of a movie star's autobiography, in which case the star at least provides the story and a working version of the facts. It was certainly not a matter of the work being shared by the two principals of the arrangement.

Such genuine collaboration seems to work out much more often for playwrights than it does for prose writers. I'm not certain why this should be true, but it may well be that theatrical writing, even when one man does all of it, is apt to have a collective aspect to it. One takes it almost for granted that rewriting will play a substantial role in the process of readying the play for production, and that any number of persons will offer input in this direction. Producers and directors will suggest changes. Actors will propose improved versions of their lines. Finally, the process of actually performing the play, first in a bare theater and then before an audience, will indicate where changes must be made if the play is to succeed.

Thus there's a long record of theatrical collaboration. This seems to be particularly true with comedy, and there are some comedic playwrights who can't seem to work effectively by themselves, George S. Kaufman having been perhaps the most obvious example.

Bill Hoffman, a playwright friend of mine, spent three years collaborating with another playwright and found the process quite successful. "One of us would sit at the typewriter and we batted each line around before it got written. The process seems to stimulate both of us. Our abilities complemented one another to a certain extent; he was a little better at storyline development and I was probably a little better at actual dialogue, but by the time something was actually written down it was impossible to say who had contributed what. Everything amounted to a joint effort."

I know two women who write novels in this fashion, Barbara Miller and Valerie Greco. One of them sits at the typewriter, the other stands alongside, and they discuss and come to agreement on every sentence before it gets typed. Curiously, I find this perfectly comprehensible as a means of producing work for stage or screen, and the image of a pair of sitcom writers swigging coffee and tossing gags back and forth strikes me as quite the way that sort of thing ought to be done. Yet I simply cannot imagine writing a short story—or, God help us, a whole novel—in this fashion.

There are, however, any number of other ways for fiction writers to share the work. A few years back Donald E. Westlake and Brian Garfield decided to collaborate on a book called *Gangway!*, a comic thriller (Westlake's forte) set in the Old West (Garfield's milieu).

Here's Westlake's description of the process: "First we sat down and discussed the whole thing at length. Then I wrote a fifteen-page outline of what we had discussed. I gave this to Brian, and he expanded it to forty pages, putting in all the historical context and everything. Then he gave it back to me and I cut it back down to twenty-five pages. At this point we were thinking screenplay, and this version was shown around as a treatment. When it didn't fly, we decided to do it as a novel first.

"I wrote the first draft, limiting myself to action and dialogue—not where they were or what they were wearing, just what they did and said. My draft ran about thirty thousand words. I gave it to Brian and he doubled it, turning each of my pages into two pages, putting in all the background and such. Then he gave me his sixty-thousand-word version and I edited it, and I gave it back to him and *he* edited it, and then we gave the whole mess to an editor."

"It sounds," I ventured, "like five times as much work as sitting down and writing a book."

"Yes," he agreed, "and about a quarter as much fun, and for half the money."

Two writers I know collaborate frequently on short stories, discussing a plot at length before one of them sits down and writes it. Since they live three thousand miles apart, one or the other of them does the actual writing unassisted. Even so, the leading profitmaker on many of their joint ventures is Ma Bell.

Years ago, I wrote some novels in collaboration, including three with Don Westlake and one with Hal Dresner, who has since gone on to write screenplays. At that time we were all earning a curious living writing soft-core sex novels, a medium that lent itself tolerably well to the collaborative process.

These collaborations could hardly have been simpler. There was no prior discussion of plot, no careful development of outline. One of us sat down and wrote a first chapter and gave it to the other, who wrote a second chapter and gave it back. The book loped along in this fashion until ten chapters had been written and it had come, as all things do, to an end.

It was all great fun. Don and I tended to leave one another with impossible cliff-hangers, killing off one another's chief characters at will. Hal and I devised a *La Ronde* form that made sex-novel collaboration almost effortless—i.e., the viewpoint character in the first chapter had, uh, a carnal connection with someone, who went on to become the viewpoint character in the second chapter, wherein he or she got it on with the person destined to star in Chapter 3. And so on.

These collaborative experiments led in due course to the ultimate *reductio ad absurdum,* the Great Sex Novel Poker Game. This ill-advised venture consisted of half a dozen of us, all writers of this sort of trash and all fond at the time of nightlong poker sessions. Operating on the premise that any of us could produce a chapter in an hour or so, we met for a night of poker during which five of us sat around the table while one of us at a time went upstairs and wrote fifteen or twenty pages of The Book. By the time the night was done—or the following day, or whatever—we would each have contributed two chapters, the book would be finished, and a division of the spoils would make us all winners, even those of us who had proved unlucky at cards.

This well-laid plan went speedily agley. After five more or less successful chapters, one of our number, his brain an object-lesson in the folly of amphetamine abuse, wrote his two chapters back to back and went home. Unfortunately, his contribution turned out to be absolute gibberish, and the writer who followed him, instead of proclaiming as much, spent hours trying to write a sensible sequel to it all. The book, in short, did not turn out well. I don't remember how I did at the card table.

Since then, I've used collaboration—or the prospect of collaboration—largely as a means of avoiding work. If there's something I really want to write, I'll probably sooner or later sit down and write it. If, on the other hand, there's something I recognize as a good idea but don't really want to mess with, I can propose it as a subject for collaboration, secure in the knowledge that I'll never have to have anything further to do with it.

"We ought to collaborate on this," a friend and I will agree, and then we'll spend a jolly hour tossing ideas to and fro, and that'll be the end of it. Because we'll each keep having other things to do, yet neither of us will feel at all guilty, because it's something we can always get around to eventually, whenever we both happen to be between books at the same time, and in the mood to collaborate, and like that.

A case in point occurred a few years ago, when I came up with an excellent if incompletely formed idea for a book involving global intrigue during World War II. It wasn't really my kind of book, yet there was a lot of strength in the basic idea, so I talked about it with Brian Garfield and proposed it as a subject for collaboration. Brian happily agreed, and we discussed it some, and that was the end of that.

Except, of course, that it wasn't. Some years later I got a handle on another element of the plot, which made it an even stronger notion, though still not really my kind of thing. I talked it over with Brian and decided to go ahead with it alone, since as a collaboration it would never have gotten written. This way it did get written, but it turned out that it really and truly was not my kind of book, and what I wrote wasn't terribly good.

At which point it turned back into a collaboration, in this case with yet another writer, Harold King. This *was* his kind of book, and he liked a lot of what he saw in my first draft and had excellent ideas of his own to bring to bear upon it, so we talked it over and he went to work on the book. And it should finally make its appearance in the stores sometime during the fall or winter.

Finally, another project in which I'm currently engaged was done collaboratively not as a way of avoiding work but to avoid avoiding it. I'd been entertaining the idea of a guidebook to vegetarian and natural food restaurants for a while, but I doubt I'd have got anywhere with it if Cheryl Morrison and I had not entered into collaboration upon it. The problem with this book was that it would require little bits of work here and there over the course of a great many months. Because I would always have a primary project on the table, the guidebook would have been lost in the shuffle. And the same thing would have happened if Cheryl had undertaken the whole project herself.

As it stands, each of us feels an obligation to the other. Thus the work gets shared, and, a little at a time, it's getting done, largely because neither of us is prepared to let the other down.

I haven't tried to tell you *how* to collaborate. Indeed, on balance I'd probably advise you against trying it altogether, unless you really and truly feel you'll write more effectively as someone's partner. There have been any number of viable partnerships—Fern Michaels, Wade Miller, Manning Coles, Ellery Queen, Burdick and Lederer—but most of the time the desire to collaborate stems from the hope of making the process of fictional creation less lonely, and most of the time that just doesn't seem to be possible. The Concerto for Four Hands and Two Typewriters has its appeal, but for most of us writing is probably destined to remain a solitary occupation. Like dying, it seems to be something we have to do on our own.

CHAPTER **12**

It Takes More Than Talent

IT CONTINUES to astonish me what a widespread and enduring fantasy Being a Writer is for the population at large. It's a rare day when I don't encounter some misguided chap who expresses the desire to trade places with me. And it's on those not-so-rare days when everything goes wrong, when the words won't come but the rejections fly thick and fast, when the bank account's gone dry again and editors don't even bother lying about the check's being in the mail, that otherwise sane folks tell me how much they envy me.

"I wish I had your self-discipline," they'll say, generally saying so on a day when I've got the backbone of a threadworm. "I envy you the imagination to keep coming up with ideas." Or they may envy me my education, which was an unremarkable one, or they'll say they wish they knew my formula for writing success, as though I had somehow unearthed an alchemist's secret for transmuting the dross of nouns and verbs into the shimmering gold of fiction.

Nobody ever says, "I wish I had your talent."

And I find that fascinating. I don't think artists in other media get the same response. I doubt somehow that people kept grabbing Picasso by the shoulder and telling him how they envied his self-discipline, standing in front of the easel day after day. I don't suppose Caruso had to listen to that kind of crap, either. Actors and singers in particular seem to be plagued by people who think talent is all there is to it, that they've been given a gift which allows them to stand up there in front of the microphone and show their stuff. The hours of training and practice, the essential will and tenacity, are somehow discounted.

With writing, it's the talent that's apt to be discounted. There are times when I tend to resent this. The unspoken premise in "I wish I had your self-discipline" is that anyone with my self-discipline could do what I do, that a persistent chimpanzee could match me book for book if he could just sit still long enough and work the space bar with his non-opposable thumb. My ego doesn't much like to hear this sort of thing.

And yet I have to admit that there are times when I think these people are onto something. It strikes me now and then that talent may be one of the least important variables in the writing business. People without a super-abundance of talent succeed anyhow. People with tons of talent never get anywhere. It happens all the time.

And it happens, I guess, in every field of creative endeavor. For years I subscribed to the popular myth that talent will out sooner or later, that all people with genuine ability in a particular field will ultimately achieve success in that field. I'll tell you, you'd be better off believing in the tooth fairy. All over America there are singers and actors and painters and composers and sculptors and, yes, writers, blessed with a sufficiency of talent but born, as Thomas G. would put it, to blush unseen, and waste their sweetness on the desert air.

If talent's not the answer, what else does it take? Why do some of us succeed while others do not? Is it just a matter of luck?

I'll tell you this much. Luck doesn't hurt. And simple luck has a great deal to do with the fate of an individual submission. When you mail off a story to a magazine, elements that have nothing whatsoever to do with the quality of that story will play a part in determining whether or not it sells. The editor's mood when he reads it is a factor, and one you have no way of controlling.

The state of the magazine's inventory is another. Competition being what it is, I'd go so far as to say that every time you manage to sell an unsolicited submission to a magazine, you've been lucky.

But I also think that luck tends to average out over a period of time. The writer who sells his first story to the first editor who sees it is a lucky writer indeed, but that first sale provides no guarantee of a second sale. Luck runs hot and cold, and nobody's lucky all the time.

What does it take, then, to be successful at free-lance writing? What, besides talent and luck, helps determine who makes it and who doesn't?

It seems to me that will is enormously important. There are any number of jobs a person can pretty much fall into, but I don't believe writing is one of them. Every once in a while somebody does become a writer apparently by accident, but such persons rarely remain writers for very long. In order to get into this business and in order to stay in it, you generally have to desire it with a passion bordering on desperation.

And the intensity of that desire doesn't seem to have anything to do with talent. A couple of summers ago I taught a seven-day seminar at Antioch College. One of my students was head and shoulders above the others. She was a middle-aged woman who had spent all her life on a farm, raising children and helping her husband with the farmwork, and she had as good an eye and ear for rural settings as I've yet encountered. Her prose was clear and clean, her dialogue was excellent, and her stories and sketches absolutely sparkled. It was immediately evident to me that she was the one person in the seminar who had more than enough ability to succeed as a professional writer.

She also had something to write about. She knew that she wanted to write fiction that derived from what she knew—life in the rural midwest. Some of us know that we want to be writers without having the faintest idea what we shall write about—I was certainly in that category—but this woman had no problems on that score.

What she did want was reassurance. Could I assure her that her prospects were good? Could I tell her it was not unrealistic to hope to make sales writing the sort of stories she had in mind? Because if such expectations were unwarranted, she explained, then she didn't want to go on wasting her time writing.

I spent quite a bit of time telling her how good she was, but even as I did so I wondered if perhaps *I* was wasting *my* time. Oh, she had the talent, all right. And there were any number of ways in which she could ultimately exploit her background and turn it into successful and commercially viable fiction. But her question suggested to me that she would never achieve her goal because she didn't want it badly enough.

Because for almost everyone the road to writing success goes through some very rocky territory indeed. If she was that worried in advance that the time she spent writing might turn out to have been wasted, how could one expect her to rise above the inevitable rejections and disappointments that just plain come with the territory?

Perhaps I should not even have encouraged her. There's an old story about a young man who cornered a world-famous violinist and begged to be allowed to play for him. If the master offered him encouragement, he would devote his life to music. But if his talent was not equal to his calling, he wanted to know ahead of time so he could avoid wasting his life. He played, and the great violinist shook his head. "You lack the fire," he said.

Decades later the two met again, and the would-be violinist, now a prosperous businessman, recalled their previous meeting. "You changed my entire life," he explained. "It was a bitter disappointment, giving up music, but I forced myself to accept your judgment. Thus, instead of becoming a fourth-rate musician, I've had a good life in the world of commerce. But tell me, how could you tell so readily that I lacked the fire?"

"Oh, I hardly listened when you played," the old master said. "That's what I tell everyone who plays for me—that they lack the fire."

"But that's unforgivable!" the businessman cried. "How could you do that? You altered the entire course of my life. Perhaps I could have been another Kreisler, another Heifetz—"

The old man shook his head again. "You don't understand," he said. "If you had had the fire, you would have paid no attention to me."

Perhaps my student had the fire. I've had no contact with her since that seminar, so I can't say whether or not she has continued to write, or if she's had any success with it. But it wouldn't surprise me to learn that she's given up. Not everyone has the will. Not everyone cares that much about writing stories and getting them published.

Will is every bit as important for those of us who have a taste of success. Several years ago a woman of my acquaintance decided to try her hand at writing. She showed me a couple of chapters of an erotic novel she'd written and I was immediately impressed by her ability. She was a natural stylist, readily able to assume the general style of any literary genre. While she tended to minimize this talent, insisting it was simple mimicry, that's what stylistic ability generally consists of at the outset of one's career.

She abandoned the erotic novel, finding it an uncomfortable genre, and took the time to read half a dozen gothics. Then, in rather rapid succession, she wrote and sold two gothics. After that she wrote a hundred or so pages of an unsuccessful mystery novel, and after that she didn't write a thing.

  She had the talent, and she had enough success to make it clear that a career as a free-lance writer was available to her. She had, too, enough drive and self-discipline to produce those two books and get them published. But, ultimately, being a writer was just not that important to her. She had drifted into it largely as a result of association with other writers, and she drifted out of it when it proved insufficiently rewarding.

  I suspect my friend has something in common with the phenomenon of one-book authors. The common wisdom holds that such writers have only one book in them, that having gotten it out of their systems they have nothing further to say. I think it might be more accurate to say that they have a very strong desire to write a particular book but no real desire to become a writer per se. Having written that book, they have slaked their hunger.

  Fair enough. Some people climb one mountain and complete one marathon and let it go at that. Others define themselves as mountain climbers or marathoners and go on climbing or running as long as they have breath in their bodies.

  And some of us go on writing.

  I have a feeling that the tendency to perceive onself as a writer is a somewhat different matter from simple will. I think, too, that it plays a big part in determining who makes it as a writer and who does not. In my own case, I decided (or recognized; it may have been more a matter of recognition than decision) that I was going to be a writer when I was in the eleventh grade. A teacher's offhand remark put the idea in my head, but once planted it grew like a weed. I had no idea how I would go about becoming a writer or what I would write about, but I somehow knew it was what I was going to do.

  I am quite certain that this self-definition had a lot to do with the development of my career. I submitted my earliest efforts to magazines, and while they came back like bad pennies, and with better cause, I took this in stride. The day came when an editor suggested a rewrite, and then another day came when he bought the story.

  That was not the end of rejection and disappointment. Sometimes it seems more like the beginning, and the end is not yet in sight. But throughout it all I have never been able to shake that perception of myself as a writer. It has kept me chained to this bloody desk for more years than I care to number, and it has made it impossible for me seriously to entertain the idea of doing anything else for very long.

  That recognition of self as a writer can happen at any age. Consider another friend of mine, who awoke eight or nine years ago to the idea of becoming a writer. He was at the time editing a scientific trade journal for little money and less glory, and he had lately become friendly with several of us who wrote fiction for a living. One weekend he realized two things—that he wanted the sort of life we were leading, and that such a life was attainable.

Monday morning he called in sick and rolled a sheet of paper into his typewriter. By the time his wife got home from her job he had eight or ten pages of a novel written. He called in sick Tuesday and did another chunk of the book. Same thing Wednesday.

Thursday he got up bright and early, ate as hearty a breakfast as the next condemned man, and went to his office. A couple of hours later my phone rang. "I just quit my job," he said. "The book's coming along nicely and I want to stay with it."

I don't remember what I said. Probably something along the lines of yeah-but-how-are-you-gonna-make-a-living?

"No problem," he said. "I'm a writer now."

I wasn't convinced of the truth of either of those sentences, but even so I figured his downside risk was limited. After all, his wife was working, they didn't have any kids, their basic overhead was low and the job he'd quit hadn't been such a much. After a little token breastbeating at having encouraged him to persist in his folly, I gave a shrug that would have gladdened a Frenchman's heart and went on about my business, such as it was.

Couple of weeks later he presented me with something like two hundred fifty pages of manuscript. Would I be so kind? Ahem. I took it home. I sat down with it. I started to read.

Page for page and line for line, his book was as bad a piece of writing as I've ever been confronted with, and that covers a lot of ground. It was not publishable, but that's the least of it. It was not rewritable, either, nor was it readable. Nor, alas, could it have been described as promising. There was nothing promising about it. No one could in good conscience read that manuscript and encourage its author to try writing anything more ambitious than a laundry list.

I was aghast. My friend had quit a job to produce this? Well, he'd better get another in a hurry. Assuming he could find someone fool enough to hire him.

I didn't have the guts to say any of this. Instead I passed the buck—and the manuscript with it—to my agent. When his judgment echoed mine we tried to figure out what to tell the author. We decided to stall, and while we did so my friend told me he was halfway through Novel Number Two.

The second book was much better. It was still nothing you'd be tempted to call good, but it was written in a language readily identifiable as English. My friend finished it, gave it to me and then to my agent, and went on to the third book.

The second book didn't sell. The third did, though, and the fourth and fifth. They were not wildly successful. They were published as hardcover mysteries, had reasonably positive reviews and mediocre sales, and did not go into paperback. One got nominated for an award but failed to win.

The story could stop right there and it wouldn't be the worst story ever told, either. But there's more. My friend went on to write several more mysteries, and these did not sell. There was a market slump about that time, and hardcover mysteries were suddenly about as much in demand as legionnaire's disease. My friend wrote three or four in a row and couldn't get arrested.

By this time he was single again, and broke. He took a job tending bar and wrote days. After a while he quit writing mysteries that nobody wanted and began doing the preliminary research for a large-scale adventure novel that would capitalize on his interests and areas of expertise. He spent a lot of time on research and more on plot development, and then he went on to spend a great deal more time writing and rewriting. Then the book came out, had a six-figure paperback sale and a six-figure movie sale, touched one or two of the bestseller lists briefly, and must have earned him something like—what? Half a million? I don't know, and it's not really important, because this chapter isn't about money. It's about writing, and the set of mind necessary to make a go of it.

At first glance, the story's point seems obvious enough. My friend had the will to succeed, the drive to keep going in the face of discouragement and rejection. He had, too, a perception of himself as a writer that refused to fade. In addition, he had a single-mindedness of purpose that enabled him to take chances. Quitting his job on the basis of a few days' production was probably ill-advised, and I certainly would not recommend it to anyone in a similar situation, but perhaps it was essential for him. Suppose he'd worked nights and weekends on that first book, taking a year or so to produce an unsalable manuscript. Would he have been as quick to plunge in again and write books two and three?

When, after having sold several books, he found himself incapable of supporting himself by writing, he might have tried to find a job rather like the one he had left. Instead he deliberately sought out a subsistence job, undemanding parttime work that let him pay the rent while he went on writing. Again, he was taking a chance instead of playing it safe.

It's worth noting, though, that the chances he took were sane ones. If he was walking a tightrope, he was not doing so without a net. If he'd failed at the beginning, the worst thing that could have happened is that he'd have had to find another job. If his big adventure novel had failed, he'd have had to go on tending bar, or look for something with more long-range promise. But no one was going to starve to death because he wanted to be a writer.

This talk of starving puts me in mind of another attitude that's important if one is to be comfortable as a free-lance writer. You have to have a pretty high threshold for financial insecurity. If a regular paycheck is emotionally essential to you, perhaps you'd be well advised to stay with a regular job.

I was very fortunate in this respect. I started writing so early in life that my ordinary expenses were extremely low. The last job I held before taking up writing fulltime was in a literary agency, where my base pay was sixty dollars a week before taxes. That doesn't sound like much money now, and it wasn't much money then, either.

My low standard of living made the small sums of money I could earn writing more significant than they'd have been otherwise. If I went home from the office and wrote a three-thousand-word pulp story and sold it for a cent a word, that was half a week's income right there. And, once I'd left the job, I didn't have to hit the bestseller list in order to match my previous income. Before very long I had a standing assignment writing a book a month for a paperback publisher. The pay was six hundred dollars a book, which was more than double what my salary had been.

All of this was helpful early on. As I grew older and acquired a wife and children and a higher standard of living, what helped keep me from going crazy was a temperament which took financial insecurity for granted. This is not to say that I find poverty a treat, or that I am not aggravated by slow-pay publishers and inconvenienced by the stretches of financial hardship that seem to be an inescapable part of the writing life. Sometimes a pile of bills and dunning letters can have a paralyzing effect on just about anyone. But most of the time my writing goes on independent of my solvency or lack thereof.

This is true of most of the people I know who function successfully as free-lance writers. But not everyone is so constituted. I know a number of established professional writers who simply lack the temperament required for fulltime free-lancing. They continue to hold forty-hour-a-week jobs, jobs which they often profess to hate, simply because they are not comfortable without the security of a regular paycheck. In several cases, there's no question but that they could earn more if they gave up their jobs. And they know this, but some of them have found out fulltime self-employment cuts their writing production to the bone because they can't work effectively when burdened with all that anxiety.

It has always seemed to me, on the other hand, that writing is infinitely more secure than any employment could hope to be. All my friends who hold jobs could conceivably be fired. Who can fire me? Even a tenured college professor could one day see his college go out of business, and then where would he be? I, meanwhile, can go on writing for a variety of publishers, adapting to changes in the marketplace, and all without a care for compulsory retirement rules or other abominations.

Of course I can't look forward to a pension, and I have to pay my own medical insurance, and I don't get any fringe benefits or sick leave or paid vacations. Nor am I guaranteed a day's pay just by showing up for work in the morning; if I don't produce anything, neither do I earn anything. I can generally accept all that. But not everybody can.

There's another essential quality in the writer's temperament, and it seems on the surface so obvious that I came close to overlooking it altogether. Quite simply, you have to like the work.

By this I don't mean that the physical act of sitting at a typewriter has to be enjoyable in and of itself. Most writers hate the process, to one extent or another, and everybody hates it now and then. (This is an anomaly of writing, and an interesting one at that. Most of the painters I know enjoy the act of painting, and almost every musician I've known loves to play so much that he goes on doing it after his day's work is done. But writers often hate writing.)

What a writer must enjoy, or at least be able to tolerate, is the utterly solitary nature of the work. When all is said and done, writing is a matter of sitting alone at a desk, staring more often than not at a blank wall, and turning thoughts into words and putting the words on paper.

I know a man who free-lanced for a while some years ago. He started off working at home, then rented a hotel room so he would have an office to go to. That structured his days somewhat, but it didn't really help because he couldn't take the solitude. He gave up the hotel room and rented space in an office so that there would be other people working around him. He enjoyed that more but it cut into his productivity because he preferred interacting with the other people to concentrating on his own work. He stopped free-lancing and got a job, and he's been gainfully employed ever since. He's published books now and then, writing them at night and on weekends, and periodically he tells me how much he hates his job and how he longs to quit it and write fulltime, but that's nonsense. He'd go nuts without a job to go to.

Even if you're the sort who finds solitude comfortable, I think it's very important for writers to make sure they have sufficient human contact when they're not working to compensate for the lack thereof during their working hours. We can't be alone all the time, nor can we expect our families to fill our needs in this area. The isolated writer loses touch with the world. He forgets what people are like. He uses up his writing source material and fails to replenish it.

In my own case, I've found that I need the occasional company of other writers. There are things about writing which people who are not in the business simply cannot share. The company of my fellows is stimulating. There's a certain amount of cross-pollination in such social intercourse, and a few hours in another writer's company serve to reinforce my own perception of myself as a writer.

At the same time, I definitely require the company of people who are *not* writers. An exclusive diet of shop talk is an unbalanced one. Besides, one wants to be occasionally exposed to reality, if only in small doses. As a friend of mine, herself a writer, says, "People who spend the most meaningful hours of their lives in the exclusive company of imaginary people are apt to be a little strange."

And that's the final requisite of the writer's temperament. We're every last one of us a little strange, a wee bit different.

And *vive la difference.*

PART TWO

Nose to the Grindstone, Shoulder to the Wheel:

Fiction as a Discipline

CHAPTER 13

Writer's Hours

I'VE FOUND over the years that the mechanics of writing appear to be endlessly fascinating to writers and non-writers alike. Perhaps because the creative process is so utterly incomprehensible, even to those of us who are personally involved in it, it is easier for us to focus on more tangible aspects of writing. Do we write in the morning or at night? At the typewriter or in pencil—or with a crayon, for those of us who are not allowed to use anything sharp? Do we outline in advance or plot things out as we go along?

Somewhere in the course of this sort of conversation, one is apt to be asked just how many hours a day he tends to put in. The answer, whether it's two or twelve hours a day, is apt to be followed by a qualification. "Of course that's just time spent actually writing. Of course that doesn't include the time I devote to research. Of course, when you come right down to it, a writer is working from the instant the alarm clock goes off to the moment when he goes to bed. For that matter, the process doesn't stop when I'm asleep. The old subconscious mind takes over then and sifts things around and sets the stage for the next day's work. So I guess it's safe to say that I actually practice my craft twenty-four hours a day, seven days a week."

I suppose most of us deliver some variation of that speech at some time or other, and I suppose some of the time we even believe it. A certain part of me, however, does not buy this load of pap for a minute. As far as that stern writer's conscience of mine is concerned, I'm only really working if I'm sitting at my desk tapping my typewriter keys and turning out pages of finished copy. Thinking about writing isn't work, and research isn't work, and reading proof isn't work, and meeting with publishers isn't work, and talking on the phone isn't work, and not even rewriting and editing are work. Unless I can actually see a manuscript of mine getting further from the beginning and closer to the end because of what I'm doing, I'm not entirely capable of regarding the task I'm performing as work.

Understand, please, that I *know* better. I realize intellectually that the non-writing chores I've enumerated above are directly related to my profession, that they take time and energy, that I can't slight them without adversely affecting the quality and/or quantity of my writing. But this knowledge doesn't seem to help me much. Unless I've put in my daily stint at the typewriter, and unless I've got something to show for it, I feel as though I've played hookey.

This attitude probably serves a purpose. My mind is sufficiently fertile that I can almost always dream up some worthwhile occupation which will keep me away from my desk. There's always a book it would pay me to read, a neighborhood I could profitably explore, a person whose expertise I should seek. None of these extramural activities is as hard as actually sitting down and writing something; thus, but for the conscience that hounds me, I could happily go months on end without wearing out a typewriter ribbon.

Sometimes, though, I find myself backed into a corner, locked into a no-win situation, damned if I do and damned if I don't. This happened quite vividly when I was working on *The Burglar Who Liked to Quote Kipling*. Bernie Rhodenbarr, the burglar of the title, had just hied himself off to Forest Hill Gardens, an upper-middle-class enclave in the borough of Queens. It occurred to me that I had not been to Forest Hill Gardens in over twenty years, at which time I had visited it very briefly. I had only dim memories of the neighborhood and had no way of knowing if it had changed in the intervening years.

I had two choices. I could trust my memory while taking comfort in the fact that every work of fiction takes place in its own alternate universe anyway. Or I could spend an afternoon zipping out there on the F train and walking aimlessly around to see what I could see.

Either way I was determined to feel guilty about it. If I stayed home and worked, I'd beat myself up for slacking on research. If I went out there, I'd accuse myself of wasting time on pointless research when I might have been tapping typewriter keys and producing finished pages. Once I was able to see that I was in a double bind, I tossed a mental coin and went to Forest Hill Gardens.

As it turned out, my memory was sound and the place hadn't changed a bit. But I felt my time had been profitably spent; I'd refreshed my impressions, picked up a little local color, and certainly enabled myself to write the scene with increased confidence.

It doesn't always work out that way. Sometimes hours devoted to this sort of research are a waste, and sometimes there's no way to determine in advance whether this will be the case. American Tobacco's George Washington Hill used to say that fifty cents of every dollar he spent on advertising was wasted. The trouble was, he went on to explain, that there was no way of knowing which fifty cents it was, so he'd go on spending the whole dollar all the same. It's that way with research, and with all the other tasks that take me away from my desk.

One factor in the operation of my personal Jiminy Cricket mechanism is, I'm sure, that I *don't* spend all that many hours at my desk. Years ago I was given to putting in long stretches at the typewriter; I was younger then, which may have had something to do with it, and I was a less meticulous writer, which must have had plenty to do with it. In any event, I could work effectively for five or six or eight hours at a clip.

I can't do that now. I don't structure my work in terms of hours, finding it more useful to aim at producing a certain amount of work, usually somewhere between five and ten pages depending on the sort of material I'm working on, the deadline I'm facing, and the phases of the moon. My work usually takes me somewhere between two and three hours. If I'm done in an hour, I'm delighted to call it a day. If I'm not done in three hours, I generally call it a day anyway, though I'm by no means delighted about it. There's a point at which it becomes counter-productive for me to continue to work, on a par with running a car's ignition when the gas tank's empty. You don't get anywhere and you just run down the battery.

Most workers, I've been told, don't really spend more than two or three hours a day actually doing anything. They take breaks, they file their nails, they daydream at their desks, they talk baseball, and two hours get stretched into eight. It's comforting to know this, but it doesn't change the fact that I think of myself as putting in a shorter working day than the rest of the world.

I've found a couple of things I can do to make my writing life as guilt-free as possible, and I pass them on for whatever they're worth.

1.   I MAKE WRITING THE FIRST THING I DO. Over the years, I've written at every possible time of day and night. For some time now I've written immediately after breakfast, and it's by far the best system for me. There are several advantages—I'm freshest then, my batteries recharged after a night's sleep—but the most important reason for me is that once I've got my day's

work done, I'm able to give myself permission to do as I wish with the remainder of the day.

2. I TRY TO WORK SEVEN DAYS A WEEK. Again, there are other reasons why this is useful. With a novel, for example, working every day keeps the book from slipping away from my subconscious mind. Whatever I'm working on, novels or short stories, daily production helps me keep from feeling profligate over working so few hours per day. By the same token, when I do take an unscheduled day off, I can do so with a clear conscience; after all, I'm still working six days that week.

3. I SAVE ROUTINE WORK FOR LATER. I'm frequently tempted to answer my mail the minute it arrives, to proofread galleys as soon as they hit my desk. These chores enable me to be practicing my profession without actually having to write anything. But they're of secondary importance, and I don't have to be at my sharpest to deal with them. They'll still be around when I've got my daily five pages finished. Lately, for example, I keep getting packages from Cincinnati, parcels chock-full of entries in the *Writer's Digest* short-story contest. My natural inclination is to drop everything and read these stories as they appear, but instead I stay at my typewriter and save those stories for late at night when I can't sleep. After I've read a couple dozen, I sleep like a baby.

Finally, I allow myself to make occasional use of that old reliable cop-out—i.e., that writers are really working twenty-four hours a day. Because in certain respects it's undeniably true. Just the other day, for example, I did my daily quota of pages in the morning, spent the afternoon in the gym lifting heavy objects, and then wandered around for an hour or so. In the course of my wandering I watched a car enter an apartment building's underground garage, and it suddenly occurred to me how Bernie Rhodenbarr could get into an otherwise impregnable apartment building by first locking himself in an automobile trunk.

Will I ever use that little bit of business? I probably will, as it happens, but almost every walk I take produces some comparable bit of woolgathering, and most of the wool I gather never gets spun into a yarn. Is it work? And does it matter if it is or not?

Points to ponder, and I leave you to ponder them. For my part, I've spent a shade over three hours writing this chapter, and I'm done now. I think I'll give myself permission to enjoy the rest of the day.

CHAPTER 14.

The Carrot and the Stick

"So you're a writer," she said, spearing a cocktail frank. "You know, I'd *love* to be a writer, but I know it's impossible. I lack the discipline."

I suppose I could have offered to supply the missing ingredient, perhaps by lashing her nude to a desk chair and flogging her with a flail, but I only muttered something inoffensive and went off in search of the stuffed grape leaves. Because everybody would love to be a writer, and everybody lacks the discipline, and it's a good thing, because the profession is crowded enough as it is.

Imagine, for instance, if every dreamer with an urge to see his byline on a book jacket actually went so far as to roll a sheet of paper into his typewriter and start filling it up with words. Imagine, further, if all the people who started novels had the effrontery to finish the bloody things. Imagine if everybody with an itch and an idea took the trouble to turn the idea into a plot, and then sat down and wrote the story.

Why, we'd be up to our nostrils in literature, for heaven's sake! Forget the trees that would be pulped to facilitate such a gush of literary productivity. Think instead of the editors who would be the recipients of it all. They all have too much to read as it is, and it takes forever to get an answer from them, and just consider how much worse the situation would be if their daily reading load were increased by a factor of ten or twenty or two hundred.

You lack the discipline to write, sir?

Well, good for you. Stick with it.

Ah, but for *you*, Gentle Reader, the situation is rather a different matter. You, let it be said, are a writer, not a bore at a cocktail party or some similar sort of ship passing in the night. The last thing I want to do is discourage you from putting words on paper. You, clearly, are Serious About Your Work. Haven't you purchased this book? Are you not reading this very page? If that's not a commitment to one's art, a dedication to one's craft, whatever is?

It's my belief that self-discipline is a problem for the vast majority of writers, however productive and successful they may be. In order to get his work done, the writer has to be every bit as much of a self-starter as the chap they're always looking for in those ads for door-to-door widget salesmen. He doesn't even have the advantage of an early morning pep talk from the divisional sales manager. He has to supply all his motivation himself. Ultimately, he has to tempt with the carrot and swat with the stick—and at the same time he's the poor old donkey pulling the cart.

Novelists are especially assumed to require a full measure of self-discipline, and for good reason. It takes a lot of hard work over an extended period of time merely to complete a book-length work of fiction. A poem can be dashed off in a matter of minutes. A short story can be hammered out at a single sitting. In both cases, inspiration can carry the writer through the completion of the work.

This is simply not true with the novel. Inspiration alone will not get the thing written, any more than sheer speed will carry anyone to the finish line in a marathon. To continue the analogy, a novelist, like a marathon runner, receives praise simply for having completed his task irrespective of how well he's performed it. No one (except perhaps the runner's mother) congratulates a last-place sprinter for having survived to the finish line of a hundred-meter dash. Nor do people hail one as some sort of conquering hero for having typed the last line of a poem or a short-short.

All this notwithstanding, I submit that the short-story writer has every bit as great a need to apply the carrot and the stick in order to be either productive or commercially successful. While seeing one story through to completion may be a less than Herculean task, it takes no end of discipline to do the same thing repeatedly, coming up with idea after idea, grinding out story after story, and working throughout at the top of one's form.

The novelist has the advantage of momentum; once into a book, he can give it its head and follow where it takes him. He knows, when he gets up in the morning, what he's going to be writing that day. The writer of short fiction, on the other hand, has to keep developing new projects and developing enthusiasm for them as he does so. And he has to do so while marketing previously completed efforts, shrugging off the inevitable rejections that are a part of that marketing process and refusing to allow them to interfere with his steady production of new stories.

Are there tricks of self-discipline? Is there a particular distance to extend the carrot, a special way to apply the stick?

I'm sure there must be, and I live in hope that one day I'll find the formula. Because I've been indefatigably productive over the years, turning out more books than anyone should reasonably have to read, people tend to assume me to be a model of self-discipline. Yet I frequently look at other more industrious writers and castigate myself for my dilatory nature. Doubtless they in turn berate themselves for falling short of their role models—the bee and the ant, I would imagine. And does the ant in turn worry that he's a closet wastrel? I wouldn't be a bit surprised.

Here are a few tricks of the trade:

1. GIVEN WRITING TOP PRIORITY. At executive training programs they like to tell the story of Charles Schwab, then president of U.S. Steel. He told an efficiency expert that he didn't have time to listen to him at length but wondered if the man had any quick suggestions for him. "Every morning," the expert said, "make a list of the things you have to do that day. List them in order of importance. Then concentrate on the first task until it's finished, without diverting your attention to anything else. Then go on to the second task, completing as much as you comfortably can in the course of the day." Schwab looked at him, shrugged, and asked what he wanted for the suggestion. "Try it for a month," the man said, "and then pay me what you think it's worth to you." Thirty days later, Schwab put a check in the mail for twenty-five thousand dollars.

The expert's advice is as good as it ever was, and as much so for writers as for steel company presidents. I would suggest that you put writing at the head of each day's list. Make it the first thing you do. Give it priority, not letting yourself be sidetracked until the day's writing is done.

2. SET GOALS FOR YOURSELF. I work mornings, generally putting in two or three hours a day; when I work more than three hours my concentration flags and the work suffers. My objective, however, is not to put in a certain number of hours but to produce a certain quantity of work. More often than not, the goal I set myself is five pages a day.

If I get my five pages written in a flat hour—which does happen now and again—I'll generally call it quits then and there. I may do an extra page or two, if the words are flowing nicely and I want to leave off at a natural stopping point. But I'll feel under no obligation to put in all the hours allotted for purpose of writing.

On the other hand, if I don't reach my five-page goal within three hours, I may stay at the typewriter a little longer and see if I can't fulfill my quota. I'm not absolutely compulsive about this, but I know I'll feel better during the rest of the day if I get my pages written, and I do so when possible.

I can usually manage it—in part because I've had the foresight to set easily attainable goals for myself. I rarely find five pages a day to be a strain; if I did, I'd adjust the quota accordingly. I avoid the trap of raising the goal as I go along, like an assembly line speedup. The object's not to test myself. It's to get my work done.

3.   STAY IN THE NOW. The most important single element in enabling me to concentrate on today's work is the ability to make that the *only* thing I'm concentrating on. If I let myself worry about tomorrow's work and next Tuesday's work, I'm not going to do my best work today. If I'm writing a short story, I can't let myself get diverted into worrying about what story I'll write next, or where I'll send this one when I'm finished with it, or what I'll do if it's rejected, or what I'll buy for myself when it sells. I can only do today's work today, so why waste energy?

4.   JUST GET IT WRITTEN. Frequently I find myself convinced that all I'm doing is turning perfectly good bond paper into garbage. Sometimes I'm right. Sometimes it's an illusion. When I feel this way, it's impossible to tell which will prove to be the case.

The answer, I've found, is simply to get it written, giving myself permission to throw it out later on if it turns out I've produced swill. This is occasionally easier said than done. It's hard to persevere when I'm convinced that the last sentence I typed is utterly wooden. But I frequently find afterward that what seemed horrible while I was writing it looks perfectly fine the next day—or at least no more horrible than the rest of my work. And, on those occasions when I do wind up tearing it up the next morning, at least I've done some work and the momentum of my writing is undisturbed.

5.   DON'T TAKE IT TOO SERIOUSLY. The work of any artist requires a certain degree of doublethink. In order to practice my craft day in and day out, I have to be very serious about it. But if I take it too seriously I'll clutch, rendering myself incapable of the relaxed approach necessary for optimum creativity.

Here's a story for illustration. Two retired gentlemen meet, and one complains that he's going nuts. "You need a hobby," the other one says. "Something to give you an interest in life and a reason for living."

The first is skeptical. "You mean like pasting stamps in a book? Doing needlepoint? What kind of a hobby?"

"I'll tell you," says the other, "it doesn't even *matter* what the hobby is so long as you got one. My hobby, just as it happens, is bee-keeping."

"You keep bees? You, living in two and a half rooms on Pitkin Avenue? How many bees do you have, anyway?"

"Oh, it's hard to say, but about twenty thousand."

"Where do you keep 'em?"

"In a cigar box."

"But . . . but, don't they get all crushed and dead and everything?"

"So? Listen, it's only a hobby."

It's only a book, I've told myself time and time again. *Sometimes it feels like the most important thing in your life, and it seems to be what you do to justify your own existence, but don't take it so seriously. It's just words on paper, it's just a pack of lies. Listen, it's only a book.*

That takes the pressure off. Knowing it's only a book, knowing empires won't rise and fall on the strength of it, I'm able to breathe in and breathe out and get the thing written.

Ahem.

Those are my professional secrets, and you're welcome to 'em. I can assure you they work for me. By applying them diligently, I've been able to get this written and in the mail—only two weeks after the due date.

Listen, it's only a column.

CHAPTER **15**

Creative Procrastination

PROCRASTINATION'S HAD a bad name ever since 1742, when Edward Young called it the thief of time. (He'd have written that line back in 1739 but he just kept putting it off.) Lord Chesterfield inveighed against putting off until tomorrow what you can do today, lumping the pastime with idleness and laziness. And Thomas DeQuincey, tongue tucked firmly in cheek, saw procratination as the end product of a chain of character deterioration that might begin with a simple act of murder.

We free-lance writers, fixed with the responsibility of scheduling our own time and temperamentally prone to procrastinate, have every reason to agree. And surely this column, designed to send its readers scampering to their typewriters, will take a firm stand against the gentle art of keeping up with yesterday.

Right?

Wrong.

On the contrary, I would submit that procrastination has its place. I'm not endorsing it out of hand, understand. In writing, as in the rest of life, the best way to get things done is to go ahead and do them. They rarely do themselves. And it has been my observation that those writers who sit down and write, day in and day out, are the very writers who get the most accomplished.

So procrastination in general is a massive liability. Creative procrastination, however, can be a definite asset. The trick is to know just when to defer action and when to get busy.

Let me give an example. When I first started writing, about the time the pterodactyl made it onto the endangered species list, I saw to it that as little time as possible elapsed between the onset of an idea and its tranformation into a piece of fiction. I was writing stories then for the surviving crime pulps, and I would typically get a story idea of an afternoon and deliver a finished manuscript to my agent the following morning. More often than not it sold. Not to a very good market, mind you, and not for much money, and the story itself would rarely be memorable in any way, but I was young and that was the best I could do.

Nowadays I do things a little differently.

A couple of months ago, for example, I got a Noteworthy Idea. I conceived of a mystery story in which the murder victim would function as the detective, solving his own murder *after* it had taken place. I had recently read *Life After Life,* by Raymond A. Moody, Jr., and his reports of after-death experiences triggered my story idea.

In the old days, I'd have gone directly to my typewriter. And, most likely, I'd have gotten nowhere with the story, because this particular idea was not an easy one to turn into a piece of short fiction. Furthermore I had no plot, no theme, no characters, no conflict—nothing but the bare idea as I've described it to you. I could have tried contriving these other elements at the typewriter, but instead I procrastinated.

I made a note to myself on the little memo pad I carry around. *Man solves own murder,* I scribbled, right between *Pick up laundry* and *Water philodendron.* Every now and then my eyes would hit those words and I'd tell myself I'd have to get around to doing the story one of these days.

Each time this happened, my subconscious got a little nudge. Gradually, these little nudges made a collective impression.

My original concept of the story, never fully formed and never committed to paper, called for the lead character to operate on some sort of spectral plane, perhaps spooking the killer into a confession, something eerie like that. After a spell of creative procrastination, I changed this. I decided the lead would die clinically in the operating room while they were removing the bullet or some such, would then have an after-death experience of the sort Moody described, in the course of which he'd be given to understand that he could not be permitted to die until he'd carried out the mission of finding out who had killed him. Whereupon he'd return to life and set about investigating the circumstances of his murder.

Much better, I decided. The story was starting to have a shape to it. But I still didn't feel ready to write it, so I put it back in a warming oven and left it alone.

A while later, I was reading poetry. I wasn't reading Robert Frost, but something reminded me of Frost, and I realized the title I wanted for my story was "And Miles to Go Before I Sleep." I wrote that on my memo pad and crossed out *Man solves own murder.* (I'd already picked up the laundry by that point.)

I like having a title before I write a story. I certainly don't insist on it but it helps. So I had the title now, and it was a good one, but I still didn't have the story.

So I put it off again.

A week or a month later, I started thinking about the lead, trying to figure out who he was. And who had killed him? And why? I wasn't sure, but I decided maybe he was a middle-aged businessman. I provided him with a wife and a business partner and a mistress and a son and a daughter, and I gave all five of them motives so they could be suspects. Vague motives, because they were still vague people, and because I had no idea which of them was the killer.

Time for more procrastination.

One day, you'll be pleased to hear, I decided I was ready to write the story. I don't know what told me this; most likely I was avoiding work on something else. At any rate, I sat down at the typewriter and got to work.

Somewhere along the way I had decided to write the story in the first person. It was trickier to do it this way, describing those after-death experiences in the lead's voice, but all that time spent living with the story convinced me it was the way I wanted to do it. And it turned out to be easier than I'd thought, because the mood and tone came rather easily to me by now.

Another interesting thing that happened is that the lead turned out to have more of a purpose than simply bringing his killer to justice. As he investigated each suspect, he found himself resolving his unfinished business with each in turn, putting his emotional affairs in order before dying for a second and final time. This change turned a simple gimmick story into something with substance.

I was pleased with the way the story turned out. It didn't seem to need substantial rewriting, perhaps because it had received so much unconscious modification and restructuring before I sat down to write it. Eleanor Sullivan liked the story and bought it for *Alfred Hitchcock's Mystery Magazine,* where it appeared as "Life After Life" in the October '78 issue, should you care to see for yourself how it ends.

My point, though, isn't that I produced a brilliant piece of work or won fame and fortune with it. It's not and I didn't, but it would surely never have reached its present form if I hadn't repeatedly put off until tomorrow work I was insufficiently prepared to do that day.

Code of Arms is another example of creative procrastination in action—or inaction, come to think of it. I first got the germ of the book a full four years ago. I was reading something about World War II and wondering, not for the first time, why on earth Hitler had halted the German armor outside of Dunkirk. That two-day respite permitted Britain to withdraw a quarter of a million troops; otherwise she might have been unable to continue the war.

Suppose some Englishman had penetrated the Wehrmacht High Command? Suppose that was the cause of the stop order?

I decided that would make the premise of a hell of a novel, and I went off and occupied myself with other things. It wasn't until years later that I suddenly remembered that idea and hit on the precise identity of the person responsible for saving the British at Dunkirk. I now had not merely an idea for a book but a compelling and commercially viable one. I promptly devoted the next six months to research, which is not quite the same thing as procrastination, although they often look alike. Then I talked to a publisher and worked up an outline, and after more work than went into Chartres Cathedral and more perils than Pauline, *Code of Arms* was published in the spring of 1981.

In this instance, I'm lucky I didn't lose the idea altogether. It's important, I think, to keep the idea visible—in a notebook, on a wall chart, whatever. That way you'll jog your memory from time to time, and when an idea or a piece of information comes along that you can use, you'll reach out and incorporate it in the story as it evolves.

When does procrastination become other than creative? When it consists of avoiding work rather than postponing it, and when my alternative to working on Project A is not working at all. Since I'm inherently lazy, I force myself to work on Project B instead.

Another thing—it was Don Marquis who called procrastination the art of keeping up with yesterday, and conscience compels me to give credit where it's due. And pretty soon I'll share with you my thoughts on the subject of Creative Plagiarism.

Perhaps we'll take up that topic next chapter. Perhaps I'll put it off for a while. Meanwhile, though, I've got to go water the philodendron.

CHAPTER

Time Out

I'LL TELL you something. The more time I spend in this writing game, the clearer it becomes to me how little I know about it. It's a rare month that goes by without my wondering that I have the temerity to go on writing for a living, let alone offer you out there suggestions as to how you can go and do likewise.

This humility attack is not the product of an insight gained from contemplation. Would that it were. On the contrary, it is the bitter fruit of experience.

Consider if you will the pattern I have established for myself over the past several weeks. Each morning, as is my custom, I awaken around seven. I get out of bed, see my shadow, and dive back into bed, where I contrive to spend the ensuing four hours with the covers pulled over my head and my eyes clenched shut. Because I'm not really tired and have already had plenty of sleep, I have to be quite relentless about this, forcing myself to stay put each time I'm moved to awaken.

Then, round about eleven, I roll out at last and put the teakettle on to boil. By that time it's safe to start the day. I'm a morning writer, and with the morning gone I can proceed directly to the non-writing portion of my day— a meal, a gym workout, a lunch date, a long walk, whatever pleasing prospect presents itself. I don't have to walk into my office, I don't have to look at my typewriter.

I've avoided work for yet another day.

I've won.

I'm not going to dignify this curious behavior by calling it writer's block. I'm not altogether certain what writer's block is, but it seems to take the form of an inability to get anything written however hard one tries. It's painfully clear to me that I have not been trying, that I have indeed done everything in my power to avoid finding out if I am or am not capable of writing by giving my typewriter a wide berth.

Regular readers of my column may well recall how I tend to stress the importance of Keeping at It. The writer who gets things done, I've pointed out, is the writer who shows up for work day in and day out. Regular hours and regular production are the keys to productivity. The hare may show a lot of early form, but the smart money's always on the tortoise.

I've argued, too, that not only one's productivity but the quality of one's work is enhanced by this slow-and-steady *modus operandi*. When I work every day—or six days a week, say—the book I'm working on stays very much in mind. I think about it during the day and let my subconscious work it over at night. I don't have a chance to lose my grasp of it.

Why, then, don't I start the teakettle going at seven, get to my desk by eight, and nail down the Pulitzer Prize?

I suppose because things don't always go as I would have them go. My best-laid plans, like those of other mice and other men, gang aft agley.

But perhaps a little background on my present situation might be instructive.

Couple of months ago I started work on a very intimidating project, a novel that's rather more ambitious than anything I've undertaken in the past. It's going to be a fairly long book, probably running four to five hundred pages in manuscript, which would make it twice as long as the mysteries I most often turn out. It will also cover a lot of ground temporally and geographically, and although I know the general shape of the plot I have no outline for this book, and don't want one. The plot is going to have to disclose itself to me as I go along.

The writing went very well at the onset. In the first month I worked five or six days a week, wrote five or six pages a day, and completed the first section of the book, a chunk of one hundred thirty pages. Then I had to switch to a different viewpoint character and pick up the story at another time and in another place. I took a week off to give myself time to get out of the first character's head and into the second's. At the week's end I hurled myself once more into the breach and wrote every morning for three days, and on the fourth day I got up and realized I could not go on.

This realization has since become a way of life, repeated each morning with subtle variations. It would be nice if I were at least enjoying this non-writing time, but of course I'm not. I constantly beat myself up for it, accusing myself of self-indulgence and sloth, and that certainly doesn't help.

What does help is if I am able to regard this time off as a part of the creative process. I'm able to take that stance when I look at some of the time-outs I've called in the past.

Last fall, for example, I sat down on schedule and wrote the first sixty pages of the fourth Bernie Rhodenbarr mystery novel. Somewhere around page sixty I got the nagging feeling that something was wrong, although I had no idea what it might be, or what to do about it. I resolved this dilemma by lapsing into the sort of paralysis I'm in now, albeit of a different style. I was then able to avoid work without staying in bed, simply by setting up dates to resume work.

"I'll get back to it after Thanksgiving," I told myself. Thanksgiving came and went, and I realized that I had the auction of the paperback rights of *Ariel* coming up in mid-December. "Well, I'll wait until that's out of the way," I allowed. "Who can work with all that hanging fire?"

Who indeed? Not I, certainly. Once *Ariel* had gone under the hammer, the holidays were upon us. Who would initiate a project at such a time? Again, not I. I decided to get back to work when the new year started.

And I did. New Year's Day I took the subway clear to Riverdale to scout a location, one I did not wind up using in the book, as it turned out. And on January 2 I sat down at the typewriter and started the book over on page one, and I swear the thing flew. I wrote the whole book in five weeks flat and was delighted by the way it turned out. The prose flowed like water from a well. The plot evolved very neatly. All I had to do was show up each morning and type it out.

What this suggests to me is that the time I spent goofing off was not wasted time at all, that those two months away from the typewriter were somehow a part of the process of literary creation. I'm sure I could not have done as good a job on the book, or had as good a time with it, if I had forced myself to hammer away at it back in October.

Why, then, can't I regard this present period of inactivity as more of the same? After all, I did the first chunk of the book quickly and easily, and I'm pleased with how it turned out. (Or at least I was, until this current indolence led me to regard everything through mud-colored glasses.) It's not illogical to supposed that my subconscious needs time to gather its forces before springing forward again. I take substantial intervals between books without second thought. Might it not be equally important to take time off between the sections of a long book?

Of course it might. Furthermore, I've been going through a lot of personal aggravation during the last two months of a sort that could in and of itself throw one's literary productivity off-stride. Isn't it fair to assume that I'll be more capable of resuming work after this emotional ferment dies down a bit?

Of course it is.

I think the first step in getting through these dry periods is one of acceptance. I don't see how we do ourselves any good by beating ourselves up for our inability to fulfill our own excessive expectations. I can always devise a schedule for myself that I am incapable of carrying out. One's reach does exceed one's grasp, inevitably, and one's life never goes quite according to the script one has written for it, and thank God for that.

Acceptance is easier said than done, however. I can accept stretches of inactivity much more easily after they're over than while they're going on. Those months of not writing last fall—I can now regard myself as having made a brilliant decision, and I have to force myself to remember what a different view I took of it all at the time. It's a lot harder to see the picture when you're standing inside the frame. Once the writing is going well again I'll very likely see my current lethargy as having been valuable, but right now, even while I'm typing these lines, I have the ambivalent feelings of a Christian Scientist with appendicitis. I want to believe, but I'm starting to get scared.

I think there are ways to avoid making a period of inactivity worse. Besides acceptance, I think it's helpful to avoid letting everything else go to hell along with the writing. This too is easier said than done, and my current miasma has been exacerbated by a stubborn refusal on my part to do anything else that might make me feel better or might render my life more manageable. I've fallen hopelessly behind in my correspondence, for example. I've let my bookkeeping slide. And I've had a difficult time keeping up with my normal routine. I always feel better, for example, after one of my thrice-weekly visits to the gym, but it is a part of my present malaise that I haven't *felt* like going to the gym.

I've been making myself go anyway. I don't want to go there, and once I'm there I don't want to *be* there, and I can't for the life of me see any point in picking up heavy iron objects only to return them to the place I found them. It seems an utter waste of time and energy. But I do it anyway, even though I don't feel like it, and then I take a sauna and a shower, even though I don't feel like that either, and afterward I feel better.

And I do tell myself, from time to time, that I'll get back to work on the book eventually, that I'm not finished forever with writing as a profession, that I'm ahead of schedule anyway and the book will get done when it gets done, and—

And sometimes I believe it.

It's not fun. One thing I've found to be true for most of us is that, whether we enjoy writing or not, one thing we enjoy a good deal less is Not Writing. Unfortunately, it seems to be true that Not Writing is occasionally a part of the writing process. And it's a lot more tolerable, and probably better all around, if I can learn to trust the process.

At least I've written this month's column—which, like everything else lately, I've stubbornly avoided doing. Like my gym workouts, I've gritted my teeth and done it in spite of all inclinations to the contrary, and whether or not it was worth doing is something I'm not equipped to judge.

But I feel better for it.

CHAPTER **17**

Do It Anyway

I'VE GOT a friend who's been calling me almost daily for the past couple of weeks. Some time ago he contracted to write the libretto for an opera and he's having a miserable time of it. He fell behind schedule, missed a deadline, and is being gently hounded by those to whom he is responsible. My experience in this area is, to say the least, limited. I've never gone to an opera, let alone written one. But we're friends, and opera librettists are evidently in fairly short supply, so I'm one of several people he calls regularly when he wants to gripe, moan, cry, beat his breast, and solicit the odd word of encouragement.

Of late my words of encouragement have grown increasingly predictable. He'll natter on about how the words won't come, how when they do come they're terrible, how he can't stand to look back at what he's written, how every time he writes something he wants to tear it up, how just sitting at the typewriter has become an anxiety-producing activity, and so on *ad nauseam.*

"Do it anyway," I tell him. "Put your behind on the chair and your fingers on the keys and get the words onto the paper. They don't have to be good words. They don't have to be the right words. You don't have to like them. You don't have to enjoy writing them and you don't have to be proud of having written them. You don't even have to believe that the whole process is worth doing. Do it anyway."

"But it's no good," he'll sometimes say. "It's wooden, it's lousy, it's *bad.*"

"Fine," I reply. "Write a bad libretto. Do it anyway."

I don't invariably proffer this sort of advice, either to others or to myself. Sometimes when a book doesn't feel right the best thing I can do is put it deliberately aside for a while and return to it when my subconscious has had a chance to sift through it and work things out. Writing, after all, is not like factory work. You can't necessarily be productive—and get paid for your efforts—simply by showing up for work and performing your allotted task. Sometimes persistence and perseverance don't amount to much more than banging the old head against the wall. The immovable wall.

There are times, though, when it is demonstrably more important to get something done than to get it done well. This would seem to be the case with my friend. His choices are not between writing a good libretto and writing a bad one, but between writing something and being relieved of the assignment altogether or failing to fulfill it.

The daily newspaper is often held up as a great training ground for writers, and there are certainly innumerable members of the profession who had their start in newspaper journalism. While newspaper experience will not in and of itself guarantee success as a fiction writer, one can't have spent much time in the game without learning to get things written and get them in on schedule.

In the newspaper business, no story is a good story if it doesn't get into the paper. If the courthouse burns down tonight, my story had better be in tomorrow's paper. It may not be a great story, it may not have the last word on the subject, and it may not be so written as to make Hemingway eat his heart out, but it's got to be in print. Otherwise it's no good to anybody.

Any daily newspaper contains innumerable stories that might have been better if their authors could have devoted more time to them. But they do their job. Sometimes awkwardly, sometimes incompletely, and almost always imperfectly, they deliver the news while it's news.

Deadlines are considerably more elastic for the free-lance fiction writer. Often the only ones that exist are of his own making. Even when all of our writing is done entirely on speculation, it's common procedure for most of us to set little deadlines, to plan to finish a particular story by a particular date. Empires will not fall if we fail to do so. More often than not, nobody but us will know.

Of course that's generally punishment enough. Most of us who manage to function productively as free-lancers tend to be quite hard on ourselves, demanding rather more than a boss would dare to demand, and beating ourselves up whenever our grasp falls short of our reach.

Thus when we set arbitrary deadlines for ourselves, we generally work mightily to meet them. However we can usually keep a saving sense of proportion on the matter. If I've decided to finish a piece of work on Tuesday, and if that's going to be achievable only at jeopardy to the quality of the work, or the state of my health, or the considerable inconvenience of others, I'm flexible enough to extend the deadline to fit the circumstances.

When our deadlines are not arbitrary ones of our own making, and when the time for flexibility has come and gone, then it's time to Do It Anyway.

A couple of observations make this particular task a little easier. First of all, let's examine the single most paralyzing element in this sort of bind, the conviction that what one is writing is beneath contempt. How can we force ourselves to go on writing when we know that what we're writing is no damn good?

It helps me to recognize that I am by no means the best judge of my own work—especially when I've just written it. There have been times when I've thought a piece of writing was coming along very nicely, only to find out when I'd finished that there was something wrong, most often a lack of tension overall that had not been apparent page by page as I was writing it.

More often, though, it's the other way around. Writing that seems unutterably labored while it's coming out of the typewriter turns out to be perfectly adequate.

Certain experiences have even left me suspecting that how I feel about what I'm doing may be the least important variable in my fiction. Some fifteen years ago I once wrote two-thirds of an adventure novel while living in marital harmony in a New Jersey city. Then my life turned abruptly and dramatically upside down, I lived through a car wreck and a capsized marriage and other trauma the report of which I'll spare you, and some weeks later I found myself in a bed-and-breakfast in Dublin with a deadline approaching.

And so I went to work. Everything was different, including my rented typewriter and the long narrow sheets of paper they sell over there. Certainly my view of everything was different. But I did manage to realize that it was more important that the book be finished than that it be perfect, and I whacked away at it every day until it was done. The publisher accepted it without revisions and published it as *Tanner's Twelve Swingers,* and when I read it for the first time after its publication I couldn't determine where the break had come. There was no seam. My life had a seam in it, all right, that was a long time smoothing out, but the book was all of a piece from first page to last.

Even when the circumstances of a book's production are less dramatic, it's a rare book that doesn't have a spot of slow going in it. Once in a while I'll write something and it'll flow like water from a well all the way to the end, but more likely there'll be occasional days—and hence occasional chapters—that come like dental extractions.

Long-distance runners say that every race has a bad patch in it. Everything hurts and the whole process seems unendurable and the runner wants nothing so much as to drop out of the race. At this time, what one has to do is call upon his previous experience, recognize that what he's going through is a bad patch, and get through it with the foreknowledge that things will get better shortly.

Books have bad patches of just that sort. The important thing is to get through them, to get the words down however ill-chosen they may seem. For myself, I find more often than not that what I write on a bad day isn't demonstrably worse than what I write on a good day, though it seems so at the time. But when I'm going through a bad patch I could type Hamlet's soliloquy and deem it stilted and wooden. I have to discount my feelings about what I'm doing and just go on doing it.

One thing that helps is to give myself permission to write badly. I tell myself that I'm going to do my five or ten pages no matter what, and that I can always tear them up the following morning if I want. I'll have lost nothing—writing and tearing up five pages would leave me no further behind than if I took the day off, and I'll have avoided guilt and at least kept my fingers limber.

Once in a great while I do wind up tearing up the day's production, but even at those times I'll have gained by testing and working through one approach to the material. Almost all the time, though, what I write (and loathe) one day looks just fine the next. I may not love it, but I can recognize it as adequate. Sometimes it may need slight revision. Often it can stand exactly as written.

When I'm really having trouble with a particular piece of writing, I can marshal extraordinary arguments against going on with it. Like my friend, I can tell myself that it's the wrong sort of thing for me to be writing, that my talent is not equal to the task, that I'm just beating my head against the wall, and that I ought to abandon the thing, cut my losses, and turn my talents in a more appropriate direction.

All of this is generally translatable as "I-don't-wanna-write-this-thing-cuz-I'm-scared-I'll-screw-it-up." This kind of fear of failure is paralyzing, and there's no way to tell in its course whether or not it's justified. Sometimes it may be. My talent, such as it is, is certainly not equal to everything I aim it at. Now and then my reach exceeds my grasp by more than a couple of furlongs.

I can only find this out, though, if I get the thing written. I sometimes sustain myself by pitting one fear against another and reminding myself that not finishing the thing at all is far more to be dreaded than finishing it poorly. This seems to be a way I can acknowledge fear and harness it to my benefit.

As I said, sometimes the fear is justified. A couple of years ago I contracted to write a book, and once I started writing it I found myself very much at a loss. It was manifestly not my sort of book. I was uncomfortable with the kind of characters indigenous to such a book. I was at sea in the plot and unfamiliar with the sets. I regretted having had the idea for the book in the first place, and wished I'd let it wither on the vine.

But I'd signed a contract, and I'd taken an advance which I could not afford to repay, and for all I knew my fear was coloring my view of things. Perhaps I could indeed write the book. I lowered my head and charged forward, five pages a day, come hell or high water, and although I kept having one bad patch after the other, I got the thing done.

And it was not good. Let there be no mistake about it; my effort was as bad in the whole as it had looked in part. But it was done. And that, in and of itself, was better than if I'd left it unfinished.

There's even a happy ending. I was able to enlist a collaborator, adventure novelist Harold King, and turned the book over to him. Our joint effort, *Code of Arms,* was published by Richard Marek and is doing very nicely, thank you. The triumph I feel on its behalf is of an odd sort. There's been nothing equivocal, though, in my having seen that first draft through to completion. If I hadn't been willing to Do It Anyway, to get the thing written no matter how much I hated writing it, there would have been no book and I would have learned none of the lessons the experience provided. And that, I submit, is in itself the most important of those lessons.

CHAPTER **18**

F U CN RD THS

YOU'VE PROBABLY seen the ads on buses and subways. "f u cn rd ths," they proclaim, "u cn gt a gd jb & mo pa." The message is as attractive as it is succinct. Who, given his druthers, wouldn't prefer a gd jb? Who, in the face of double-digit inflation, couldn't make use of mo pa?

What they're selling, of course, is instruction in Speedwriting, an alternative to shorthand employing ordinary letters and taking the form of verbal arcana of the sort quoted above. The implication is that if you can read that sort of thing you can in due course learn to *write* that sort of thing and to do so at such a pace as will enable you to take dictation, with ensuing improvement in your employment, your salary, and, one assumes, your posture and your love life.

Did you have a question, Rachel?

I was just wondering what all this had to do with writing, sir.

We'll get to that, Rachel.

Because if you're seriously suggesting that we'll be better writers by leaving out vowels and stuff—

Don't get your vowels in an uproar, Rachel. What I'm getting at is the whole question of increasing one's writing speed. The faster we produce our books and stories, it would stand to reason, the more books and stories we'll be able to write over the months and years. Similarly, if we can halve the number of hours it takes us to turn out a particular piece of work, we shall be doubling our hourly rate of compensation in the process.

There are a couple of implicit assumptions here, chief among them the notion that an increase in writing speed will not be accompanied by a drop-off in writing quality. And it's quite natural to believe that the opposite is true, that the faster one writes something the more slipshod and imperfectly conceived and developed it is likely to be. Don't you get out of something what you put into it?

I think the question's an interesting one. Joseph Heller's second novel, *Something Happened,* was some ten years in the writing; would it have been a poorer piece of work had it been accomplished in five? At the other extreme, Voltaire is supposed to have written *Candide* in three days. Would he have made a better job of it by allowing a full week for its composition?

It's certainly possible to contend that an increase in writing speed can adversely affect the quality of one's work. One might rush through the work before ideas have had a chance to develop. But it is also possible to argue that sometimes a book or story will be better for having been written more rapidly.

I think there's a definite gain in intensity, for one thing. If I write a book in a month, for instance, it's likely to be all of a piece. The way I feel about my characters—and, consequently, the way they feel about things—is likely to remain the same from start to finish. Furthermore, if I write that book in a month it's going to be very much a presence in my mind throughout that month. If the same amount of writing is spread out over a year, it will probably claim a correspondingly smaller portion of each day's conscious and unconscious attention.

Similarly, fast writing helps keep a book from going stale. If a book seems to be taking forever in the writing, I'm likely to be bored by the process of writing it. While it is not necessarily axiomatic that a book which bores its writer will have the same effect on its reader, it's rare that a writer's disenchantment with his work doesn't show up on the printed page one way or another.

This is not to say that the faster a book is written the better it will be. For one thing, there is a trade-off. A gain in intensity may be offset by a loss of that quality that comes of living in and with a book for an extended period of time. If I rush too rapidly through what I'm writing, I don't give myself time to explore its possibilities, time to learn more about its characters. And I find myself in the position of an aggressive general who has outrun his supply lines; by covering literary ground at too swift a pace, I'm unable to replenish the energy required to allow each day's work to be of optimum quality.

How fast is too fast? This is a hard question to answer, because the answer seems to vary not only from one writer to the next but from one book to another.

The fastest book I ever wrote took three writing days. My second daughter had just been born and I thought it would be nice to be able to settle the hospital bill. I accordingly arranged to write an extra book that month for my regular publisher, a soft-core sex novel of the sort I was then doing monthly at a usual pace of ten working days over two weeks. I wrote from nine in the morning until six or seven at night for two days, then worked from nine to three on the third day, and completed a two-hundred-five-page manuscript by that happy hour.

I don't know that the book was any better or any worse than what I generally turned out in those days. I do know that I forgot each scene as I wrote it, that my words seemed to pass onto the page and out of my mind simultaneously, to the point where I could never recall from one page to the next what color hair my characters had, or anything much beyond their names. The names, too, were forgotten within a day of finishing the book, and I now recall nothing whatever about it except the speed of its production. I don't own a copy, and it's not improbable that I could read the thing now without recognizing it.

That book, I would say without hesitation, was written too rapidly.

On the other hand, I wrote a book called *Ronald Rabbit Is a Dirty Old Man* in four consecutive days, and while nobody ever mistook it for *Candide,* I think it worked out rather well. The ideas kept coming as fast as I could type and I simply couldn't tear myself away from the book. Another book, *Such Men Are Dangerous,* took eight or nine days and was similarly written in white heat; a lot of people consider it my strongest novel.

I can't write at that pace any more, not merely because I'm older but because my writing has become more deliberate. Really fast writing demands that one wear blinders like a racehorse; thus attired, one plunges singlemindedly toward the goal, undistracted by alternative possibilities. There was a time when I rarely envisioned more than one way to write a sentence, or construct a scene, or fabricate a plot. Now, considerably more aware of my options, I need the time to select among them.

And yet the latest Bernie Rhodenbarr mystery, *The Burglar Who Studied Spinoza,* took a mere month to spring from my typewriter, much to my own surprise. And its admittedly biased author thinks it's the best of the series.

Go figure.

There are, it has been said, two kinds of people in the world—those who divide people into two categories and those who don't. Ahem. There are, I have come to believe, two kinds of writers in the world, fast writers and slow writers, and transmutation of metals is a cinch compared to turning either into the other.

Still, we often make the attempt. If we hadn't been dissatisfied with ourselves to one degree or another we very likely would not have become writers in the first place, so is it surprising that we're often dissatisfied with the kind of writer we seem to be?

Most commonly, a naturally slow and contemplative writer will try to soup up his engine out of a natural desire to get more accomplished, or to get the same amount accomplished but have the summer free, or whatever. Now and then, however, a fast writer decides to slow down.

Evan Hunter, a born speedwriter, is supposed to have made such a decision some years ago. He'd become acquainted with Stanley Ellin, whose work he understandably admired, learned that Ellin worked at a very slow and painstaking pace, and concluded that his own trouble lay in writing too fast. He resolved to change, and at their next meeting told Ellin with some jubilation, "It's working! I'm down to eight pages a day!" Ellin at that time thought eight pages was a healthy output for a week, so the idea of holding oneself down to that many pages a day didn't strike him as—yes, Arnold?

Sir, is this all some elaborate build-up for the old to-thine-own-self-be-true number?

You do provide one with the makings of a humility attack, Arnold. I suppose part of today's lesson is indeed the suggestion that you seek to be the sort of writer you truly are, which may not be that far from what Polonius was saying. But I have a few more specific thoughts as well.

I was hoping you would, sir.

1. DON'T ASSUME TOO MUCH. Most professional writers tend to aim for a daily production quota, one or two or five or ten pages of copy a day. This quota system seems to be generally useful—I know I've always found it so—but I think it's a mistake to assume that a particular magic number will remain a constant through all the books or stories one writes or through all one's states of mind.

In long-distance running, one is advised to pace onself "at the edge of one's breathing"—i.e., run so that running faster would leave one short of breath. I think a writer can find his maximum safe speed in much the same fashion.

2. QUIT WHEN YOU GET TIRED. The work I do after a certain point is work that might better be left undone. When I'm tired, I'm just not at my best; if I continue to stay at the typewriter I'm either wasting my time or doing something distinctly counter-productive. Again, avoid assuming you're tired because you're always tired after X number of pages. Instead, concentrate on developing an awareness of how you actually feel.

3.   AVOID CHEMICAL ASSISTANCE. There are cunning little pills available which banish fatigue, stimulate the central nervous system, and seem to sharpen creativity while extending performance. Sooner or later these magic pills rot your kidneys, calcify your liver, leach the calcium out of your bones and teeth, and lead in the fullness of time to dependency, madness, degeneration of the nervous system, and death.

There are writers who take them anyway, at their peril. I did so, at one point, and I do not do so any longer. I found that the psychic damage alone was too high a price to pay for whatever service the drugs seemed to provide.

The story is told of the college student who took a hit of speed and proceeded to write the most brilliant exam paper in the history of the department. Unfortunately, he wrote it all on one line.

Yes, Arnold?

You wouldn't happen to remember where he bought the stuff, would you, sir?

Speed kills, Arnold.

Oh, I know that, sir. But couldn't I take it until I need glasses? Just a joke, sir. Just my little joke.

CHAPTER **19**

Washing Garbage

THERE ARE writers who enjoy rewriting. At least they say they do, and a feigned passion for revision would seem as unlikely as a pretended carnal enthusiasm for chickens, so I'm perfectly willing to believe them. These people say things like, "My books aren't written; they're rewritten." Or, "Once I get a first draft hammered out, then the real fun begins—the second draft. Then comes the third draft, and the fourth draft, and finally the joys of the final polish. Of course sometimes it's not really final because I just can't resist running the manuscript through the typewriter again."

Well, *de gustibus non disputandum est,* as the old lady said when she kissed the cow. For my part, I can't imagine too many things more resistible than running a manuscript through a typewriter for the fifth or sixth time. I'd sooner run a camel through the eye of a needle. Or vice versa, come to think of it.

Other writers regard revision as a chore, and an unpleasant chore at that, but they seem to accept it as an inescapable part of the game. In the first draft, one is given to understand, the writer simply tries to "get it down on paper." The second draft realigns the plot, smooths out inconsistencies of character, and otherwise gets the writer's ducks in a row. In the third draft scenes are restructured, plot and character refined. In the fourth, paragraphs and sentences are hammered into shape, dialogue is sharpened, commas are dropped here and inserted there. And, sooner or later, the abominable first draft emerges transformed into something divine and imperishable.

The late Jacqueline Susann frequently told television audiences how she rewrote every book four or five times, using yellow paper for one draft, green for another, pink for a third, blue for a fourth, and finally producing finished copy on white bond. I don't seem to recall what the point of this rainbow approach to revision may have been, nor am I sure I believe Susann actually did this; anyone as good as she at self-promotion might well have been capable of embroidery.

But that hardly matters. What's relevant, I think, is that Susann knew her audience. The public evidently likes the idea of reading books over which writers have labored endlessly. Perhaps it's somehow galling to shell out upwards of eight ninety-five for a book that flowed from its author's typewriter like water from a cleft rock. The stuff's supposed to *read* as though it came naturally and effortlessly, but one wants to be assured that a soul-satisfying amount of hard work went into it.

Well, the public be damned. The same public goes to prizefights to see boxers flattened and attends auto races hoping desperately to witness a crash. If they want hard work from writers, well, we can tell them we sweated our tails off. But do we actually have to rewrite our books and stories over and over?

There is, let it be said, a persuasive argument *against* rewriting. It can be advanced in either of two ways, depending whether one's approach is that of the artiste or the cynic.

The former might hold that a piece of creative work should indeed be all of a piece, that its artistic integrity is in part a function of the artist's mood at the moment of creation, that the verve and passion involved in writing could only be diluted by rewriting. Jack Kerouac took a position along these lines, explaining that he was trying to create a "spontaneous bop prosody" that amounted to a novelist's equivalent of a jazz musician's creative improvisation. This approach seems to have worked for Kerouac better in some books than in others—I found it generally effective in *The Subterraneans,* less so elsewhere—and I'm willing to entertain the hypothesis that the man's novels would have been watered down rather than spruced up by another trip or two through their author's typewriter.

A cynical rendition of the same argument may be found in a novel about a hack science-fiction writer who is enormously contemptuous of his own work and of the people who read it. He never rewrites anything, we are informed, because he knows revision would rob his crap of the only thing it has going for it, its freshness. Once you start rewriting, he argues, you're not able to stop. With each draft the fundamental banality and worthlessness of the material becomes more evident even as its vitality and spontaneity are drained from it. All you wind up doing is what William Goldman, discussing in *The Season* the agony of restructuring and rewriting an inadequate play prior to its opening, called "washing garbage."

Personally, I've always detested rewriting. When once I get to the end of a piece of work, whether it's a quickie short-short or a ten-pound novel, I bloody well feel finished. When I write The End, I mean it.

Years ago I hardly ever did any rewriting. I was churning out appalling quantities of pulp novels and my first drafts were publishable as they stood. I had enough natural facility so that my prose and dialogue got by. Plot and characterization barely existed in these books, so revision wasn't necessary to rectify inconsistencies in those departments.

My attitude at the time was a cavalier one. "I never rewrite," I was apt to say, "because I make it a point to get it right the first time around. It does seem easier that way."

Ah, the brashness of youth. I'm older now, and a shade less arrogant, and the books and stories I write come less like the torrents of spring and more like molasses in January. They are more ambitious and they take a good deal more of my time.

And they involve considerably more rewriting than they used to.

But I still don't enjoy the process. And I still try to get it right the first time around. Because, all things considered, it still seems easier that way.

Unless you're one of those souls who was born to rewrite, you'd probably prefer to spend less time redoing your work and more time writing new things—or working in the garden, or watching sunsets, or whatever. Toward that end, let me offer a hint or two.

1. DON'T TAKE REWRITING FOR GRANTED. It may very well be that

everything you ever publish will make two or more trips through your typewriter on its way to immortality. That's okay. What's not okay is writing your first draft with the assumption that that's all it is, a first draft, a piece of unfinished work, and thus an excuse for you to be utterly sloppy about what you're doing. "It doesn't matter how rough it is, I just want to get this down; later on I can worry about turning it into English." Well, no. Sorry, but I don't buy it. All a sloppy first draft teaches you is to be sloppy in your writing.

What's useful in this regard is a sort of doublethink process. You *know* you're going to have to rewrite the piece, but in the course of your first draft you *act as if* the version you're doing will be final copy, ready for the printer. This way you'll produce a cleaner, more artfully crafted first draft—and, every once in a while, you'll find that it can stand as written, that you honestly don't have to rewrite it. And even when you do, it's a whole lot easier to remodel than something that reads as though you typed it with your toes.

In this vein, do your first draft on decent paper, not second sheets. Set your margins, use carbon paper, the whole bit. This trick of *acting as if* is the best way I know of learning to clean up your act.

2. Revise as you go along. This is handy in novels especially, but I also find it a useful practice in short stories. Often when I'm writing I'll get an idea somewhere along the way that sends the plot off on a previously unanticipated turn. This will frequently necessitate some changes in the material I've already written—a scene changed around, a bit of plot business planted earlier, whatever. The natural impulse is to go ahead with the book or story until it's finished, then backpedal and fix up the rough spot.

You'll make things considerably easier for yourself if you return to do this back-and-fill work as soon as possible, *before* going on to complete the manuscript. You may not want to break off the forward progress of your work immediately, but as soon as you reach a convenient stopping place, and when the revision work is clear in your mind, go back and do it.

There're a couple of reasons why this makes sense. First, you don't have the prospect of ultimately going back and revising constantly nagging at you. Once you've done the work, you can feel good about the portion that's written and devote your complete attention to what's coming up next. Second, the changes you make in the early part of the script may spark additional developments later on. This kind of revision is like fence mending; the sooner you see to it, the less elaborate a job it winds up being in the long run.

3. Keep your mind on your work. This is always good advice. While it may not be quite as crucial for a writer as for a demolitions expert, it's still good policy. As far as rewriting is concerned, or avoiding rewriting, it's very

important. A lot of the sloppy habits that make comprehensive revision necessary result from paying insufficient attention to what you're doing and to what you have done. If what you've just written isn't fresh in your mind, you're apt to repeat phrases you've recently used, or contradict something you've previously established. The blond in Chapter 3 is suddenly a brunette in Chapter 7. Chapter 5's orphan is talking to his mother in Chapter 9. If you're lucky, this gets attended to in your second draft. If you're not so fortunate you never do spot it. Then an editor spots it, and that's embarrassing. Or no one spots it until it's published, whereupon five hundred readers write in and you really feel like the southern end of a northbound horse.

The first remedy for this is concentration. Avoid writing when your mind is tired. Don't work behind any kind of mood-changers—alcohol, marijuana, ups, downs, tranquilizers.

If you're doing a piece of work that takes more than a day to finish, start each day's stint by rereading the previous day's production. More to the point, don't just read what you wrote yesterday. Proofread it, making those minor pen-and-ink corrections that are required. This gets details fixed in your mind, and it also gets you into the flow of the narrative. If you're working on a book and you've been away from it for more than a few days, don't just read the last chapter. Read the whole thing—and, if you've been away from it for a long time, read it more than once.

There's another advantage, incidentally, in proofreading as you go along. It increases your confidence in what you have produced while saving you from the eventual chore of proofing the entire manuscript all at once.

Just as you look at what you've done yesterday before going to work today, you should get in the habit of looking at the preceding paragraph or two whenever something comes up that breaks your concentration. This will help keep you in the flow and avoid repeating words and phrases unwittingly. This factor alone will keep me away from dictaphones and tape recorders forever, incidentally. I want to be able to see what I've done, and if I can't immediately check out how it looks on the page I can't have any confidence in what I'm doing.

4. DO YOUR FIRST DRAFT IN YOUR MIND. I've written a lot of things, from short stories to full-length novels, without knowing where the hell I was going. Sometimes I've begun a short story without knowing anything more about it than the first paragraph. This sometimes works out fairly well, but it's no way to produce finished copy.

Lately I find that the time to rush to the typewriter is not at the moment of inspiration but the following morning, or perhaps the morning after that. In the meantime I'll play the story idea through my mind any number of times, and I'll have one or two nights to sleep on it. I may even dream about it, as a happy alternative to my usual dream about being naked at the Annual Bake Sale of the Jamestown (N.D.) Grange. By the time I actually get around to writing it, I'll know a whole lot more about it than I knew at the beginning, so that what comes out of my typewriter isn't really a first draft at all. It's a second or third draft and it's a lot less likely to need revision.

5. DON'T GO OVERBOARD. This last point is a necessary counterbalance to the preceding four. Don't go crazy striving to avoid the need for revision. Don't be so intent on getting it right the first time that you never do get the first draft written. Don't back and fill so many times that the manuscript ceases to get longer and merely gets older. Don't be so intent on getting the story right in your mind that you never get around to writing it at all. Don't read your stuff over and over to the point where you're all bound up in what you've done and can't think about what you're going to do.

In other words, moderation. Moderation in all things, including moderation.

When Stanley Ellin was writing short stories almost exclusively, he was almost compulsive about rewriting. And he liked to do it as he went along. He couldn't move on to page two until page one was perfect. Once, he recalls, he rewrote page one upwards of forty times before moving on to page two. And so on, page by page, through the story.

Now that's madness. But so are most of our approaches to rewriting—or, for that matter, to writing itself. If we weren't at least a little bit mad we'd probably have found our way into a saner line of work altogether. In the final analysis, my suggestions for avoiding revision are just suggestions, and I offer them only because they work for me, just as other approaches may prove more useful for other writers.

One thing, though. I'd hate to have to tell you how many times I've washed the particular piece of garbage you've just finished. . . .

CHAPTER **20**

On Being Read

SOME YEARS ago, when we were both comfortably ensconced at a small midwestern college, he presumably teaching and I presumably studying, Judson Jerome declared that there were two varieties of undergraduate writers to be found upon a college campus. The first sort, he explained, grew a beard and cultivated an intense scowl and told everyone who asked (and almost everyone who didn't) that he was a writer—but never went so far as to *write* anything.

The other sort, he went on, was apt to dash off any number of fitful little poems and rush about pressing them upon people like urine specimens, crying out, "Look at this! It is a part of me!"

I had, as I recall, a foot in both camps. I did have a beard and a scowl, both of which were destined to endure for twenty years, and I certainly told the world that I intended to be a writer when I grew up. But at the same time I also wrote a great deal, fitful poems and feckless short stories and whatever else recommended itself to me, and I did indeed force these schoolboy efforts on my friends, my mentors, and indeed virtually anyone who had not yet learned to duck out of sight when he saw me coming.

The beard's gone, and the scowl's a seldom thing. I don't write many short stories these days and I haven't perpetrated a poem in donkey's years.

But some things don't change. I still want very much to be read. Not merely by the reading public, upon whose reception of my work my income and professional standing ultimately depend, but as well by that handful of close friends to whom I still scuttle like an Antioch sophomore, urging my work upon them and demanding that they read it and report to me as soon as possible.

For a great many of us, I suspect the urge to be read is inherent in the urge to write. Some of us are exceptions, writing only for the inner satisfaction of

114

transforming our experience into an orderly and artistically successful entity; once we've done so, it matters not a whit whether anyone ever looks upon our work and says yea or nay. God alone knows just how many such private writers exist, keeping notebooks of poetry and fiction in locked drawers, telling no one of their efforts, and leaving instructions that their work be destroyed unread upon their demise. I rather doubt that many writers of this sort are regular readers of *Writer's Digest;* the magazine's concentration upon such matters as improving one's communicative ability and increasing one's chances of publication very likely strike such a writer as irrelevant.

The rest of us want to be in print, and while the desire for publication embodies as well a desire for money and recognition, at its core is the pure and simple desire to be read. Bishop Berkeley posited that the tree falling where no human ear hears it fall makes no sound, that vibrations only constitute sound when they are heard. Similarly, most of us regard our works as silent screams unless someone somewhere hears us.

Are there real advantages to having friends and associates read one's work? And whom can one best press into service in this capacity? And what attention ought one to pay to the response one receives?

In my own case, I only rarely show unfinished work. More often I'll wait until I've completed a story or a novel before handing it around. I then tend to select as readers persons who have liked my work in the past, and who strike me as apt to like this present piece of writing in particular.

I suspect I do this because what I really want is praise and adoration. Most of us claim that what we want is criticism, and most of us, I'm afraid, are terrible liars. While I may claim to want criticism, and while I may indeed be grudgingly grateful for advice on how to improve something I've written, I no more want criticism than does the proud parent holding up an infant for one's inspection. When I show you my child, the flesh of my flesh and blood of my blood, don't tell me the little bleeder's head's too big. Tell me rather that he's the most beautiful baby who ever drew breath, with the wisdom of Solomon shining in his unfocused eyes, and I'll love you and treasure you as a sage.

The need for praise, or at least for enthusiastic acceptance of one's work, is quite real for many of us. Writers, after all, work very much in a vacuum. A nightclub comic knows how he's going over; his audience laughs or doesn't laugh, and he lives or dies, succeeds or fails, with every punch line. We don't have this kind of mechanism available to evaluate our work even as it is composed.

Those of us who are established in our profession will have our work read in due course by our agents and editors, and their professional opinions are enormously valuable, but there is a special value, too, in the specifically less professional opinions of trusted friends. Those of us who submit our efforts over the transom can wait months for nothing more responsive than a form rejection slip or a stock letter explaining that "Your present effort does not meet our needs."

Most of us have big egos to begin with. We have to in order to sit down and make up stories in the expectation that other people will want to read them. But at the same time we are generally insecure about our work. We need to be reassured, and this need doesn't seem to wane in the presence of critical and commercial success.

When I attempt something different from my usual work, I require someone's assurance that I haven't struck out in the wrong direction or bitten off beyond my masticatory capacity. Conversely, when I write a new volume in an established series, I need to be persuaded that I have not fallen off from my previous standards, that I have not merely repeated myself, that I have not lost the touch, and that the world will not gaze upon my work and yawn.

The most useful readers of my work are those people who give me something beyond this praise and reassurance. They may call to my attention weaknesses which I can then attend to. They may spot errors of fact which, uncorrected, might damage my credibility in an editor's eyes. They can tell me whether a particular scene works as I'd hoped it would, whether they found a particular character sympathetic or noxious, whether a surprise development in my fiction struck them as insufficiently foreshadowed or altogether too obvious.

In *The Burglar Who Studied Spinoza* there were three surprise elements at the end, two of them having to do with the discovery of the murderer. Of the book's several readers, almost everyone anticipated one or another of these developments, while no one saw all three of them coming. I found this reassuring.

When an editor at *Savvy* found the ending of a short story of mine ambiguous, I went to a friend who had read the story. She had noted this ambiguity, although she'd not much objected to it; her perspective helped me see that the editor's objection was not unwarranted, and I was able to revise the ending accordingly.

Some years ago, I dashed off an erotic novel with the intention of publishing it pseudonymously as a paperback original. There were things I liked about it, and I began urging it upon friends for a reading. They were all so enthusiastic about it that I withdrew it from the paperback house and submitted it to hardcover publishers, the second of whom elected to publish it as

Ronald Rabbit Is a Dirty Old Man. There's no whirlwind ending to this story—the publisher did not promote the book effectively, the critics did not pay it much attention, and it sold like ice in the winter, but the point is a simple one; but for the reactions of my friends, I would never have thought to publish it in hardcover under my own name in the first place.

Other writers make the best audience, and most of the friends to whom I show my work are either writers themselves or at least peripherally involved with the business of writing. As such, they're better equipped to appreciate matters of technique, and I'm more inclined to value their reactions. I'm similarly concerned to have the reactions of non-writer friends, whose opinions are at least as important; after all, the mass of one's audience consists of non-writers. But I'm more likely to wait and let them read the work after it's published.

Sometimes I think the main function of writer's clubs is to provide unestablished writers with a peer audience for their work. People commonly organize themselves into such groups with the expectation that the criticisms they receive from one another will have a salutary effect upon their writing, and sometimes this may be true. But I suspect it's more important to have a fellow writer read your work than that he say anything particularly incisive about it.

Something even more useful, incidentally, is not what one learns from another's reaction so much as what one perceives by noting the strengths and weaknesses in the other's work. It is easier to detect the mote in a fellow's eye than the beam in one's own, as I am scarcely the first person to point out, and by observing what does and does not work in a friend's story, I have often been able to sharpen my own technical skills.

A couple of suggestions:

1. DON'T LEAD WITH YOUR CHIN. Some people are going to have a vested interest in tearing your work apart. For one reason or another, they are not going to like what you write and are going to delight in telling you so. That's their problem. If you persist in showing your work to them, you make it your problem.

2. DON'T SHOW UNFINISHED WORK. If you can avoid it, don't make people read work in progress. Especially avoid doing this if the work is going along well. You merely give yourself an excuse to interrupt your progress on the work, and you risk throwing yourself off-stride.

3. IF YOU DO SHOW UNFINISHED WORK, BE CAREFUL. Sometimes my insecurity about a novel is sufficient to make me break Rule #2. If I'm paralyzed by self-doubt, a quick reading and a reassuring word can loosen me up and enable me to continue. When this is the case, I try not to take chances. I

try to pick someone who's reasonably sure to like the thing and unlikely to express serious reservations even if he has them—unless there's something so inescapably wrong that it cannot be overlooked, in which case I'm probably better off knowing about it then and there.

4. DON'T KILL THE MESSENGER. The genuinely useful reader supplies something beyond simple praise. He furnishes an honest response. While he is presumably sympathetic, and favorably inclined toward your work generally, he is not going to be uniformly and unequivocally nuts about everything you write. Sometimes his reaction will be lukewarm. Sometimes it'll be downright chilly. And, because nobody's perfect, he may dislike something of yours not because of its intrinsic worthlessness but because it's just not his kind of thing, or because he read it on a bad day.

Don't react by hating him, or deciding he wouldn't know a good story if it bit him, or suggesting an anatomically impossible course of action he might profitably pursue. If you can't stand the heat, stay out of the kitchen. If you don't want the peaches, leave off shaking the tree. And if you can't bear disapproval, keep the stuff in a locked drawer.

CHAPTER **21**

Burning the Raft at Both Ends

IMAGINE, IF you will, a chap adrift upon a huge wooden raft in the icy waters of the North Atlantic. In order to keep from freezing to death, he periodically chops off chunks of the raft and burns them for warmth. As the days pass, the raft grows smaller.

Sooner or later, this guy's gonna have a problem.

I submit that we writers are in much the same situation. For each of us, the capacious raft is the background and life experience we bring to our writing, and we burn up pieces of it every time we roll a fresh sheet of paper under our typewriter platen. We consume our past in order to fuel our writing. Day by day, the raft shrinks.

Sooner or later, we're treading water.

This is a common problem, very nearly a universal one, for writers of fiction. Interestingly, its effect is particularly noticeable upon the most successful practitioners of our profession. It has been said for several generations now that success in America is frequently devastating, and devastation of one sort or another is commonplace for successful American writers. Even if one (to prolong the nautical metaphor) steers one's ship between the Scylla of alcoholism and the Charybdis of suicide, the successful author is left with the very real prospect of running out of things to write about, of writing more and more about less and less. Increasingly isolated by his success, both from his own past and the world around him, the writer has an audience hanging on every word and, sadly, nothing much to say to them.

You don't have to be a great success to find yourself on the same raft, or up the same creek, or whatever. Some years ago I first became aware of the way this particular dynamic was operating in my own life. I had begun writing early, dropped out of college (albeit at the dean's suggestion) to practice my own profession, and but for a year's interval in the mid-sixties never did anything but write for a living. My pre-writing past hadn't amounted to much in the first place, and every year's passage made it that much more remote. As time went by, my circle of friends tended to be composed more and more of other writers, agents, publishers, and sundry persons in the industry. While one could not ask for a warmer, brighter or more interesting group of people, and while the shop talk of such a circle is something I have come to regard as indispensable, this represented yet another way in which the raft was shrinking.

The effect of this shrinkage of the past was less dramatically evident in my own case because my work has never derived directly and obviously from my experience. Some writers, like Thomas Wolfe, produce their novels by fictionalizing their own lives. Others can do their best writing only when they concentrate on a particular subject; James Jones, who only wrote at the top of his form when dealing with World War II, comes quickest to mind.

While most of my work, like all valid fiction, is in one way or another a distillate of my experience, I have rarely drawn directly from life. Still, I could see a pattern in the making. One way or another, I was running out of things to write about.

I was throughout these years a highly productive writer—burning the raft at both ends, if you will—and I was a fulltime writer, unable to draw input from a job situation. Yet I suspect parttime writers and weekend writers face very much the same dilemma. The office worker, after all, goes every day to the same office, performs essentially the same tasks, interacts with the same people, and very likely travels to and from the office by the identical route day after day. Even if the job itself is interesting—even if it's *fascinating*—it can provide limited input at best for future writing.

Looking back, I don't recall making any specific attempt to create additional input. As it happened, I wound up doing the right things—or some of them, anyway—for the wrong reasons.

Like many people who wind up writing, I've always tended to be interested in a great many things. I'm given to intense if short-lived enthusiasms, taking up hobbies and areas of interest with a passion, reading everything I can get my hands on about them, pursuing them relentlessly for three months or so, then shelving them and moving on to something else. I used to regard this fickleness as a character defect, but have come instead to view it as a useful aspect of my personality in that it has enabled me to learn a fair amount about a curious mix of subjects.

This tendency, combined with general dissatisfaction with my living situation at the time, led me to wander down various paths during the hours I spent away from my typewriter. One example should suffice. Nine years ago I had the temerity to open an art gallery in New Hope, Pennsylvania. To say that it was less than a commercial success is vastly to understate the case. Mine was a veritable *Titanic* of art galleries. Nor was the business of running it the exhilarating experience I'd hoped it might be. On weekends it was so mobbed with tourists and their small destructive children that customers couldn't have bought anything if they'd wanted to—which none of them did. And on weekdays it was deserted; you could shoot deer in the place.

All of this notwithstanding, owning and operating the art gallery was of enormous direct benefit to me as a writer. During the single year of its existence, I met innumerable people in New Hope. My circle of acquaintances included artists, tradespersons, tourists, hippies, freaks, druggies, and assorted area residents. I learned quite a bit about both the artistic and the commercial sides of painting. I learned a lot, too, about the manner in which potential customers responded to art. While I certainly can't say I learned to paint, I did turn out some geometrical abstracts, if only to have something to do on deer-shooting afternoons. In this fashion I learned something of what it's like to be a painter, and when some of my efforts actually sold, I learned again that anything's possible in this universe, and that Barnum was right.

The most obvious result of my year as an art dealer manqué was a long novel set in New Hope and drawn almost entirely upon my experiences and observations. Understand please that I had no intention of writing such a book when I opened the gallery. I was not doing research. I was pursuing another end entirely, but my year's experience turned out after the fact to be input for a novel.

But it amounted to much more than that. Long after the novel has vanished from print, my whole frame of reference remains changed and enriched by my experience. Aspects of the people I met during that year have taken shape as characters in any number of other books. In short, my experiences added new planks to that tedious metaphorical raft I sail on.

Since then my life has taken innumerable curious twists and turns, and sometimes it has seemed to me that my circuits have been so overloaded with input that I might blow a fuse at any moment. For the past couple of year, however, I've lived in the same place and with the same person—and, God willing, both my landlord and my consort will pick up my option for the foreseeable future.

This stability has not diminished my writing input, perhaps because I've found a few ways to increase the flow. They work for me, and I suspect they'd work as well for anyone.

Here are some of them:

1. STAY OUT OF RUTS. Easy as it is to get into a rut, it's by no means inevitable, and I think it's worthwhile to make a deliberate effort to avoid ruts. There's a place eight blocks from my house that I walk to at least once a day, and I make it a point *not* to follow the same route every time. In fact, whenever I have to get from one place to another, I deliberately select an unfamiliar route, even if it takes me a slight distance out of my way.

May I urge you to reread Robert Frost's "The Road Not Taken"? I always try, both literally and metaphorically, to take the road less traveled by—and have found it makes all the difference.

2. LOOK WHERE YOU'RE GOING. Some routes are ruts because we stop paying attention; overfamiliarity keeps us from noticing even those things we haven't noticed before. I've found that if I keep myself open to new experience, if I use my senses, I walk every path as if for the first time and invariably see something I've never seen previously.

3. DON'T STOP LEARNING. Recently I've noticed that I seem to respond to architecture in a way I never have in the past. I find myself paying attention to the shapes of buildings and various architectural details. I deliberately fueled this interest by picking up a copy of *The City Observed,* Paul Goldberger's enchanting guide to the architecture of Manhattan, and before long found myself looking around me with sharper and more knowledgeable eyes. The book has changed my way of seeing my surroundings, so much so that I've decided to continue the process by taking a course at the New School on New York architecture.

And how will that course benefit my writing? Most importantly, by changing my way of seeing, by enlarging and enhancing my perspective. Perhaps my increased awareness will be reflected in what I write. Perhaps something I learn will lead directly to a plot or a scene or the development of a character. Perhaps, serendipity being what it is, I'll meet someone else taking the course, or at the water fountain in the corridor, who will tell me something which will serve to springboard a future novel. I don't know how the course will benefit my writing, and I don't *have* to know, because input is a different thing altogether from research. The latter looks for answers where the former isn't even aware of questions.

4.   HANG OUT. Art Spikol, *Writer's Digest*'s non-fiction columnist, raised a few eyebrows a while back by telling housewives to try hanging out in bars as a means of augmenting input. For my own part, I found over the years that the time I spent in saloons tended to decrease input by shutting me off from the world around me, but I think Art's general point is well taken. I can't be certain that anything's going to come along to broaden the base of my experience if I spend a few hours riding around in the squad car with my cop friend, or go sit on a bench in St. Vincent's emergency room, or rub elbows with the drug dealers and three-card-monte hustlers in Washington Square, or take in the scene at the Port Authority Bus Terminal. But I can be fairly sure nothing much is going to happen if I stay home and watch reruns of *I Love Lucy.*

Travel's broadening. I try to keep the fresh-eyed awareness of the traveler, not only when I'm out of town but when I walk the familiar streets of my own neighborhood. The rafts we all float upon need never be consumed. We can burn their planks for fuel indefinitely, secure in the knowledge that new boards will replace them. The possibility for experiential input is infinite— as long as we remain open to it.

CHAPTER 22

Creative Plagiarism

SOME MONTHS ago I got a call from a writer friend of mine, whom I'll call Brian Garfield. He mentioned that he'd recently read a novelette of mine in *Alfred Hitchcock's Mystery Magazine* and that he thought it was a nice piece of work. It will very likely not surprise you to learn that this news pleased me greatly.

What he said next was faintly unsettling, however. "I liked it so much," quoth he, "that I managed to figure out a way to steal it."

"Steal it?" said I. *"Steal it?"*

"Oh, it's a legitimate sort of theft," he assured me. "You'll see what I mean when it comes out."

I countered by quoting Oscar Levant. " 'Imitation,' " I pointed out, " 'is the sincerest form of plagiarism.' "

"Couldn't agree with you more," said Brian, and rang off.

My novelette, *Like a Dog in the Street,* concerned the capture of a daring international terrorist by Israeli security forces. His confederates counter by planting a bomb in the United Nations Building in New York and threatening to blow up half the eastern seaboard if the terrorist isn't released. The Israelis do release the man, but while processing him for release they give him an injection of rabies virus; the symptoms won't appear for about thirty days, and once they do appear death is inevitable.

That little gambit with the rabies virus was one that I'd been carrying around for years before I found the right story to support it, and I was not entirely happy with the idea of Brian's having stolen it. In due course his story appeared and I read it and relaxed. In his yarn, a U.S. intelligence service has to release an enemy agent in response to a terrorist demand. They don't want to lose him, so before the ransom demand is met he's given poison which begins acting after he's in East Berlin, or wherever. Once the symptoms show up he gets in touch and is told the antidote is available—all he has to do is surrender himself again, which he does, only to learn he's been tricked, as the poison was non-lethal all along.

Brian was absolutely right—what he'd practiced here was legitimate theft, or what I prefer to call creative plagiarism. His story derived directly from mine, but he had so adapted the idea as to create a completely different story.

And, thinking about the way his story had grown out of mine, I remembered how my story had developed in the first place. Back in 1961 I saw a *Ben Casey* TV show, one of the first episodes, in which Vince Edwards gets scratched by a rabies victim and for some medical reason can't risk taking the series of Pasteur shots. He has to wait thirty days to see if symptoms develop, knowing that the disease will be fatal if they do. The fragment of medical information, and the idea of making dramatic use of it, hung around in my mind for a long time before it took fictive form. When I got around to using it, I wasn't stealing it from the producers of *Ben Casey,* any more than Brian was stealing anything from me.

Most writers are readers, and I think it's natural enough that our reading should be the source of a substantial portion of our story ideas. There is a line to be drawn between legitimate and illegitimate theft, between simple and creative plagiarism. The acid test, it seems to me, is whether the plagiarist contributes something significant of his own devising to what he has borrowed.

Milton made essentially this distinction three centuries ago in "Iconoclastes." "For such a kind of borrowing as this," he wrote, "if it be not bettered by the borrower, among good authors is accounted Plagiarè."

Writers, good or otherwise, are often quick to suspect they've been plagiarized, and not creatively, either. I've had this experience myself a couple of times. For example, I wrote a book called *The Canceled Czech* in which my hero goes behind the Iron Curtain to liberate an imprisoned Czech who had collaborated with the Nazis during the war. He accomplishes this by putting the Czech into a cataleptic trance, smuggling him across borders in a coffin, and then indulging his own sense of justice by conveying the man, comatose in the coffin, to a crematorium.

A couple years after the book came out, I ran across a novel called *Mills,* which opens with the hero smuggling a war criminal from East to West Berlin in a coffin, disguised as a corpse, and then indulging his own sense of justice by conveying the man, still in the coffin, to a crematorium.

This did not make me terribly happy. I can't be sure that the man who wrote *Mills* ever read *The Canceled Czech;* even if he did, I can't be certain the theft was deliberate. A good friend of mine discovered to his horror that he'd committed grievous plagiarism in a novel, having stolen the plot of a well-known short story in considerable detail. He knew he'd read the story many years previously, although he had no conscious memory of it. The author of the short story never sued him and no reviewers ever remarked on the coincidence, but he still winces at the memory of this unintentional larceny.

These things happen. More than a few times, an editor has recognized unintentional plagiarism in time to nip it in the bud, and quite a few authors have simply discarded stories and novels when they learned they'd duplicated someone else's plot. But the creative plagiarist, using someone else's work as a point of departure for his own, has no worries on this score.

Discontent will often serve to initiate an act of creative plagiarism. Much as the oyster copes with an irritating grain of sand by coating it so as to form a pearl, so may an author deal with an irritating film or story by refashioning it into a more satisfying story of his own. When I watch a character behave stupidly, I find myself calculating what he should do, and what the effects of this proper behavior will be. Occasionally my solution to his problem is sufficiently different from the author's, and seems to me to constitute a sufficient improvement, so that I'll go ahead and write a story of my own.

I've come up with other plots by trying to figure out the endings to somebody else's stories. Television is handy for this sort of thing, and the old *Alfred Hitchcock Presents* program was ideal. Every once in a while I'd see the trick ending halfway through—but some of the time I was wrong, and my version was completely different from what the writer of the teleplay had come up with. A couple of times I sat down and wrote out my version, since it amounted to a completely different story from what I'd seen.

I have known some authors who, when stuck for an idea, will specifically set out to steal a story. I used to know a science-fiction writer, for example, who would systematically read through back issues of S-F mags, looking to find a story that he could alter enough so that he could feel free to steal it. I've made occasional attempts at this sort of thing with crime stories, and it never seems to work out for me.

With one exception, which I guess I'll tell you about.

Twenty years ago, I read a story of Fletcher Flora's in *Manhunt*. The plot ran something like this: a friend of the narrator's had been arrested for committing a series of homicides, having strangled half a dozen young women with identical shoelaces. (He used identical shoelaces to strangle various young women, that is. He didn't seek out women wearing a particular variety of shoelace and wring their necks. Just wanted to clear that up.)

The narrator visits his friend in jail, sees that the case against him is over-powering, then returns home where there's another shoelace that he found in the friend's closet. Not only does he not turn this evidence over to the cops, but, with his friend safely alibied by being in prison, he goes off to use that shoelace to commit murder, all as a way of freeing his friend.

For twenty years I had a yen to steal that story. I guess there was some-thing I really liked about it, but what the hell, Fletcher Flora wrote it first, so I didn't do anything about it. But often when I was stuck for a plot the idea would come to mind and I would put it regretfully aside.

Then, a little less than two years ago, I happened to reread the story in an old copy of *Manhunt*. And I began to play with the plot idea, trying to find a way to change it enough so that I would feel sanguine about stealing it.

I changed the shoelace to a necktie, which didn't amount to much of a change. Then I made the man in jail not a multiple murderer but a rejected suitor who strangled his former fiancée with his old school tie. I had his mother seek the help of a criminal lawyer I invented for the occasion, a very unusual lawyer who collected fees only when he succeeded in winning his clients' freedom.

And I made the lawyer a criminal—i.e., I had him, operating offstage and inferentially, fly over to England to purchase a batch of ties identical to the murder weapon and then commence strangling a slew of women similar in appearance to the original victim, so as to transform her death from a moti-vated murder to the first episode in a multiple homicide.

By the time I was finished, I don't know that Fletcher Flora himself would have spotted the theft. And the little lawyer—I named him Martin H. Ehrengraf—emerged as a sufficiently compelling character to appear in half a dozen stories to date. The series has been running in *Ellery Queen's Mys-tery Magazine* over the months and I've greatly enjoyed writing the stories.

And Fred Dannay, editor of *EQMM*, commented that my man Ehrengraf had obviously derived from Randolph Mason, the creation of pulp writer Melville Davisson Post. Mason, you see, was a lawyer who used criminal methods to get his clients off the hook. Fred didn't think I was stealing from Post, but that Ehrengraf had obviously been inspired by Randolph Mason.

Well, I'll tell you a secret. I never *heard* of Randolph Mason, never read any of those stories. If I had, I'd probably never have dared come up with Ehrengraf. Interesting, don't you think? Because Ehrengraf grew out of creative plagiarism, but not the creative plagiarism people have assumed.

Some notes, finally, on what does not constitute creative plagiarism. It's not CP to steal an element from each of half a dozen stories, put them all together and pass them off as your work. It's not CP to turn a western into a piece of science fiction, or a Shakespearean play into a modern story, if you do no more than change the costumes and external trappings. (*West Side Story* is CP, for example, but in a recent short-story contest I judged there were three or four S-F versions of western gunfights, with the principals riding blue dragons and drawing blasters, and they were all just awful.)

Finally, it's not creative plagiarism when you're writing non-fiction. In fact, it's not plagiarism at all.

They call it research.

CHAPTER **23**

"Where Do You Get Your Ideas?"

IN THE past fifteen years I have established two incontrovertible if unrelated facts. One: glass-topped coffee tables can really hurt your shins if you're not careful. Two: admit you're a writer and someone will immediately ask you a foolish question. I avoid glass-topped coffee tables insofar as possible, and for a time I stopped admitting I was a writer, generally attempting to pass myself off as a gentleman jewel thief. I stopped this when I found that the questions they ask jewel thieves are even more unsettling than those they ask writers.

Questions, questions, questions! *Have I read anything you've written?* I wouldn't know, sir. I'm a writer, not a mentalist. *Have you had anything published?* Why, no, madam. As I've told you, I've been doing this for fifteen years, and have written somewhere in excess (oh, wretched excess!) of a hundred books. And not a one of them published, madam. I am a compulsive masochist, you see, and I live in the woods upon roots and berries. *How long does it take to write a book?* Long enough to get from the beginning, sir, to the end. Like Mr. Lincoln's legs, don't you know.

Say, where do you get your ideas?

Indeed.

There, to be sure, is the rub. Because for all the banality of the question, it is one every writer asks himself often enough, one which ought to be answerable, and one which evidently is not. The writer clearly requires ideas. Precious little gets written without them. In many types of writing, once a certain level of professional competence is granted, it is the strength or weakness of the idea itself which determines the success or failure of the finished piece of work. It is this absolute need for ideas which one generates onself that makes the process of literary creation wholly incomprehensible to a great many people not engaged in it. The writer is not buying widgets from Mr. A and selling them to Mr. B. He is making something out of nothing, out of thin air. He is getting ideas, and it would seem to follow that he must be getting them somewhere.

But where?

Or, more important for our purposes, how?

Because every writer knows what it's like when the mind is as fertile as a field of Illinois bottomland, with ideas sprouting at every turn. And sooner or later every writer knows the other side of the metaphor, wherein he languishes in a vast Dust Bowl of the mind, barely able to type his name at the top of the page. "I've been rich and I've been poor," Sophie Tucker said, "and believe me, rich is better." I believe her, and you may believe me that ideas are better than mental stagnation.

Where does one get one's ideas? I had a friend once who told askers of this particular question that there was a magazine published twice a month called *The Idea Book,* or some such nonsense. "It's loaded with excellent plot ideas," he said. "I have a subscription, of course, and as soon as I get my copy I write in and select half a dozen ideas and get clearance on them, so that no other subscriber will go ahead and write them. Then I just work up stories around those ideas and Bob's your uncle."

An encouraging number of oafs bought this premise, and of course they all wanted to subscribe to the magazine. "You have to be a professional writer," my friend said, dashing their hopes. "Have to be a member of Author's League and have a dozen sales to your credit. But keep plugging away by all means."

Enough. Let us address ourselves to fundamentals. Obviously, a substantial number of ideas spring from the subconscious, lodged there by means of various phenomena from the trauma of birth onward (or back into the collective unconscious of the race, if your outlook is Jungian), and liberated therefrom and directed along creative lines by other processes impossible to understand.

I submit, though, that enough ideas turn up in less abstruse ways, and that a look at them might help us to encourage the development of ideas.

So where do I get mine?

Bits of fact can fit together. Almost all of the successful fiction writers I know share a tendency to retain odd scraps of data to no apparent purpose. Sometimes these orts prove useful, sometimes they do not. I know, for example, that in 1938 the state of Wyoming produced one-third of a pound of dry edible beans for every man, woman and child in the nation. I should be roundly surprised if I should ever build a story around this nugget of information.

But perhaps a dozen years ago I read an item in one of the newsmagazines about a handful of people in the world who seemed to exist without sleep. I digested this item, and went on to study a bit about sleep, and then I set it aside. Shortly thereafter I was reading about the British House of Stuart in the encyclopedia and learned that there was still a Stuart pretender to the English throne, though he certainly didn't work at it very hard. Happily enough, he seemed to be a Bavarian. I now had the notion of a permanent insomniac with a madcap scheme to restore the House of Stuart, and that didn't add up to a story, either, so after some more speculation on the sort of life a sleepless man would lead, I found other things to think about.

Two years later I spent an evening doing some moderately serious drinking with a numismatic journalist who had recently returned from Turkey, where he'd spent a couple years earning a very precarious living smuggling ancient coins and antiquities out of the country. I found his conversation fascinating, especially when he spoke at length about a rumor he'd tracked down about a cache of gold coins in the front stoop of a house in Balekesir, where the Armenian community had hoarded its wealth at the time of the massacres in Smyrna. He and some associates actually located the house as described by a survivor, broke into the stoop in the dead of night, established that the gold had been there, but established, too, that someone else had beaten them to it.

Aha!

A couple of weeks later I began a book about a young man, his sleep center permanently destroyed by a shrapnel fragment, and a devotee of all lost causes, restoration of the House of Stuart just one among many, who goes to Turkey and damn well finds that Armenian gold. I called him Evan Tanner,

I called the book *The Thief Who Couldn't Sleep,* and I wrote seven books about the chap before he quit on me and stretched out for forty winks.

If I'd tried writing about Tanner when I first got the idea of insomnia as a character trait, I'd have had no story for him and my mind wouldn't have had time to keep him on the back burner while his character defined itself. If I'd forgotten him entirely, if I'd dropped the insomnia notion once I failed to find an immediate use for it and had let it stay permanently dropped, the item about the Armenian gold cache would have led at best to a routine foreign-intrigue chase with stereotyped characters. But everything came together, and I had as much fun writing those seven Tanner books as I've ever had with my clothes on.

People give you ideas. In the vast majority of cases, those who say they have great ideas for stories are quite wrong. They don't. The people who do provide good story ideas are almost invariably other writers or people in publishing.

What? Other writers give away good ideas? Are they crazy or something? Oh, yes, they'll give away ideas, and they're not crazy at all. Everybody does it. The fact that I might have an idea that ought to make a good novel or short story is not reason enough in and of itself for me to write it. It might be the foundation of a good story without being my kind of story. Either I wouldn't have any fun with it or I wouldn't do a good job with it—or most likely both. So I'll give it to someone else.

Publishers are far more likely to give away book ideas. In a sense they're not giving anything away; they supply the author with the idea and contract to publish the book once he's written it. This happens rather more frequently than the reading public realizes. There are quite a few writers who spend most of their time working up novels from ideas supplied by publishers. I'm not just talking about lower-level writers knocking out formula paperback fiction to order, but carefully calculated and well-promoted bestselling novels the ideas of which, and sometimes a fair portion of plot and characterization, originate with the publisher.

There is a very real danger in working from an idea that is spoon-fed to you in this manner. When an idea is your own, the odds are that it's been kicking around in your subconscious for a long time, and as you work on it you'll be bringing all of that subconscious concentration to bear on it. When you're working with someone else's idea, *unless you like it a great deal right from the start,* you won't improve it as you go along. That's why so many books developed in this fashion, written by good writers and based on commercially sound ideas, turn out flat and mechanical.

I wrote one book which I stole—with permission—from another writer. He had a premise, a bride is raped on her wedding night and the groom hunts down the bad guys. And he had a title, *Deadly Honeymoon.* I stole them both.

I waited over a year to do it. Then, when I couldn't get to work on anything else and couldn't get *Deadly Honeymoon* out of my mind, I called him up and asked him if he was going to do anything with the idea—he wasn't—and did he mind if I did. He didn't. I had the bride and the groom hunt the villains, and Macmillan published it and Dell reprinted it and the movies kept optioning it and dropping it and it was like an annuity for a while there.

Writers get ideas the way oysters get pearls. There are those who would hold that all creative ideas are spun out of one's neurotic defenses. That may be going a little far, but sometimes the process is fairly obvious. Several years ago I was in a state of depression that made Schopenhauer look positively giddy. Every day I got up a little after noon and played solitaire until it was time for dinner. Then I played solitaire for a few more hours and then I drank myself to sleep. I must have been sensational company.

I would try to write now and then but I couldn't seem to motivate a character. I couldn't think of a sound reason for anybody to do anything. Ever. I would get a plot notion and think, "Hell, why doesn't he just turn over and go back to sleep?" And I would do just that.

So I wrote a book about an ex-Green Beret, a burnt-out case turned down for employment by CIA, who just can't get it together and can't think of a reason to do anything at all, who finally winds up all by himself on an island in the Florida Keys, fishing for his meals and living a rigidly controlled life. Then somebody from Central turns up and gets him involved in an operation, but by that time the character's set and the book virtually wrote itself. (It was published as *Such Men Are Dangerous,* by Paul Kavanagh.)

Ideas turn up on television. I suspect television is a great source for story ideas. I'd use it more often if I could bear to watch it, but I generally can't.

I don't mean that you take what you see on television and write it down. That's called plagiarism, and it's a no-no. What you do—and you can't set out to do it, it just happens now and then—is you rewrite what you see on the screen. You improve on it, which, given the state of the art, is not by any means a Herculean task.

I probably did this several times unconsciously, but there is one time I recall when I knew just what I was doing. (Which is rare for me in any area of human endeavor.) I was watching *Alfred Hitchcock Presents* and there was this man who was not getting along with his wife, and he seemed to be having episodes of madness.

"Ha!" said I to my future ex-wife, "I see how they're going to end it. He's pretending to be mad, establishing a pattern, and after he's got a mental history he'll kill that bitch he's married to, and he'll get off easily on a temporary insanity plea, while actually he's been planning it from the beginning."

Wrong. Dead wrong.

I don't remember how the silly thing ended, but I wasn't even in the ballpark. He wasn't pretending to be nuts. Maybe his wife was making him think he was nuts, or making other people think so, or something. I don't remember. Actually, I didn't pay too much attention to their ending. I was busy working out mine.

I didn't even wait for Hitch to come out at the end and explain that the criminal didn't really get away with it. I went straight to my typewriter and wrote the story my way, tagged it *If This Be Madness,* and sold it first shot out of the box to *Alfred Hitchcock's Mystery Magazine.* I figured they deserved first crack at it. Fair is fair.

That brings up a point. I wrote that story immediately upon getting the idea. In that instance it worked out fairly well because I got the whole story in mind in the course of the program. But I've written a lot of stories that way, getting to the typewriter as soon as I have the idea, or shortly thereafter, and I've come lately to the conclusion that it's a great mistake.

One idea may carry a short story, but for the story to be at its best it should be played out in the right setting by a cast of well-realized characters. The sort of alchemy that gets place and background and characters to the right spot at the right time will occasionally take place while you're at the typewriter, and certainly *some* of the creativity that makes a story work will happen during the writing of it.

But I have found that, if I take a couple of days to mull a plot notion over, other ideas will spring to mind to complement what I've started out with. I'll get characters, I'll get plot complexities, I'll get whole slabs of dialogue. I may not use all of this, but I'll have it in mind so that I can sift through it all while I'm at the typewriter doing the actual writing.

My present routine lends itself to this practice admirably. I don't live anyplace, but spend my time traveling from place to place, following the sun around and endeavoring to leave a town before I'm asked to. I get up in the morning, put in a couple of hours at the typewriter, then either drive a couple hundred miles or, if I'm going to stay in the same spot another night, wander around looking at things, talking to people, and fishing. All that time with myself for company lets plots and situations develop so that they're well-formed by the time I tackle them in my morning's stint. And all those new places and new people are productive of ideas.

Ideas come out of conversation. I was in a gift shop on the North Carolina Outer Banks a couple weeks ago. The woman whose shop it was and I got into a rap about recycled jeans, which she sells a great many of at six dollars a pair. What I wondered was where they came from, and I learned that she ordered a hundred pair at a time from a firm which is one of the nation's chief suppliers of this commodity. I learned, too, that all the jeans thus supplied were just at the broken-in stage.

Now where does the company get them from? Who on earth sells jeans that have just reached the comfy stage? And what can the company *pay* for them if they retail at six dollars? A buck a pair?

Curious.

So we talked, and I said maybe I'd write a story about an agent of the firm murdering young people for their jeans, and we laughed over that, and I went on my way. Now here's a good argument in favor of giving an idea time to develop. If I'd written the story right away it would have been thin, and there was also the fact that it's hardly worth murdering someone for jeans that will retail for six dollars. But by the time the story got written, the jeans-recycling operation was just a sideline for the company; their major business, you see, is the manufacture of dog food.

Well, I might not sell that one. It's a little grisly. But I *like* it.

When I lived in New Jersey, my neighbor's father ran the local animal shelter. They had an incinerator for disposal of dead animals, and my neighbor told me how a couple of local cops were eyeing the machine longingly. "That dope peddler we can never make anything stick on," one said. "Just pop him in there one night and there's nothing left but a little envelope of ashes, and nobody'd ever know, would they?"

And, said my friend, they were dead serious.

I almost turned that into a story but it was missing something so I forgot about it. Quite a while later my friend's dad had to close the outdoor animal compound where he kept farm animals penned up for kids to feed and play with. For the nth time, vandals had come over the fence at night and slaughtered animals for the thrill of it. So he closed up.

And now I had a story. In my story, the operator of the shelter traps a kid who has slaughtered a sheep, gives him a tour of the place, then pops him in the incinerator and cooks him. Hitchcock's magazine published it as "The

Gentle Way" and Al Hubin selected it for *Best Detective Stories of 1975,* and neither plot component would have been worth dust without the other.

Ideas, ideas, ideas. An idea doesn't do you much good if it's not right for you, however good it may be in and of itself. The idea of casting Dashiell Hammett as the detective in a period murder mystery is nothing less than brilliant, but how many people besides Joe Gores, himself a San Franciscan and ex-private eye, could have begun to do the book justice? (It doesn't hurt a bit either that Joe writes like a dream.) Why, if I'd had that idea I'd have given it away—or more likely simply forgotten about it.

On the other hand, when Brian Garfield told me a book idea of his some time ago I had an overwhelming urge to knock him over the head, lock him in a closet, and not let him out until I'd stolen his idea and written the book. But I suppressed the urge and Brian wrote the book and decided he'd call it *Death Wish.*

I should have locked him in that closet. Where did he ever *get* that idea, anyway?

Brian got the idea one night when he found his convertible top slashed; he turned his own righteous rage into the raw material of fiction. This chapter, I might add, was my first piece for Writer's Digest, *written somewhere in the Carolinas. About a year later I sat down with John Brady and proposed a column on fiction. Meanwhile, "A Pair of Recycled Jeans" did sell to a magazine and was in due course anthologized.*

PART THREE

Oh, What a Tangled Web:

Fiction as a Structure

CHAPTER 24

Opening Remarks

ANYONE WHO *starves in this country deserves it.*

Relax. The above is not this author's sociopolitical opinion. It is, rather, the opening sentence of the first short story of mine to see print, published in *Manhunt* just a year or two after Grant took Richmond. The story wasn't a bad one, but no one could call it the greatest ever told. I suspect its opening lines had a great deal to do with its acceptance for publication.

Well, openings are always important. Writers of non-fiction are well aware of the importance of getting things off to a good start. In a straight news story, the lead is literally everything, embodying in a sentence or two the who-what-where-when-why-how of it all. In a magazine article the lead is no less vital, although there may be less urgency about jamming all the facts at the reader right off the bat. In any event, the lead has the job of catching the reader's attention, involving him in the story, and establishing that the paragraphs to follow will be sufficiently useful and interesting to warrant his reading them.

Short stories and novels have leads, too, and their openings perform much the same functions. It's said that you never get a second chance to make a good first impression, and that old bromide is as valid in fiction as it is in life itself. And, in fact as in fiction, a good first impression is essential.

I think this is even more the case for the beginner than for the established professional. When an old pro submits a story, the editor who reads it knows who wrote it. It's brand-name merchandise. Even if the first paragraph's a wee bit blah, the editor knows the story's likely to get better as it goes along. He may well wind up rejecting it—old pros get rejected left and right, just like everybody else—but at least he'll probably read it all the way through.

The beginner, coming in cold over the transom, had better connect in the first paragraph. Because that is very often all an editor will read. Anyone who's read slush will tell you that it is a fundamentally unpleasant way to spend one's time, and that only a masochist reads unpublishable material through to the end. Editors are a busy lot, and it's essential that they wade through the slush as quickly as possible.

Your story, of course, is not garbage, to be returned unread to whence it came. And, while every sentence you write must be designed to convey this message to the reader, the first sentences have the most work to do.

Such as—

1. GETTING THE STORY MOVING. The worst thing about the openings of most stories by new writers is that they take more time getting started than an old Studebaker on a cold morning. This flaw was very much in evidence among the entries in the *Writer's Digest* short-story contest; I couldn't tell you how many stories began with the lead character getting out of bed, taking a shower, getting dressed, and going through a quarter or more of the two-thousand-word maximum length before presenting the reader with the story's central problem.

In contrast, here's how Richard Stark opened his novel *The Outfit:*

> When the woman screamed, Parker awoke and rolled off the bed. He heard the plop of a silencer behind him as he rolled, and the bullet punched the pillow where his head had been.

Stark gets things going, doesn't he? He opens with action—right in the middle of action, as a matter of fact—and you're caught up in what's going on before you even have time to wonder who these people are. He'll tell us in due time who Parker is, who the woman is, and why all of this is taking place. And we'll keep reading until then, because he's done a good job of attracting our attention.

This sort of opening doesn't have to consist of action. Here's how Joyce Harrington starts *The Old Gray Cat* by letting us listen in on a conversation:

> "I should kill her. I should really kill her."
> "Yeah, yeah. But how, how?"
> "I could find a way. I bet I could."
> "Oh, sure."
> "You don't think I could? I could put poison in her cocoa."

"What kind of poison?"

"Ah, you know, arsenic. Something like that."

This is a teaser—two characters are discussing the murder of a third and we don't know anything more about them than that the prospective victim is female and drinks cocoa. But the situation's compelling and we keep reading.

2. SETTING THE TONE.

> The elevator, swift and silent as a garotte, whisked the young man eighteen stories skyward to Wilson Colliard's penthouse. The doors opened to reveal Colliard himself. He wore a cashmere smoking jacket the color of vintage port. His flannel slacks and broadcloth shirt were a matching oyster-white. They could have been chosen to match his hair, which had been expensively barbered in a leonine mane. His eyes, beneath sharply defined white brows, were as blue and bottomless as the Caribbean, upon the shores of which he had acquired his radiant tan. He wore doeskin slippers upon his small feet and a smile upon his thinnish lips, and in his right hand he held an automatic pistol of German origin, the precise manufacturer and caliber of which need not concern us.

The paragraph above is the opening of a story of mine, "This Crazy Business of Ours," which concerns a meeting of two professional killers. I could as easily have opened it this way:

> When the young man stepped off the elevator, Wilson Colliard was pointing a gun at him.

Neither opening is necessarily better than the other. I chose the one I did because I wanted to begin by setting a particular tone for the story. I used the image of the garotte at the start to suggest that the story would be a grim one, then described Colliard at some length to give him a particular presence. I wanted the reader to get a sense of the man before finding out that he had a gun in his hand. The final clause in the paragraph is an arch touch deliberately designed to remind the reader that he's reading a story; I use this kind of distancing device now and then because I think readers have an easier time enjoying a grim story if they know they're not supposed to take it too seriously.

For all of that, this opening does get things going; by the end of the paragraph we've got two men facing each other over a gun.

Sometimes a particular detail, perhaps one which has nothing much to do with the story to follow, can serve to set the tone. Here's how Russell H. Greenan begins "The Secret Life of Algernon Pendleton":

> On Beacon Street near the corner, a mutilated ancient elm tree stands. Having been shorn of all its limbs by the Brookline Forestry Department, it is now only a tall stump. Soon the stump too will be amputated, but meanwhile a twig has started to grow out of the raw chain-sawed surface at the top, and from it a few tender ovate leaves are sprouting.

This visual detail inspires the narrator to meditate on the nature of life and death, and life in the midst of death, and so on. The image of the tree stump, so vividly described for us, prepares us not only for the narrator's rumination but for the ensuing narrative. It sets the tone, and we're ready to be drawn into what follows.

3. ESTABLISHING THE PROBLEM. Sometimes a writer's foremost concern in opening a story is to present the central plot-problem to the reader as expeditiously as possible. Here's how Jack Ritchie uses dialogue to acquaint the reader with a complicated situation:

> I had just returned from my vacation and Ralph began filling me in on the case assigned to us.
> "Three members of the jury were murdered," he said.
> I nodded wisely. "Ah, yes. I see it all. The jury convicted a felon and he swore he would get his revenge."
> "Not quite," Ralph said. "Actually it was a hung jury. Four for acquittal and eight for conviction."
> "But of course," I said. "So the criminal promptly proceeded to kill three of the jurors who had voted for his conviction."
> "Not that either, Henry. All three of the jurors murdered had voted for his acquittal."
> "Why the devil would he want to murder three jurors who voted for his acquittal?"
> "He didn't really murder anybody, Henry. He couldn't because he was dead."

The problem here is extremely complex; Ritchie's opening draws us in simply by having one detective explain things to the other.

In "The Problem of Li T'ang," Geoffrey Bush gets things going by summing up the problem, one that can be stated much more simply than Ritchie's:

I had a problem. I had sixteen midterm papers from my course on Chinese painting, the first papers from the first course I'd ever taught, and one of them was brilliant.

In a sense, of course, most effective openings do several things at once. They get the action going, set the tone, and establish the problem—and while they're at it they may sketch a character or two, convey some important information, take out the garbage and sew a button on your cuff.

The opening's not everything. You can start off with *Call me Ishmael* and still lose your reader down the line if you're not careful. But your opening *has* to be good—or the rest of the story won't have a chance because nobody'll stick around to read it.

CHAPTER **25**

First Things Second

NEVER EAT *at a place called Mom's. Never play cards with a man named Doc. And never lie down with a woman who's got more troubles than you.*

These precepts, according to Nelson Algren, are What Every Young Man Should Know. I came upon them at an early age and never forgot them, and indeed I've never ordered an omelette at Mom's Café or dealt aces and eights to Doc McGee.

I figure two out of three ain't bad.

All the same, Algren's admonition isn't the best advice I ever received. That designation has to be reserved for a watchword I was given many years ago by Henry Morrison, boon companion and my erstwhile agent. Candidly, I feel a certain amount of reluctance about sharing this kernel of wisdom with you. It's stood me in such good stead over so many years that I'm not altogether certain I should let the world in on it.

Oh, what the hell. We're friends, aren't we? We're members of that international brotherhood of hacks and scribblers, so why shouldn't we share a trick of the trade. There are indeed tricks to every trade but ours, as the carpenter said while hammering a screw, so don't blab this one around. Keep it to yourselves, gang.

Don't begin at the beginning.

Let me tell you how I first came to hear those five precious words. I had written a mystery novel which I called *Coward's Kiss,* and which Knox Burger at Gold Medal in his finite wisdom retitled *Death Pulls a Doublecross.* The book is mercifully out of print and we can all be happy about that. It was a reasonably straightforward detective story featuring one Ed London, an amiable private eye who drank a lot of Cognac and smoked a pipe incessantly and otherwise had no distinguishing traits. I don't believe he was hit on the head during the book, nor did he fall down a flight of stairs. Those were the only two clichés I managed to avoid.

As I wrote the book, it opens with London being visited by his rotten brother-in-law, whose mistress has recently been slain in such a way as to leave the brother-in-law holding the baby, or the bag, or what you will. In the second chapter London wraps the young lady's remains in an Oriental rug, lugs her to Central Park, unrolls the rug and leaves her to heaven, or to whatever necrophiles are prowling that expanse of greensward. Then he sets about to solve the case.

I showed the book to Henry. He read it all the way through without gagging. Then we got together to discuss it.

"Switch your first two chapters around," he said.

"Huh?" I said.

"Put your second chapter first," he said patiently. "And put your first chapter second. You'll have to run them through the typewriter so the transitions work smoothly but the rewriting should be minimal. The idea is to start in the middle of the action, with London carting the corpse around, and then go back and explain what he's doing and just what he's got in mind."

"Oh," I said. And looked up quickly to see if a light bulb had perchance taken form above my head. But I guess it only happens that way in comic strips.

Now this change, which was a cinch to make, didn't convert *Death Pulls a Doublecross* into an Edgar candidate. All the perfumes of Arabia wouldn't have turned that trick. But it did improve the book immeasurably. By beginning with Chapter 2, I opened the book with things already going on. There was action. There was movement. There was tension and suspense. The reader had no idea who Ed London was or why this young lady was wrapped up in her Bokhara like cheese in a blintz, but the reader had plenty of time to learn this later on. After he'd been hooked.

I'll tell you something. As far as writing is concerned, I've learned a tremendous amount from reading what other people have done. And I've learned quite a bit from my own work. But over the years I've rarely been *told* anything about writing techniques that has done me much good. The outstanding exception is this one precept, which I'm going to say again to lessen your chance of forgetting it.

Don't begin at the beginning.

In the suspense novels I've written since I saw the light, I've followed that advice far more often than not. At the risk of doing an And Then I Wrote number, let me page through some books to give you an idea of how all of this has worked out in practice.

After the First Death concerns a college professor who is sentenced to a life term for murdering a prostitute during an alcoholic blackout. He goes to prison, his wife divorces him, and after a couple of years he gets released on the grounds that his confession was improperly obtained. He returns to a drifting kind of life, and one morning he wakes up in a Times Square hotel room and finds he's not alone. On the floor is a hooker with her throat cut. He thinks, *God, I've done it again,* and bolts. Later, threads of memory return and he becomes convinced he didn't commit this crime and sets out to discover who framed him.

The book opens with him waking up in the hotel room. I think it's the most effective first chapter I've ever written.

The Girl With the Long Green Heart concerns a retired con man who's euchred into going back to his trade for one last operation. It's a caper book; the con job goes through until a wheel comes off and various people betray one another and so on. I opened the book with the lead and narrator arriving in Olean and setting the job in motion, then flashed back and said who he was and how he got there. If I were writing this book today, I'd have opened the book a little further along in the story.

I wrote seven books about a whimsical adventurer and secret agent named Evan Tanner, and every last one of them followed this pattern. Each book began with Tanner involved in some kind of tense situation, then paused to explain how he'd managed to get into such a bind, generally out of friendship or as a result of his penchant for championing lost causes.

In *The Thief Who Couldn't Sleep,* Tanner starts out in a Turkish jail. In *The Canceled Czech,* he's on a train in Czechoslovakia, where he's the most *non grata* of *personae,* and a cop asks him for his papers. *Two for Tanner* opens with our hero suspended in a bamboo cage like some giant canary bird; he's about to be informed that they're going to lop his head off come sunrise. Tanner gets buried alive in the first chapter of *Me Tanner, You Jane.* He slips through the Iron Curtain in *Tanner's Twelve Swingers.*

In *Tanner's Tiger* he's prohibited from entering Canada. And in *Here Comes a Hero* . . .

Enough. You get the idea. Sometimes I've simply opened with a chapter with Tanner in a tight spot, then flashed back to a chapter of explanation. In other books the action has gone on for two or three chapters before the explanatory material is provided. In these books, a secondary purpose was served by this technique. The opening chapter or chapters generally left Tanner up against the wall to a greater or lesser extent, and this tension was maintained and even heightened by forcing the reader to pause for a flashback.

This business of beginning after the beginning is a natural for novels of suspense, for novels of adventure and action in general. But it also works very well in an altogether different sort of novel. Innumerable examples of mainstream fiction of the highest order are structured along these lines. They open with a scene that is dramatic or revealing or in some other way serves to get things off to a good start. Indeed, I've read a slew of novels in which the first chapter poses a crisis, the ensuing thirty chapters recount the hero's entire life up to that crisis, and the final chapter resolves it. (*The Enemy Camp,* by Jerome Weidman, is a vivid example of this approach.) By and large this strikes me as too much of a good thing; if the problem can be stated and resolved in ten thousand words, what's the point of wading through another hundred thousand words of background?

Ahem. I've also written quite a few suspense novels which do not follow the pattern I've described. While I think it's a wonderful way to structure a book, I certainly don't think it's the only way, and there have been many occasions when I've deliberately begun at the beginning.

For example:

Deadly Honeymoon features a honeymoon couple. On the first night thugs kill a man at a nearby cabin. Almost as an afterthought, they beat up the husband and rape the bride. The two do not report this to the cops; instead they hunt down the villains themselves. Here the rape is of paramount importance. It supplies the motive for everything that follows and makes their vigilante activity acceptable and even praiseworthy. There are no flashbacks in this book.

Such Men Are Dangerous is about a burnt-out case on the verge of a breakdown who hies himself off to an island in the Florida Keys and lives a hermit's existence. Then a CIA type drops in and involves him in a caper. This would have been a natural for the second-chapter-first approach but I was more interested in establishing the lead's character at the beginning since that to me was the most important single element of the book.

The Sins of the Fathers, the first of three books featuring ex-cop Matthew Scudder, opens with Scudder hired by a murdered girl's father. The action which follows is gradual and I felt the book would build most effectively if events were dealt with in chronological order. Flashbacks are a component of the other two Scudder books, however.

The Specialists is a caper book, a crew of ex-Green Berets and their legless colonel banding together to right wrongs and make money by doing in the evil-doers. I elected to open it with what the movie people call a pre-credit sequence: a hooker in Vegas is abused by a hood and she goes to one of the guys in the group and tells him about it. That's set off as a prologue and then the action begins.

(And I'll insert a confession here. Some books have spun themselves out in chronological order because I didn't know where they were going when I started writing them. Their plots just growed, Topsy-style. And occasionally topsy-turvy style. When the resulting narrative seemed natural enough I left it alone.

But whether your novel ought to begin at the beginning or not, just how and where it does begin is vitally important. All article writers know the importance of getting the lead paragraph absolutely right, and short-story writers know that a lead is every bit as important in fiction. (I think it's more important: a reader may stay with an article because the subject matter's interesting to him, but a weak lead will make him skip a short story nine times out of ten.)

Well, your first chapter is the lead paragraph of your novel. Mickey Spillane has said more than once that the first chapter sells the book and the last chapter sells the next book. I wouldn't dream of arguing with that.

A novel, as we've all heard far too often, ought to have a beginning and a middle and an ending.

No question about it.

But not necessarily in that order.

CHAPTER **26**

Spring Forward, Fall Back

ONE, TWO, three, four, five, six, seven, eight, nine, ten, eleven . . .

Well, if you were going to take the numbers one through eleven and put them in order, that's probably the order you'd put them in—unless you happened to be perverse, ignorant, psychotic, or wildly original. Most of us, however, while a wee bit perverse, ignorant, psychotic, and original, tend to arrange things in their natural order. When it comes to arranging events in a prose narrative, fictional or otherwise, the order we select is chronological order. We relate events as they happen, one after another.

I suspect human beings have always told stories in this fashion, ever since the first cave dweller embroidered the truth a bit in describing a hazardous altercation with a sabre-tooth tiger. By relating the events in the order in which they took place, the storyteller best holds the attention of his audience and maintains the highest possible degree of suspense. Will the tiger sense the man's approach? Will the beast attack? Will those keen fangs draw blood? Will the hunter's skill prevail? These questions become substantially less urgent if the narrator begins by describing the process of gutting and skinning the tiger, because by so doing he answers them before they can be asked.

There are other risks involved in departing from straightforward chrono-logical narration. A major one is confusion. When you play games with the temporal order of things, you run the risk of leaving the reader wondering just what the hell is going on. In *Writing the Novel: From Plot to Print* I dis-cussed two works that skipped artfully to and fro in time, Sandra Scoppet-tone's novel *Some Unkown Person* and Stanley Donen's film *Two for the Road.* While both gain something aesthetically from this reshuffling of time, both lose some of their audience in the process.

A story, it has been said far too many times, has a beginning, a middle and an ending. I think it's high time I admitted that I for one don't understand what this particular sentence means. One might as well announce that a story has a first page, a last page, and some pages in between the two. Or that a football game has a first half, an intermission, and a second half. Or that a golf tournament has a first round, two middle rounds, and a fourth round. Or that—

Enough. It might be more useful to point out that a story has two beginnings, its beginning on the first page and its chronological beginning. Sometimes they coincide. Sometimes they do not.

The chronological beginning of the chapter you are now reading lies in a memo from John Brady. I'll reproduce a part of it here, not only because it is pertinent but because I delight in retyping an editor's words and selling them back to him:

> When I teach magazine article writing, I always say, "Start in the middle and end at the beginning." It's rigid, it's handcuffs; it also works. Start full steam with a topic, get the reader involved and interested; then backtrack, fill in, move through the research, the topic, build, build, build . . . then, when you get to the end, look back at what you suggested in the beginning and round it out.

Magazine article writing is a different discipline from the writing of short or long fiction, and the process John describes here is better geared to nonfiction. The trick of starting in the middle, however, is extremely useful in fiction. By beginning at a point where events are already in motion, you involve your reader in the flow of action and get him caught up in your fiction right away. Then you can back off and let him know what it is he's gone and gotten himself interested in.

In the preceding chapter we saw how this principle works in opening a novel. The basic gimmick of switching one's first and second chapters is as simple and useful a one as I've learned.

And it's as useful in short fiction as it is in the novel. Short stories have to get to the point quickly, and one way to manage this is to begin them with the story already in motion and the action in process.

For illustration, the example that comes to mind is a negative one. Some months ago I happened on an ancient magazine story of mine, a crime-pulp yarn that begins with a guy coming home from the office only to find that the bar he always goes to is closed for alterations. So he wanders around until he comes to another bar, where he has a drink and meets a beautiful woman, and one thing leads to another and he becomes a dope dealer, as I recall.

Now it may be significant that he's in that second bar by coincidence, that the whole thing never would have happened if his usual watering hole had been open for business as usual on that particular evening. But that don't butter no parsnips. What's more significant is that I had this clown wandering around for perhaps a thousand words before much of anything actually happened.

If I were writing this story today—and I won't, because it was a pretty lousy story in the first place—I'd begin much further along in the story's chronological flow. Perhaps I'd start with the lead's initial contact with the woman. Perhaps I'd begin with the two of them already engaged in some illegal transaction. In any event, I could go back later and fill in, letting the reader know who the guy is and how he got in this mess in the first place. I could do this in a full-scale flashback, or, more likely, in a briefer summary.

This basic technique of starting with action and filling in later on is applicable to more than the openings of stories and novels. It can be employed effectively over and over again in the course of a prose narrative. By springing ahead and falling back, a writer can create any number of new beginnings and avoid dull patches that would slow down his story.

Any transition may be the opportunity for a new beginning of this sort. If one chapter ends with the lead character going to bed, the succeeding chapter doesn't have to start with him getting up the next morning.

Here's an example from *The Last Good Kiss,* a particularly fine private eye novel by James Crumley. The narrator, who has just learned that the woman he's been seeking has died some years ago, is beaten up in his motel room and left trussed up in the bathtub. One chapter ends like so:

> Then his associate gagged me with a sock. I was thankful that it was clean, thankful that after they left I was able to shove the water control off with my foot, and thankful too that when the maid came in the next morning, she jerked the sock out of my mouth instead of screaming . . . I tipped the maid and told her to tell the desk that I would be staying over another day. I needed the rest.

Here's how the next chapter begins. Notice how Crumley starts things off not only after a spring forward but right in the middle of a new scene:

> "It's just not true," Rosie said for the fifth time.
> "I'm sorry," I repeated, "but I saw the death certificate and talked to the woman she was living with who saw the body. I'm sorry, but that's the way it is."
> "No," she said, and struck herself between the breasts, a hard, hollow

blow that brought tears to her eyes. "Don't you think I'd know in here if my baby girl had been dead all these years?"

It was an early afternoon again in Rosie's, soft, dusty shadows cool inside, and outside a balmy spring day of gentle winds and sunshine. . . . After a quick visit to the emergency room for an X-ray and some pain-killer, I had left Fort Collins and driven straight through on a diet of speed, codeine, beer, and Big Macs, and had arrived at Rosie's dirty, unshaved, and drunk. . . . Fireball woke up long enough to slobber all over my pants, but when I didn't give him any beer, he slunk over behind the door. Rosie wouldn't look at me, though, not when I came in, not even when I told her the news.

"I'm sorry," I said, "but she's dead."

This business of springing ahead and falling back is a timesaver, but Crumley could have handled the material in the same number of words without this mini-flashback. The chapter might have begun "After a quick visit to the emergency room" and covered the trip to Rosie's in the same abbreviated form. Instead, Crumley jumps directly into the scene at Rosie's. We want the scene to go on, want to know what will happen next in it, and thus are glad to receive the recapitulated material in the summary fashion in which it is presented.

The technique's a useful one in all manner of fictional narrative. In a long novel spanning many years, a jump into action can bridge a gap neatly and effortlessly. In a story with continuous action, like *The Last Good Kiss*, the same technique helps establish the novel as a collection of vivid scenes.

Spring forward, fall back. A good maxim to remember. If you don't get to apply it in your writing, at least it'll help you remember how to reset your clock when the country goes on or off Daylight Savings Time.

CHAPTER 27

Don't Take the D Train

IN AN early novel, written in my salad days (they were mixed and green, heavy on the oil and vinegar), I wrote, after intense deliberation and painstaking research, a passage that read something like this:

> I hung up the phone, thought for a moment, then got my topcoat from the hall closet. I let myself out of the apartment and used the key to lock the door after me. The elevator took me down six flights. I walked through the lobby to the street and headed west on 77th Street.
>
> At Broadway I turned downtown. There was a newsstand at the entrance to the subway station at 72nd and Broadway. I bought a paper and read it while I waited for the train. I took the downtown local to Columbus Circle where I walked through a passageway to the IND platform. I caught a Brooklyn-bound D train and rode it to DeKalb Avenue where I transferred to a local. At the Avenue M stop I got off the train and walked up a flight of sooty steps to—

Enough!

I trust you get the idea. The passage is imperfectly recalled, as well it might be, but the point is that I used to do this sort of thing all the time. Like the biography that told the high school girl more than she cared to know about Queen Victoria, I was telling my readers considerably more than they cared or needed to know about something that was neither germane to my story nor interesting in and of itself—i.e., the subway system of the city of New York.

Now this sort of detail might have been relevant in, say, *The Taking of Pelham One Two Three,* where the action of the story specifically concerns the hijacking of a subway train, but my narrator was using the train solely to get from Point A to Point B. So all I had to do was write something like this:

I hung up the phone, thought for a moment, then got my topcoat from the hall closet. Forty minutes later I stepped off a subway train in Brooklyn and walked up a flight of sooty steps.

Ah, those sooty steps. . . .

Well, transitions are tricky. Getting your characters in and out of the room is as complicated a problem for the novice fiction writer as shuttling them on and off the stage is for the neophyte playwright. While an increase in skill and confidence at this sort of thing does come with experience, transitions continue to demand that the writer make a choice, deliberate or intuitive, as to just how and where he will interrupt the narrative action and how and where he will pick it up again.

In multiple-viewpoint stories, this is just a matter of closing down one scene and skipping across space and time to open up another. The author still has choices to make as to just how much must be reported to the reader, but he's rather less likely to spend eternity on the subway. But in single-viewpoint narratives, whether told from the first or the third person, there's a natural tendency to account for every moment of the lead character's time and to tell the reader far too much.

Sometimes, of course, you'll want to tell the reader a great deal. Even the subway sequence at the beginning of this article might be appropriate, for instance, if you wanted to convey a sense of the tedious passage of time, the monotony of dragging oneself here and there beneath the city streets, and the dogged persistence of the narrator in carrying out his task, whatever it may be.

If, on the other hand, you want to stress action and pace, you might prefer to make your transitions as abrupt as possible. No one does this better than Mickey Spillane. His detective, Mike Hammer, just never spends any time getting from one scene to another. In one sentence he's stuffing some chap's head into a men's room toilet; a sentence later he's clear across town shooting a girl in the stomach. He may waste time now and then at lovemaking or thinking aloud but he never wastes it getting from place to place, from one piece of action to another.

Spillane started out writing comic books, and I think that's where he learned to make fast cuts. While I'd personally rather read the label on the little bottle of Worcestershire sauce than check out Mike Hammer's adventures, there's no getting around the fact that Spillane, especially in his early books, had an immediacy and a gut instinct for the dramatic that won him a large and genuinely loyal readership, and there's a little more to his success than sex and sadism.

In Spillane's books and writing of that sort, the story's action is all more or less continuous. Fast abrupt transitions are easy enough because what is skipped is pretty much routine. In stories that cover a great deal of time, though, you have to skip over days or weeks or months or years, and when you do the transitional passage sometimes reads like this:

> Summer mellowed into fall and fall into winter. The days grew shorter and the nights colder. The holidays came—Thanksgiving, Christmas, New Year's Day. Then, as the days lengthened again and the sun's rays once more began to warm the receptive earth. . . .

Years ago filmmakers used to do this sort of thing by showing us hands spinning merrily on a clock or months flipping by on a calendar. Or they'd hurl a montage of newspapers on the screen, their headlines advancing history from, say, Armistice Day to the attack on Pearl Harbor.

Without flipping calendar pages, you can make faster cuts and still give the reader a sense of the passage of time. You might simply take up your character in the middle of a new scene and add a sentence somewhere along the way to establish the scene, like so:

> Susan slipped out of bed, moving silently to avoid waking Howard. She put on a robe and hurried downstairs, mindful of the board two steps from the bottom that would groan if you stepped in its center. It was January now, they'd been in the house for three months, and he still hadn't found the time to fix the creaking stair.

The transitional information here—that it is January and they've been in the house for three months—is slipped in here in a quick sentence that lets Susan whine to us about Howard's procrastination and perhaps tells us something about their relationship. We've advanced the action and told the reader what time it is in unobtrusive fashion.

Here's another way to cover a lot of time quickly, in this case through a long-range weather report:

> The next two winters were mild ones. Then, when the boy was four years old, frost came the last week in September and the first snow fell before Thanksgiving, and it was well into April before the ground was warm enough to plow.

Suppose your story involves a relationship between the narrator and another character. You might have a transition along these lines, simply bridging the gap between two wide-spaced meetings of the two:

I shook his hand and smiled. "I'll see you," I said, but in fact it was nearly three years before I saw Waldo Gordon again. I thought of him from time to time, though not too intently or too often. Then one May evening on the way home from my club I turned a corner and there he was. The first thing I noticed about him was that he'd put on weight. He was jowly and he'd taken on a bit of a paunch, and my eyes registered this before I happened to note that his right arm was missing from the elbow down. Indeed I had already reached out to shake his hand when . . .

But let's go back to the D train for a moment. One reason that it's permissible, and indeed desirable, to skip all that garbage is that *nothing much happens in its course*. It's no real challenge to get from place to place by subway—at least it's not supposed to be—and this particular passage is uneventful.

It's a temptation for novice writers to over-report such subway rides because they're easy to write about while skimping on more important scenes which are trickier to write. When that subway ride's important—when the hero gets beaten up in its course or shinnies up the third rail or whatever, that's when you can't cheat. You've got to write about it.

Here's a good example of the way prose differs from film. A film, unlike a book, moves at a predetermined pace. The viewer has to put up with the cuts that the director has made. He can't set the film aside for a moment and frown, then pick it up again, back it up a few frames, and examine it for inconsistency. As a result, films can be wildly inconsistent and illogical, and their cuts can get the characters in and out of unexplained trouble.

But you can't get away with that in a book or story.

Some years back I wrote a book called *The Thief Who Couldn't Sleep,* about a sort of whimsical adventurer who played hopscotch all over the map of Europe in the course of chasing down some long-buried treasure. A lot of the plot business was devoted to his crossing borders surreptitiously through diverse stratagems abetted by various odd characters. While I never got a Pulitzer Prize for this, it worked well enough as a book.

A while later, after many a summer had melted into fall and the Jets won the Super Bowl, it became my job to transform this book into a screenplay. (Of which, sadly, nothing ever came.) Well, a lot of those border crossings, amusing enough on the page, clearly would *not* work on film. Too slow, too talky, not enough happening visually. So, having previously established the resourcefulness of the character, I took to showing his achievements. I had him cornered in an alleyway in France, wearing a three-piece suit and carrying a briefcase. Then I cut to an interior shot of a busful of Italian workmen in Milan, laughing and singing and eating their lunch, and the camera moved in to reveal that one of their number, dressed like them and behaving like them, was our hero. No explanation, because this was film and *how* he dunnit didn't matter much.

Film and television techniques have made readers more sophisticated. We don't have to have things spelled out for us as thoroughly as we once did. But this still doesn't mean you can cheat in prose, and that cut to the bus in Milan is something I'd never dream of doing in cold print.

Transitions are interesting. It can be instructive to see how other writers handle them, for better or worse, and you might want to take special note of this sort of thing in your own reading. But whatever you do, *don't* take the D train. Mr. Ellington says you should take the A train instead.

It's still the quickest way to get to Harlem.

CHAPTER **28**

The I's Have It

SOME TWENTY years ago, when I was earning a dishonest living criticizing manuscripts for a schlock agent, a stock paragraph in my letters of rejection cautioned hopeful writers against the use of first-person narration. The first person, I was quick to point out, was fraught with pitfalls for the inexperienced writer. It served as a barrier between the reader and the story itself, limited the scope of the narrative, and, as I recall, caused dental caries in children and skin cancer in laboratory mice.

Now this admonition to shun the first person was by no means my own private aberration. It still seems to be part of the conventional wisdom of writing courses to inveigh against this narrative form. I recall hearing all these warnings at an impressionable age and thinking what a shame it was that the first person was such a bad thing, since it was at the same time the most *natural* way to write.

Hmmmmm.

Now that I think about it, I wonder if this bias against the first person isn't very much a part of our Puritan tradition. Mencken defined Puritanism as the haunting fear that someone somewhere may be happy, and I don't think he'd mind our amending the definition to include the fear that someone somewhere may be doing what comes naturally. After all, if something's easy to do, if it comes naturally and simply and works like a charm, there must be *something* wrong with it. It'll give you hair on your palms, or make you blind, or something.

About the same time that I was telling people not to write in the first person, I came upon a how-I-do-it piece by David Alexander, a reporter for the old *Morning Telegraph* and the author of a series of excellent private eye novels featuring Bart Hardin, a Broadway type who lived upstairs of a flea circus, wore flamboyant vests, drank nothing but Irish whiskey and never took a drink before four in the afternoon. In order to give his writing a feeling of immediacy, Alexander explained, he wrote all his first drafts in the first person. But, in order to avoid hairy palms, he then rewrote them start to finish in the *third* person.

Mr. Alexander's no longer around so I'll never be able to ask him whether he really did this. I've a hunch he was having us on. Any man who deliberately writes a book in one voice with the intention of rewriting it in another is a man who makes government projects look like the invention of an efficiency expert. But it hardly matters what Alexander actually did. The fact that he could even conceive of this approach points up the two significant aspects of first-person narration—it provides a sense of immediacy, and it's somehow considered reprehensible.

Well, I myself may have joined the club and warned other clods not to use the first person, but that doesn't mean I was fool enough to take my own advice. My own first novel was written in the first person, and most of my mystery and suspense novels, including all those books involving series characters, have been so written. At the beginning I felt I was running grave risks, and that I was at the same time taking the easy way out, but I decided I'd just write this way, so to speak, until I needed glasses.

I haven't gone blind yet, although I'm moving into the foothills of Bifocal Country. And over the years I've received support in my addiction to the first person from sources as diverse as Somerset Maugham and the Ogallala Sioux (and I'll bet you a nickel no one ever put them in the same sentence before).

Indians first. An acquaintance who was raised on a reservation told me how Indian oral history, involving the repetition over the centuries of the stories of important battles and buffalo hunts, is always couched in the first person. While his listeners are aware that the tribal storyteller is recounting incidents that happened hundreds of years before his birth, it's an accepted convention for him to speak in the voice of a participant or observer. *And then as I lay in the tall grass I saw Carries Two Spears riding from the mountains, and I felt the ground shake at his approach. . . .*

Maugham explained that as a young man he wrote with the stunning confidence of youth, adopting the omniscient third-person viewpoint. But when he grew older, he reported, he found it much more secure to write in his own voice and from a fixed point of view. (In Maugham's particular case, the limitations of the first person have less effect than gravity on a soaring hawk. If you want to see the agility with which a master can bend the first person to his ends, dealing with events at which his narrator is not present, swimming to and fro in the currents of time, give some attention to *The Razor's Edge, Cakes and Ale,* and *The Moon and Sixpence.*)

I've also noted my own tendency as a reader, when confronted with a rack of unknown paperbacks, is to select a book written in the first person in preference to one written in the third. All things being equal, a first-person book is more likely to have a sense of reality about it and the lead character is more apt to come alive for me.

As a writer, one of the things I like most about first person is the way it enables me to convey character easily and rapidly. In *Burglars Can't Be Choosers,* my lead's a sort of gentleman burglar who finds himself framed for murder and has to solve it to save himself. I wanted to get across right at the onset that this chap was a rather arch sort, so I wrote the first paragraph like this:

> A handful of minutes after nine I hoisted my Bloomingdale's shopping bag and moved out of a doorway and into step with a tall blond fellow with a faintly equine cast to his face. He was carrying an attaché case that looked too thin to be of much use. Like a high-fashion model, you might say. His topcoat was one of those new plaid ones and his hair, a little longer than my own, had been cut a strand at a time.

Hardly an immortal bevy of sentences, but they do limn the character and get things going. If the same paragraph were recast in third person, I don't think it could do the job nearly as well.

Characterization in general comes more easily for me in first-person books because it's such a natural matter. You don't observe from without. Instead, you get under your character's skin and speak to the reader in his voice, and by doing this you not only make the character come alive for the reader. You make him come alive for your own self as you write.

A standard objection to first person is that you can't describe your narrator. You can, of course, have him look into a mirror and report on what he sees, but I really hope you'll restrain yourself in this regard. Without an actual description you can convey some information about your lead's appearance—in the sample above, for instance, we have an idea what the lead's hair is like.

Anyway, I've long felt that there's a great advantage in *not* furnishing a physical description of a viewpoint character, and this is true whether you tell your story in first or third person. The story, after all, is seen through his eyes and over his shoulder, and you often come out ahead letting the reader make up his own mind what the lead looks like. (Often, I suspect, the reader winds up seeing the narrator as looking rather like himself. That's as vital a process in fiction as transference is in psychoanalysis, and the last thing you want to do is impede it.)

While first-person narration comes easily to most beginning writers—it is, after all, the natural voice one employs when telling a story to a friend— there are certain undeniable pitfalls which may come into play. Perhaps the most common is the tendency to tell the reader far too much about what is running through the narrator's mind. If reading a first-person story is like hearing a story at a party, reading a story with this fault is like being cornered by a crashing bore who won't let go of one's coat.

I don't know exactly how one sets about avoiding this. You might simply bear in mind that it is not necessary to report to the reader every thought that goes through the narrator's mind, any more than you would report every single act the narrator performs in his day-to-day existence. (You don't have to mention every time your lead shaves, or goes to the toilet, or freshens her makeup, or whatever.)

Along the same line, it is possible for *significant* things to happen to the narrator without their being reported to the reader. This can be important in suspense fiction. While it's not fair or dramatically satisfying to withhold important information forever, you can pick your time to reveal it. In *The Sins of the Fathers,* for instance, I have Matt Scudder enter an apartment illegally to look for evidence. He reports:

> The window wasn't locked. I opened it, let myself in, closed it after me.
> An hour later I went out the window and back up the fire escape. . . .

Now what Scudder found in the apartment is important, and a couple of chapters later he lets the reader know about it. But it would have slowed things down to report on his discoveries when he made them, so I postponed the revelations accordingly. More important, in the same book, there's a point where he figures out What Really Happened—but that explanation's postponed until a confrontation with the evil-doer rather than disclosed by having Scudder think aloud.

There is one long-term hazard in first-person writing, and I had that brought home to me when I gave a writer friend a manuscript of mine called *The Triumph of Evil.* He reported that he liked it. "Of course I knew how it was going to end," he said, "but I don't think anyone else would have known."

Why, I asked, had he known?

"The book wasn't multiple viewpoint. But you wrote it in the third person."

So?

"So I figured the only reason *you* didn't use first person was the lead character was going to die at the end, so I wasn't exactly awestruck when he did."

Hmmmmm.

CHAPTER **29**

The Plot's the Thing

DEAR MR. BLOCK,

I read your column in *Writer's Digest* regularly and can't understand your statement that the plot is the single most important element of a story or novel. Either you're wrong or the cards are truly stacked against the beginner in this writing game. Many's the time I've put in long, hard hours writing a story to have it rejected. Agents will criticize the story as trite and explain to me what's wrong with the plot. Then a matter of months or years later I'll see a story with the identical plot published in a major magazine, but with the byline of a "name" writer. So I don't think plot is as important as you claim it is. Maybe it's a question of writing style. Mine may not be as smooth as some people's, although Lord knows I try. Or maybe, as I strongly suspect, it's largely a question of who you know. . . .

For myself, I've always felt that it's not who you know, it's what you've got on 'em. But that's by the way. The letter quoted above is a fabrication, although it certainly echoes any number of letters in my files. It also echoes thoughts of my own that have come to me over the years. Ages ago, when I labored in the vineyards of a literary agent, my job consisted of criticizing the efforts of amateur writers who had submitted them with reading fees. I was under instructions to stress in each instance that the story's plot was at fault, so as to avoid reflecting adversely upon the client's writing ability and to encourage him or her to send us more stories—and more reading fees.

I felt at the time that this was palpable nonsense. Here I'd be reading the effort of someone who couldn't write his name in the dirt with a stick and instead of telling him as much I'd talk about the fundamental inadequacies of the story's plot—knowing all the while that O. Henry once wrote a story with the identical plot and did just fine with it, thank you. I began to suspect that plot was the least important component of a story, that the only real question was whether the writer could write.

Basic writing ability is essential, to be sure. Facility with prose and dialogue is vital, and when it is lacking one knows on the very first page that a story is not worth finishing. I was made freshly aware of this while judging entries in *Writer's Digest*'s recent short-story contest. It was not necessary for me to scan more than a page of half or more of the entries in order for me to determine that the writing ability of the entrant was insufficiently high to rank the story among the prizewinners.

Some writers fooled me, however. They had the ability, and there was a spark in their prose and dialogue that kept me reading all the way through, nearly certain I held a winner in my hands. Then, like as not, I wound up shrugging and sighing or ranting and raving—and in any event shredding the story and moving on to the next entry. Because, time and time again, the plot would prove to be a washout. "No impact!" I'd rant. "No conflict!" I'd rave. "No story!" I'd lament, and tear the offending manuscript in half.

As this happened in story after story, I was struck anew by an old truth. The plot is the most important single element of a story. Indeed, the plot *is* the story. Unless it works, all you've got is words.

But wait a minute. Isn't there a contradiction here? We've all seen writers succeed with plots with which we've failed, and it's not always a matter of style—or of who or whom you know. What gives?

What gives, I suspect, is a confusion of plot and idea. An idea, as I see it, is the premise of a story. A plot is the structure by means of which that idea is transformed into a work of fiction.

Sometimes an idea, if it's good enough, will make a story successful in and of itself. This is especially likely to be the case with short-shorts, which are often little more than ideas in prose form. In the *Writer's Digest* contest, for example, I awarded a high prize to one entry just a few hundred words long because it was a legitimate surprise and a wholly original notion. It was also nicely developed, but there's no question that the idea was primarily responsible for the story's high placement.

Perhaps we can most effectively distinguish between idea and plot, and understand the subtle importance of the latter, by looking at a case in point. I only recently made the acquaintance in print of one William Trevor, a short-story writer of uncommon excellence whose work I recommend to you without reservation. Mr. Trevor, an Irish writer now living in Devon, not only writes involving and affecting stories but is also infintely variable in theme and subject matter. His stories do not run to type, and their only common denominator is their unflagging quality.

Having said as much, I'm going to ruin one of the best of his stories for you by telling you about it. The story in question is "Last Wishes" and it appears in *Angels at the Ritz,* a collection of a dozen of Mr. Trevor's stories currently available in paperback from Penguin.

And here's the plot:

Mrs. Abercrombie, an old woman, is both a recluse and a hypochondriac. She rarely leaves her bedroom, where she is attended by a flock of faithful servants who are devoted to her and who love their work. Her only contact outside her own household is with the doctor who makes regular visits to her bedside.

Suddenly and unexpectedly, Mrs. Abercrombie dies. The servants are threatened with the loss of their living situation, until one of their number realizes that they can go on indefinitely as long as no one knows of the woman's death. No one has seen her outside the house since her husband's death decades ago. They can bury her on the property and proceed as if she were still alive, living out their own remaining years in peace and harmony—if only they can get the doctor to countenance their deception.

That's the story's idea, its premise, and while there's a good measure of ingenuity to it, it is William Trevor's considerable ability which makes "Last Wishes" as good as it unquestionably is. Writing style and characterization play their role, but plotting craftsmanship is also abundantly evident.

The story begins with our introduction to life at Mrs. Abercrombie's house. We're given some background on the woman, then introduced to the servants in turn, with a paragraph or so about each to show us how ideal the Abercrombie household is for them all. Plunkett, the butler, is sleeping with

Tindall, the housemaid. The two gardeners love their silent work, and the cook rejoices in having her meals appreciated after a lifetime of institutional cooking. We at once like these people and like the way they get on together. We want them to continue in this fashion forever.

Next we meet Mrs. Abercrombie, who has her breakfast, looks at her mail, recalls the circumstances of her husband's death, and quietly dies in her bed. It is a peaceful death, and we perceive it as no tragedy; for years Mrs. Abercrombie has been waiting to die that she might be reunited with her husband in heaven.

The servants are shaken by her death, especially when Plunkett reveals that Mrs. Abercrombie had been in the process of altering her will. The estate is to pass to an institution for the study of rare grasses, but Mrs. Abercrombie's solicitors just that morning had written to her about her projected change of will, by the terms of which her servants would have life tenancy on the property prior to its passing into the hands of the research institution. But the woman has died before the revised will could be prepared.

All of the servants begin to see what their lives will be like elsewhere, and the outlook for them is uniformly unpleasant. It is at this point that Plunkett conceives of burying the woman on her property and concealing her death, and he begins trying to sell this plan to the rest of the household. He starts with the rationalization that they would merely be carrying out her actual wishes and before long reaches the point of lying, telling the assembled company that Mrs. Abercrombie expressed the wish to be buried on her own land. He argues that the doctor can be gotten round, painting the picture of the doctor as an incompetent responsible for deaths in the past, virtually senile, and something of a toper. Gradually he begins to win them over, overcoming the objections of the cook, but having a hard time getting round Miss Bell, the second gardener. Eventually, with the doctor ringing the doorbell, Plunkett's rationalizations have become increasingly desperate, acrimony between him and Miss Bell has been unsheathed, and the man's excitement even leads him to a grammatical lapse, this last the first such failing which Tindall, his occasional bedmate, has known him to make.

Enter the doctor. Plunkett takes him to the bedroom, then reveals his plan—and it is at this point that we the readers realize his plan is absurd. We've accepted it wholeheartedly up to this point, but now we are hearing it as it were with the doctor's ears, and it's nonsense. Nor is the doctor the bumbler Plunkett has led us to expect—the bumbler we've *wanted* him to be. Plunkett's plan to blackmail him into silence, which struck us as just and reasonable when it was hatched in the kitchen, now comes across as base and impossibly ill-conceived. Of course the doctor won't go along with this, and of course he shouldn't, and how could we have ever thought otherwise?

So much for the plan. The doctor's opening the door has let the cool air of reality into the house. But more has happened than that a plan has been proposed and dashed. The delicate relationship between the parties in the house has been forever changed. They who had been a family are now a collection of strangers ill at ease with one another.

But Mr. Trevor has one more zinger for us. Because the doctor realizes from a glance at the solicitor's letter that all of this has been for naught. Mrs. Abercrombie's instructions to her lawyers would be honored despite the fact that the will has not yet been drawn and signed; her intent was clear and her untimely death will not prevent her wishes from being carried out. Plunkett did not realize that, none of them did, and thus the flaws in their characters ruined their prospects, and it's far too late for the woman's last wishes to change things; these people, forever changed by their moral weakness, cannot possibly go on living together.

Do you see what I'm getting at? It's not the *idea* of "Last Wishes" that makes it a powerful experience for the reader. It's what the author has done with the idea, primarily in terms of the structure of its plot. I'm afraid I've ruined the story for you in order to provide this illustration, but in a larger sense I have not; a story as good as "Last Wishes" is not easily ruined. If you've an interest in short fiction, I would strongly urge you to pick up a copy of *Angels at the Ritz* and read the story for yourself. And read the rest of the stories while you're at it; Mr. Trevor makes a habit of this sort of thing.

CHAPTER

No More Mr. Nice Guy

I'M NOT much on Hitler jokes as a general thing, but here's one from some-body's old nightclub routine that has lingered in the mind. The fuehrer's in the bunker, see, in the spring of '45. Messengers bring him one piece of dreadful news after another. German forces are reeling back from catastrophic defeat on every front. The Allies are advancing in the west and the Russians are on the outskirts of Berlin. The Third Reich, built to last a thousand years, is collapsing.

"All right," Hitler snarls. "All right! They have gone too far! From now on, no more Mr. Nice Guy!"

Ahem. Levity aside, boys and girls, the subject of today's class is motivation, and it would seem to me that—yes, Arnold?

Could you define motivation for us, sir?

I suppose so, Arnold. Motivation is the business of supplying your fictional characters with plausible reasons for them to act as you would have them act in order for your stories to be dramatically effective.

And motivation is not something which can be merely taken for granted, like blue eyes. You can just say that a character has blue eyes and let it go at that. You don't have to explain that his mother also had them, that her ancestors came from a village in Sweden where everyone was blue-eyed. You may mention as much if you want, but the reader will generally accept most of the physical aspects of your characters as given. He'll take your word for it.

He won't take your word that such a character feels a burning desire for revenge, or to right a wrong, or to get a better job, or to steal a car, or whatever you would have him do. He'll accept the ordinary—if your lead character is an accountant, let us say, he may add a column of figures without provoking a quibble from the reader. It is an ordinary part of an accountant's day to add a column of figures. But if he rushes off to British Columbia to extinguish a forest fire, or to light one, you'd better have furnished him with a reason for so doing.

Then motivation is necessary when a character does something extraordinary?

Hmmm. I guess that's as good a way as any to put it. It might be of more practical value to say that motivation is important at those points in a narrative where a reader might wonder why the characters are acting in a certain way when they might act in another, or not act at all.

There have been times in my own life when I have had particular difficulty supplying my characters with adequate motivation. One time, I recall, I went for several months without writing anything because I couldn't think of a single reason for any character to care strongly enough about anything to take any real action in any direction. Plots just wouldn't form themselves in my mind, or wherever in a person's anatomy they tend to take shape. On another occasion, I began writing several novels in succession, each of which died on the vine somewhere around page sixty, perishing out of a massive failure of the author's imagination. I couldn't summon up a reason for any of the characters to Go On, or dream up anything for them to say or do if they did.

Did you want to say something, Rachel?

Just that we're all glad you're feeling better now, sir.

Why, thank you, Rachel. Now where was I?

No matter. I read a book recently that will serve us as a particularly good example of how a skillful author can motivate his characters and make us believe the dramatic validity of their actions. How many of you have read *Wilderness,* by Robert B. Parker? Raise your hands if you've read it. Haven't *any* of you read it? Arnold?

I guess the general feeling, sir, is why buy hardcover suspense novels?

I see.

Well, let me tell you about *Wilderness* then, since you haven't had a chance yet to read it for yourselves. The hero is a writer named Aaron Newman. He runs and lifts weights to keep in shape, and is passionately devoted to his wife of twenty years, this notwithstanding the fact that their marriage is rather crumby.

One day, while jogging home from the gym, Newman witnesses a murder. An honorable man, a man *concerned* with honor, he goes to the police and agrees to testify against the murderer, a notorious hoodlum. He returns from the police station to find his wife tied naked in their bedroom, a warning from the hoodlum. She has not been raped, merely violated optically and emotionally.

His code of honor notwithstanding, Newman promptly knuckles under, earns the contempt of the police by retracting his identification of the killer, and sets about trying to live with himself and his wife. This is made rather more difficult by his recognition of the fact that the sight of his wife, bound and helpless, has had an undeniable aphrodisiacal effect on him. Furthermore, his inability to protect his wife from these savages makes it harder for him to live with himself and accentuates his wife's propensities to reveal contempt for him in any number of ways, and—yes, Edna?

I think you're trying to say she's a ballbreaker, sir.

Thank you, Edna.

Now comes a test of Parker's ability to motivate his character. The plot he's devised calls for Newman and his wife to launch themselves upon a mission of revenge, to expunge the humiliation they have suffered by taking the law into their own hands and committing an uncharacteristic act of homicide. They are taking vengeance out of proportion to the injury inflicted upon them; although their adversary is unquestionably a murderer himself, all the Newmans have suffered at his hands is intimidation.

Mr. Parker makes this work by motivating his character a little at a time, and by arranging plot developments that derive naturally and directly from the characters and situation he has established. The idea of killing the hoodlums first comes up in a drunken conversation, with Newman throwing it out with macho bravado. The wife seizes on the idea—she wants these men dead and seems to have no trouble articulating the desire. And Chris Hood, a bar owner and friend of Newman's, takes up the idea.

Hood is an important character. He killed men in wartime, and rather liked it. His life since then hasn't come to much. The Newmans' mission of vengeance is an opportunity for him to live intensely as he has not been able to live in years. Furthermore, Hood has the skills for this sort of thing. With his assistance, the whole operation becomes conceivable.

The Newmans want to get the thing over and done with as quickly as possible, to kill their enemy and get away with it. Hood, however, has an infinite capacity for taking pains that ultimately amounts to a delaying tactic—he'd like to devote a lifetime to planning and reconnaissance and rehearsal, because once the dirty deed is done his *d'être* will no longer have any *raison*. This is excellent for plot purposes, in that a problem in many novels of vengeance is that the logical thing for the characters to do—i.e., take revenge quickly and directly—would bring the book to an abrupt and unsatisfying conclusion some twenty thousand words down the road, while a more circuitous route leaves the reader wondering why the characters aren't brighter and more to the point. Hood's vacillation, like Hamlet's, is not unreasonable, and it is Newman who is frustrated by it, not the reader.

Right about this point Mr. Parker boosts the ante a little. Although we may have accepted the Newmans' motivation in desiring revenge, it's been something they want, not something they need. Revenge might help their relationship, but the notion of killing some stranger to bolster your marriage is not something you're likely to encounter in Dear Abby. Indeed, we might have trouble avoiding some sympathy for their opponent as he goes through life as an unwitting target.

No problem. We learn that the hoodlum has elected to make assurance doubly sure by hiring a killer to hurry Newman off to kingdom come. We meet the killer as he plans his crime, and he's himself killed on Newman's own doorstep by Chris Hood, whom we've seen before on solitary, secret night vigils in the Newmans' yard, vigils which have seemed absurd until now.

See how the stakes have gone up? It's now kill-or-be-killed, because it's to be expected that their adversary will hire another killer when he learns of the failure of the first. This incident, too, makes the whole thing much more real for the Newmans. They have to take it seriously.

The locale shifts to the wilderness, where their quarry goes on a hunting trip along with his son and the two henchmen who violated Ms. Newman. Our trio is in pursuit, and it is in the wilderness that Hood is able to indulge his passion for war games and strategy sessions. His skills have never been more valuable, yet paradoxically he becomes a liability here, missing opportunities for an easy kill because he cannot bear to see the game end.

Hood dies, finally, in a skirmish with the hoodlums. At the same time, Newman is recognized; again the stakes are raised, in that their opponent knows Newman's identity and will not rest until Newman is dead. And Hood's death has disarmed the Newmans. They have to rely on their own resources now, on resources they may not in fact possess.

At this point—yes, Rachel?

Don't spoil the story for us, Mr. Block.

I wouldn't dream of it. I don't know that I could, even if I were to carry this plot summary to the book's conclusion, because the excitement in *Wilderness* lies not merely in what happens but in how it happens, and in how the characters act and react and how they are affected by their actions and reactions.

I see our time's almost up for today. I hope I've given you a glimmering of the way an author's ability to motivate his characters affects the reader's response to the story, not merely creating suspense along the way but making us care what happens to these people. There are other elements of the book I'd discuss if we had more time—the cameo relationship between the hired killer and his woman, for instance, which is a provocative contrast to the Newman marriage. I hope you'll read the book and see for yourself.

I hope, too, that I've answered your question, Arnold.

What question was that, sir?

"Why buy hardcover suspense novels?" And I'm sure you won't have too much trouble uncovering my motive for so doing. My own most recent hardcover suspense novel is readily available wherever good books are sold. I expect all of you to go right out and buy it.

CHAPTER 31

Think You've Got Problems?

WANT TO hear a terrific idea for a story? Just listen to this. After a war, a whole bunch of guys are anxious to get back home to their wives and sweethearts and aged mothers. So they get on board their ship, have a nice smooth voyage, and the next thing you know they're all back home, safe and sound, and everybody's happy.

You don't like it?

I don't know why not. It worked pretty well a while back, when a guy named Homer wrote it and called it *The Odyssey*. It's worked well any number of times since then, its latest incarnation being Sol Yurick's recently filmed novel, *The Warriors*. Homer was writing about veterans of the Trojan War, Yurick about members of a teenage gang, but the problem in both stories is the same—i.e., getting home safe.

And problem, after all, is what a story is about. To one extent or another, every story or novel involves a lead character's attempt to cope with a problem. If the lead is well drawn and human and believable and sympathetic, if he's the sort with whom the reader can strongly identify, then the reader will want things to work out for him. And, if the problem is believable and significant and urgent, the lead's successful resolution of the problem becomes important to the reader.

You couldn't ask for a better hero than Odysseus, and returning safely and swiftly to Ithaca is a fine central problem, whether you're a bunch of Greek soldiers or the Cornell football team. But what has made that voyage a memorable one for readers down through the millennia is the fact that it was never smooth sailing, not for a minute. From the time they left Troy, Odysseus and his merry men were constantly in hot water. They no sooner stared down the Cyclops than they had to steer between Scylla and

167

Charybdis. If the Sirens weren't calling them, Circe was turning them into swine. The tension never stopped.

The title characters in Yurick's novel don't have it much easier. Their central problem is returning safely from the Bronx, no easy task for any New Yorker at the best of times. It's especially difficult for the Warriors because members of dozens of other gangs are dogging them every step of the way, determined to kill them. For Yurick's Warriors, as for those ancient Ithacans, life is just one damned thing after another.

Pay attention.

Because we are about to fasten upon an essential truth.

Fiction is just one damned thing after another. If your hero, however likable he may be, confronts his problem, however desperate it may be, and just plain goes ahead and solves it, you have not got something *Publishers Weekly* is going to call "a real page-turner." But if he keeps dodging one menace only to rush headlong into the jaws of another, and if his prospects keep getting worse, and if he winds up with more perils than Pauline, then you just might be on the right track.

Understand, if you will, that I am not just talking about adventure stories. A problem, in fictional terms, need not be quite so heart-pounding an affair as a voyage through hostile waters. It might be obtaining a master's in comparative linguistics, or coming to terms with one's sexual identity, or getting out of a bad marriage. And the perils along the way need not be of the lashed-to-the-railroad-track variety; they are whatever incidents complicate the story, render its successful outcome in doubt, and force the hero to overcome them in order to survive.

When I first started writing fiction, just a couple of months after the boys made it back to Ithaca, I had trouble with troubles. I might be able to limn a suitably heroic hero, and I might confront him with a sufficiently dire problem, but then I tended to let him go ahead and solve it cleverly and expeditiously and lickety-split.

I knew what I was doing wrong but I didn't seem to be able to do anything about it. I knew there was no real tension if a character fell into a pit and then hopped back out again. I knew that things had to get worse before they could get better, that my hero's efforts to solve his problem had to lead him deeper and deeper into trouble before he could finally win through to glory. I knew all that, and knowing helped me a little, but I still tended to make things easy for my hero. The result of this was two-fold; my stories rarely went on for more than fifteen hundred or two thousand words, and they rarely developed much in the way of tension. When they sold, it was to minor markets.

Well, time passed, as it tends to do, and my writing developed, albeit slowly. For a couple of years I turned out a soft-core sex novel every month, and those potboilers certainly taught me how to keep the pot boiling. While my lead characters may not have been getting into hot water in every chapter, they were at least getting into something, or vice versa.

My early suspense novels, now that I think of it, suffered from a lack of ever-heightening tension. In *Deadly Honeymoon,* for example, a bride and groom join together to hunt down and kill the thugs who raped the bride. There's tension, and they have problems along the way, but I can see now that the book would have been stronger had there been an increasing threat to them developing even as they contended with these problems.

The seven books I wrote about Evan Tanner were faintly similar in structure to *The Odyssey,* in that my ardent insomniac played a sort of global hopscotch in the course of solving a problem or two and finding his way back home. In a typical novel, Tanner would cross half a dozen international borders illegally, confronting pitfalls in seven languages before he was back home again on the Upper West Side.

Detective novels have a more confined structure. They don't ramble around so much, and the story is essentially over when the main problem—the identity of the murderer—is solved. This notwithstanding, the more effective books are generally marked by pitfalls and stumbling blocks which the lead keeps encountering, developments which he is unable to anticipate, and any number of elements which make the problem more difficult and its solution more urgent and imperative. A suspect turns out to be innocent. A key witness turns up dead. A murderer strikes again. The detective finds himself framed for the killing. An important item—money or jewelry or a Maltese falcon—disappears. One way or another, things get worse before they get better, and they hold the promise of getting even worse, and of not getting better at all.

To do this sort of thing effectively, you have to be your lead character's best friend and worst enemy all at the same time. You send your hero on a walk through the woods. Then you have a bear chase him. You let him climb a tree. You chop the tree down. The bear chases him into the river. He grabs onto a log. It turns out to be an alligator. He grabs a floating stick and uses it to jam the beast's jaws open. You give the bear a canoe and teach it how to paddle—

Well, you get the idea. At least I hope you do, because I'm not going any further with a bear in a canoe.

Although he has not yet to my knowledge placed a bear in a canoe, Robert Ludlum is a master at keeping things hot for his lead characters. A typical Ludlum novel—insofar as the books run to type—has his hero confronting a shadowy conspiracy of monumental proportions. From the onset, even before he's more than peripherally involved, Ludlum's hero is in Deep Trouble. Cars leap curbs at him. Safes fall from high windows and crash at his feet. Bullets whine overhead. Before he even knows who's doing what or why, the Ludlum lead has to do something in order to save himself.

And this sort of thing keeps happening. Some of it, in the final analysis, may not make absolutely perfect sense. You might finish a Ludlum novel, properly breathless and ready for bed. A couple of hours later you might wake up hungry, and on the way back from the icebox it might occur to you that there was no reason for the Estonian nationalists to put cyanide in the hero's peanut-butter cookies. That kind of icebox thinking may make it hard for you to get back to sleep, and it might even move you to write the author a letter demanding a full and proper explanation. But it can't negate the fact that the author and his poisonous Estonian villains kept you reading way past your normal bedtime. The incidents themselves were sufficiently involving, and the tension they generated sufficiently gripping, that your objections didn't manifest themselves until you'd finished reading the book—and enjoyed every page of it.

Does this mean you shouldn't worry about keeping your own plots sound and logical? Certainly not. You can't be sure that the reader won't spot your flaws until he's made a trip to the fridge. He may detect them immediately, in which case he may very well stop buying the whole premise of your story then and there.

It does mean you can take a few chances, trusting that you'll figure out a way to pull things together later on. This sort of thing happened in *The Burglar Who Liked to Quote Kipling*. Bernie Rhodenbarr, the very hero indicated in the title, has filched a rare book from a home in Forest Hills. Now, the following afternoon, he has just arranged to deliver it to the person on whose behalf he pilfered it.

It occurred to me that something dramatic ought to happen. So, while Bernie is standing behind the counter of his second-hand bookstore, the door opens and in walks a bearded Sikh with a turban. The Sikh points a gun at him and demands the book. Bernie gives it to him and out he goes.

When I wrote that scene, I hadn't the foggiest notion who the Sikh was, where he came from, or how he was going to fit into the book's future development. But he did liven things up, and I figured I'd burn those other bridges when I came to them. Later on, in the course of fitting him in and making sense of his actions, I got some ideas that enriched other elements of the book's plot.

There's a moral here. When things flag a wee bit, do something dramatic, Put a bear in a canoe or bring in a bearded, turbaned Sikh with a gun in his hand. Or work your own variation of this procedure. Try it with an Estonian bear, say, who walks into the bookstore with a canoe in his pocket. Instead of a turban, have the bear wearing one of those Smoky hats. Make the canoe an ocean liner. Make the bookstore a bakery so you can fit in those poisoned peanut-butter cookies. Make the Sikh a girl, but first get rid of the beard, and—

You don't like it? Maybe we can turn it around. There are a whole bunch of bears, see, and they've just finished fighting a war, and they're anxious to get back home to their wives and sweethearts and aged mothers. . . .

After the foregoing was written and set in type, I learned that The Warriors *was based not on* The Odyssey *but on* The Anabasis, *Xenophon's account of the Greek retreat after a disastrous military engagement in Persia. Rewriting it accordingly just seems like more trouble than it's worth, especially since it would require my reading* The Anabasis. *I beg the reader's indulgence for my Xenophobia.*

CHAPTER **32**

Judging Distances

HAVE YOU ever noticed how some writers draw you in close to their characters while others keep you at arm's length? The distance between a reader and a character is to a large extent a question of identification. The more the reader finds a character sympathetic, and the more he is able to relate to that character, the narrower the gulf between them becomes. When identification is intense enough, the reader may feel as though he's experiencing the story along with the character, seeing it through his eyes or over his shoulder. When identification is minimal, it's as if he's observing the action through the wrong end of a telescope.

But identification isn't all there is to it. On innumerable occasions I have found myself drawn close to unsympathetic characters and kept at a remove from sympathetic ones. Harry Bogen, the protagonist of Jerome Weidman's *I Can Get It for You Wholesale,* is certainly an unpleasant sort, with little of the charming rogue about him. Yet I can still remember how close I felt to him while reading that novel. On the other hand, although I identified strongly with Larry, in W. Somerset Maugham's *The Razor's Edge,* I never felt that kind of close proximity.

There are certain things you as a writer can do to draw the reader in or push him away from your lead character. The first thing to consider is how you're going to refer to the guy.

Let's say your lead character's a mining engineer named Lucian Hapgood. Well, as the fellow on television might put it, you could call him Lucian, or you could call him Hapgood, or you could call him Lucian Hapgood, or—

Enough. What you call him does make a difference in terms of distance. If you wanted the reader to be drawn closer to him—not necessarily in terms of liking him so much as in terms of sharing his experience—you wouldn't refer to him as "mining engineer Lucian P. Hapgood" except when you first introduced him, or when he's reintroduced after having been absent from the narrative for an extended period of time. You won't go on calling him by his full name, either. It'll have to be either Lucian or Hapgood.

Once you make this choice, I think you ought to stick with it. Not every writer does, however. In the early Ellery Queen novels, authors Manfred B. Lee and Frederic Dannay took turns at the typewriter, with the result that their hero is called Ellery in one chapter and Mr. Queen in the next. Other writers haven't needed to collaborate in order to bounce back and forth between first name and surname, and one of the elements that make Russian novels impenetrable for me—one of many elements, I'm afraid—is the tendency of their authors to make a guy named Dmitri Ivanovitch Glinkov, say, and call him one thing in one paragraph and another in the next and a third on the following page, until I really don't know who we're talking about.

The conventional wisdom holds that your reader will feel closer to your lead if you call the lead by his first name. I think this is probably true, but I think the decision of whether or not to call the character by his first name is more complicated than that.

Sometimes, it seems to me, you diminish your lead character by calling him by his first name. You reduce his statue and undermine his importance.

In a book called *The Triumph of Evil,* which I wrote under the name of Paul Kavanagh, I had to decide what to call Miles Dorn. On the one hand he is the presumably sympathetic lead from whose viewpoint the entire story is perceived. On the other, he's a professional assassin, a middle-aged terrorist with a lifelong history of violence who murders a great many people in the course of the book. While I wanted strong reader identification, I was leery of drawing Dorn's fangs by making him someone you'd call by his first name.

Writers almost always get on a first-name basis with female characters, and with juveniles. I'm not sure why this is, though I'm willing to believe that it's consciously or unconsciously patronizing, and that, in respect to female characters, sexism is at the root of it. For the time being, I'm afraid fiction writers are stuck with this situation. I may decide that I'm lessening a character's dignity when I call her Susan, but if I start calling her Ackerman instead I'm going to confuse readers. Furthermore, that sort of stylistic departure creates yards and yards of distance between character and reader.

In multiple-viewpoint novels, a frequent auctorial trick consists of calling your hero by his first name while calling other characters by their last names, even in scenes where they are the viewpoint characters. Robert Ludlum generally does this. It's a way of putting a white hat on the good guy, telling the reader whom to root for. Sometimes I find this device awkward, but sometimes it seems perfectly natural.

Come to think of it, I have a hunch the first-name-last-name question is one that is most effectively settled intuitively. I didn't consciously decide to call my man Dorn instead of Miles, making the decision for good sound reasons. I just recognized that I was more comfortable with him that way and acted accordingly.

At least as important as what you call your lead is the extent to which you call him anything at all. The more you use any name, the more distance you create. If you want to draw the reader in close, the trick is to use pronouns at all times except where to do so would result in confusion. Use the name to establish who we're talking about, and often enough throughout to avoid unclarity. At all other times, stick with *he* and *she*. You'll probably find that you don't have to use names very often.

In dialogue passages, you can cut down the distance even more by eliminating everything but the dialogue itself. Whatever else you include calls the reader's attention to the fact that he's not really overhearing a conversation but reading something that somebody wrote. Some of the distance is eliminated when you use *said* instead of substitute verbs, when you use pronouns instead of names, and when you cut out modifiers. "Jennings ruminated archly" is a more distancing phrase than "he said." When you drop the *he saids* and *she saids* as well, slipping one in now and then only when it would otherwise become hard to keep straight who's speaking, you make the conversation that much more intimate and bring the reader that much closer into it.

It's not hard to understand why a writer would want to reduce this kind of distance. Sometimes, however, it's desirable to *create* distance between the reader and the story.

A frequent device in mystery novels, for example, involves the use of a Watson, so called after the narrator of Sir Arthur Conan Doyle's Sherlock Holmes stories. The obvious functions of a Watson include keeping the reader in the picture while hiding certain things from him; he knows only what the Watson knows, not what the Great Detective is thinking or observing. Additionally, the Watson character can marvel at the brilliance and eccentricity of the Great Detective, who would appear egomaniacal were he to mutter such self-aggrandizement directly into our ears.

But I think another important advantage of the Watson device is the distance it creates, distance from the Great Detective but not from the story. That character, with his quirks and idiosyncrasies, is more commanding if we are made to stand a bit apart from him. Let us peer over his shoulder and we can see his feet of clay.

The use of a subordinate character as narrator is by no means limited to mystery fiction. Consider Maugham's first-person narrators in *The Razor's Edge, The Moon and Sixpence,* and *Cakes and Ale,* John O'Hara's Jim Malloy, or Melville's Ishmael. These voices are hardly Watsons, but their functions are not all that dissimilar.

In a handful of stories I wrote about a criminous criminal lawyer, I used several techniques to keep the reader at a distance from my character, Martin H. Ehrengraf. For example, I frequently referred to Ehrengraf as "the little lawyer" or "the diminutive attorney." The purpose of this was not so much as to fix Ehrengraf's appearance in the reader's mind as to make the reader aware that he was reading a narrative, that this was a piece of fiction about an imaginary character.

Why did I do this? For one thing, the Ehrengraf stories were by nature unrealistic, the character a dapper eccentric who fabricates evidence and murders people in order to exonerate guilty clients. Write something like that and make it genuinely realistic and, paradoxically, readers react by failing to come through with the voluntary suspension of disbelief which fiction requires. By distancing the reader from Ehrengraf, I was effectively saying, "Relax, this is just fiction, this disagreeable madman doesn't really exist, so it's okay to unwind and pretend that he does long enough to enjoy the story."

Similarly, the Ehrengraf stories were illogical and implausible—or would have been if seen from up close and treated realistically. At a remove, they could be allowed to have their own mad logic.

I generally feel a little funny writing about specific fictional techniques. I think it's enormously valuable to know how writers get the effects they do. I know that my own reading is marked by a good deal of reflection as I notice the particular technical choices a writer makes and their various effects.

At the same time, it is exceedingly rare that I consciously apply the fruits of this analysis in my own writing. I have just now been reflecting on those Ehrengraf stories, and I cannot recall ever deciding to keep the reader from stepping on Ehrengraf's heels. The techniques I employed were selected intuitively, without thought; it simply seemed the natural way to tell a particular story. Once in a great while I make this sort of decision purposefully, but the rest of the time it's an unconscious one.

This makes it no less a choice, but it does make me feel wary of overexplaining this sort of thing to you. If you were to gain anything from this column, I would hope it would be just a little more awareness of your options as a storyteller, and perhaps a touch more analytical perspective when you read other writers' work. And perhaps this will ultimately improve your ability to make choices of your own, on the unconscious intuitive plane where most creative decisions seem to be made.

CHAPTER

It's a Frame

GOOD MORNING, class.

Good morning, Mr. Block.

As you may recall, last week we were discussing—yes, Arnold?

Actually it's afternoon, sir.

So it is. Thanks so much for bringing that fact to my attention, Arnold. Ahem. Last week we were discussing distance in fiction, and the various ways in which the distance between the reader and the story may be either diminished or increased. There was one rather interesting distancing device I didn't mention at all. It's called a frame. Anyone know what a frame is? Rachel?

Yes, sir. it's when you're innocent but the police fabricate a case against you anyway. Or the real criminal leaves false clues so that you'll be suspected. Or—

Thank you, Rachel. I'm afraid the frame I'm referring to is a different matter. A frame as a literary device is a way of setting a story—either a short story or a novel—within a fictional superstructure of one sort or another. In its simplest form, such a story might consist of two men running into each other in a bar, say, and—yes, Gwen?

Why do they have to be men, sir?

They don't. They could be women. They could be one man and one woman. No reason, actually, for them to be human beings at all. Let's say two Venusians encounter each other in a bar, all right? They're having a friendly drink together, and one says something and the other is reminded of a story. Which he—or she, Gwen—tells at considerable length. When the story's finished they have one last drink and go their separate ways.

See how this works? The actual core of the story is whatever the one Venusian relates to the other, and the reader's in the position of a person on the next barstool, eavesdropping on their conversation. That barroom sequence encloses and sets off the true story just as a picture frame surrounds a canvas.

If the story's worth telling in the first place, it could stand by itself, unsupported by a framing device. What one Venusian tells the other could be related directly to the reader, either by the Venusian in the first person, or through third-person narration. What do you suppose are the effects of using a frame?

You mentioned distance, sir.

Indeed I did, and that's the most obvious result of building a frame around a piece of fiction. You create distance between the story and the reader. Right off the bat, you make him—or her, Gwen—conscious of the fact that this is indeed a story. Fiction owes a lot of its impact to the fact that we lose sight of this while we're reading. Our voluntary suspension of disbelief enables us to become convinced that the story is happening as we are reading it.

Let's consider a frame of another sort, one in which the framing device is not a conversation but the passage of time. An example that comes quickly to mind is *True Grit,* the novel by Charles Portis. The book takes the form of the first-person narrative of a fourteen-year-old girl's pursuit of her father's killer, but we are being told the story years and years after the fact, by the woman into whom that fourteen-year-old girl has grown.

You would think that this would gut the book of its suspense. Mattie, the heroine, is in danger of death at the story's climax, yet we know with absolute certainty that she is destined to survive for at least another half-century. It is a measure of Mr. Portis's considerable skill that Mattie's story remains highly suspenseful in spite of the fact that we know she has lived to tell the tale.

Still, distance is distance. There's no frame in the film version of *True Grit,* and I'm sure it was an easy decision to dispense with it. I think we would have to acknowledge that some suspense and some immediacy is lost as a result of the frame device. Are there gains to offset this loss? And what might they be?

It seems to me that there's a significant gain in *dimension.* In Portis's novel, we see Mattie's whole life, not just the portion she tells us about. We learn by means of occasional asides that she never married, that she has become a rather hard-nosed businesswoman, that her neighbors and associates have come to regard her as somewhat eccentric, and by learning this while watching her perform as an adolescent we are seeing an illustration of Wordsworth's observation that the child is father of the man (or, in this case, mother of the woman). We watch the unfolding of the story itself through Mattie's fourteen-year-old eyes and from her vantage point as a mature woman, and this gives the book scope that it would not otherwise have.

A Covenant With Death, by Stephen Becker, is similar in that the narrator, a middle-aged judge, recounts a case that took place early in his legal career. Again, how that experience looks from the perspective of age, and how it shaped and colored the intervening years, is part of the story.

The frame is not a device I employ frequently, but I did write one which appeared not long ago in *Gallery.* It's set in an unnamed island in the South Seas, where two brothers, a planter and a trader, are trying to get the better of one another in an exchange. One has a legendary bottle of 1835 Cognac, while the other has as his ward a nubile young woman of mixed ancestry. Each consults the local doctor in the hope that he can devise a method by means of which the other may be cheated, and this the cunning old doctor does.

It would have been simple enough to tell the story without a frame. Instead I elected to surround it with a fictional superstructure. I had as my narrator a younger man, a writer on the rebound from a broken relationship, who in the course of his travels finds himself as the doctor's dinner guest. As they sip a postprandial brandy, the doctor offers to recount an incident in which he played a part, one which he thinks the younger man might be able to turn into fiction.

The doctor then tells the actual story. At its conclusion we return to the frame, and the doctor explains how he actually tricked both men in the course of pretending to help them, thus winding up with the Cognac himself and enjoying the first embrace of the young lady.

Why did I use the frame? I may have done it in part as an act of homage to Maugham and other writers who used to do this sort of thing all the time. It seemed to me that a South Seas story just plain belonged in a frame. I was using a sort of old-fashioned plot, and by telling it in a similarly old-fashioned manner I felt I was following in hallowed footsteps.

Another reason I used the frame—or at least another effect of having used it—has to do with distance. Of course the frame created distance between the reader and the actual story of the doctor's machinations with the two brothers. I felt, though, that such distance wouldn't adversely affect the story's impact. The story is one of plot, and its appeal is more intellectual than emotional. Distance doesn't hurt it.

At the same time, a frame cuts one sort of distance while creating another. Remember a few moments ago when we were talking about those two Venusians in the bar? The reader, I pointed out, was in the position of an eavesdropper on a nearby barstool. If he's distanced from the story, he's simultaneously brought closer to the two people who are having the conversation.

The frame device I used had a similar effect. Assuming for the moment that the story does what I wanted it to do, the reader is drawn into that tropical dining room. Like the narrator, he sits at the doctor's table, sipping brandy and listening to the older man's dry voice.

O. Henry sometimes used frames to great advantage. I'm reminded of a story called *The Man at the Top*. The narrator is a professional gambler, and he tells how he and two other crooks, one a burglar and the other a con artist, came into a sum of money. The burglar used his share of the proceeds to open a casino, and the narrator tells how he rang in decks of marked cards to cheat the burglar out of every cent he had. He concludes by boasting that he has invested the proceeds in something solid, and we learn that the signature on his stock certificates is that of the third criminal, the con man. The frame device gives that surprise ending an impact it could not otherwise possess.

Every story within a story does not represent a use of a frame. I can recall a story of mine, for example, in which one of a pair of lovers tells the other a fairly lengthy apocryphal anecdote. The anecdote makes a point about the lovers' relationship, and as a result of her telling it, the relationship is brought to a conclusion. That's not a frame, however, because the real story is what's going on between the two of them. The story within the story is conversation, something to move the plot, and no more a central element than the play within the play of *Hamlet*.

I wouldn't advise any of you to use frames for your stories, not for the time being, at any rate. The risk is usually greater than the potential reward. But it might be valuable for you to notice how some other writers do make use of this device, while avoiding it yourselves unless you should happen to hit on a plot that demands this type of treatment.

Do you have a question, Arnold?

More of an observation, sir.

Oh?

You might say, sir, that you've used a frame in this chapter. Drawing the reader in by casting the chapter in the form of a dialogue with an imaginary class, and then cutting out the interruptions once you've got him hooked and getting directly to the heart of the matter.

You might say that, I suppose. Yes, Rachel?

And then you bring us back at the end to finish off the frame, eh, sir?

Something like that. Yes, Gwen?

Did you hear what Arnold just said? "You've got him hooked." Why not make it "him or her?"

Why not make it Venusians? Well, it looks as though our time is up, and not a moment too soon. Good morning, class.

Good afternoon, sir.

CHAPTER 34

Documentary Evidence

Saxtons River, Vermont
26 August 1979

Mr. John Brady
Writer's Digest

Dear John,

It's a reasonable facsimile of Paradise up here. Fresh air, cool temperatures, green hills, no billboards, no litter. We've got four days before we head back to the city, and I don't wanna go.

I've been thinking of writing a column on experimental narrative techniques—writing novels and stories in the guise of diaries, collections of letters, etc. There were several contest entries of that ilk this year, some good and some bad, but one thing I noticed during the judging was how quickly those narrative forms draw you in. The special pleasure, I suppose, of reading someone else's mail or sneaking a peek at another's diary.

I myself became very much interested in these approaches to fictional narrative ten years or so ago, when I found myself souring on the whole concept of the novel, which came to have an artificial feel to me. For a while there I even found conventional novels hard to read because they seemed unreal. Whose was this disembodied voice with omniscience over the lives and thoughts of all these characters? And, even when I read a first-person narrative, I found myself quibbling. When was it that the narrator was recounting all of this? How did he remember such minutiae as what so-and-so was wearing months previously? My bout of extreme literal-mindedness put me off novels of the usual sort, and I found myself drawn to books which pretended to be actual documents—letters, diaries, journals, whatever.

This sound like a viable topic to you? I'll spend the next two weeks kicking it around. I may not come up with enough to fill a whole column, but I think there's something here worth dissecting for *WD*'s readers.

Best to Rose and all the gang. Hang in there, big fella.

Larry

DATE: 28 August 1979
PLACE: Saxtons River, Vermont
TIME OF RUN: 7 p.m.
DISTANCE COVERED: 6 miles

Comments: I'm going to miss running in the country. Another couple of days and it's back to grinding out the miles on the West Side Highway, pounding the concrete and gulping down the smog. I'll miss the fresh air and the scenery, but I won't miss the dogs. If I ran around here all the time I think I'd wind up carrying a gun.

Spent most of today's run musing about the next *WD* column, which will probably concern experimental narrative techniques. Question: why call them experimental? When I first thought about doing a book in diary form, I thought of it as an experiment; ditto when I started writing a book in the form of a collection of letters. Why? There's nothing new about it. The technique's as old as these hills I've been running through. Consider—the first novel written in the English language, Samuel Richardson's *Pamela,* took the form of a collection of letters from the titular heroine to her sister. (Q— was it her sister? Should probably check this. This is what comes of having taken a course in the eighteenth-century novel without reading a majority of the assigned books. Such chickens always come home to roost.)

Defoe's early novels were similarly "experimental." *Journal of the Plague Year, Robinson Crusoe,* etc. *Moll Flanders,* while closer in form to the conventional first-person narrative, was deliberately cast in the form of a memoir.

I suspect early novels took the form of fake documents because readers weren't prepared yet for fictional prose narratives. These transitional forms prepared the eighteenth-century reader for the novel as it came to evolve. *Goal for Tomorrow's Run:* Same six miles. And if that Airedale chases me again I swear I'm gonna kick his face in.

New York City
4 September 79

Mr. John Brady
Writer's Digest

Dear John,

Hope your Labor Day weekend was a good one. Mine was, well, laborious. We got back from Vermont and ran headlong into a mound of correspondence for the vegetarian restaurant guide.

Midway down the pile was your response to mine of 26 Aug. I was dismayed to learn you think the column topic is too slight and specialized, as I've been having further thoughts on it and feel it's a solid one. It seems to me there are a lot of angles I can cover.

For example, just how important is verisimilitude? On the one hand, the reader *knows* that the book he's holding in his hands is a novel, that some myopic fictioneer made up the whole thing and penned (or more likely typed) all the letters or diary entries. This being the case, one might argue that all other considerations should be subordinated to Telling the Story.

This certainly was the case in the first English novel, Richardson's *Pamela*. It's hard to believe Pam would have written at such length. The form is simply a device by means of which the author tells the story.

Same thing goes for two contemporary successes, Ring Lardner's *You Know Me, Al*, and John O'Hara's *Pal Joey*. While the narrative voice of each conveys the writer's character perfectly, we can't really believe that Lardner's baseball player or O'Hara's nightclub entertainer would actually write letters of this sort. Yet the books work, and could hardly work better.

On the other hand, there's a special treat for the reader when the writer does try for verisimilitude. When I can read a book and *believe* (in the sense of that voluntary suspension of disbelief essential for the success of fiction) that I'm reading real letters or a real diary, my enjoyment is greatly enhanced.

Example: Month or so ago I read *A Woman of Independent Means*, by Elizabeth Forsythe Hailey, a so-so seller in hardcover which word-of-mouth has made a paperback bestseller. The novel takes the form of a selection of a woman's correspondence over her entire lifetime. The lead character strikes different attitudes depending on the person to whom she's writing, omits certain points, bends the truth, and is thus revealed between the lines of her own letters and emerges as one of the most wholly realized characters I've met with in many years.

Another example, in a lighter vein: Some writers have enormous fun with this sort of format, especially in a couple of books that come to mind featuring not merely the letters written *by* the lead character but letters written to him as well. *Wake Up, Stupid,* by Mark Harris, is a wonderful example, as is Hal Dresner's *The Man Who Wrote Dirty Books.* I made a modest attempt of my own in a book called *Ronald Rabbit Is a Dirty Old Man,* but since it sold perhaps eighteen copies I don't think I'll bother referring to it in print.

Donald E. Westlake's *Adios, Scheherezade* deserves mention in this context. His narrator is trying to grind out a formula sex novel, but keeps wandering off the subject and typing fifteen-page letters to himself and/or the world instead of the fifteen-page chapters he's supposed to be writing. His desperate attempt to make himself write the book, and the sense you get of him hammering away at an out-of-control typewriter, helps make the book the delight it is.

Well, I'm rambling. I hope you'll reconsider and approve, even if grudgingly, a column on—what's the generic term for this sort of book, anyway? Novels in letter form are epistolary novels, but is there a term to cover them and diaries and similar gallimaufries? *Documentary novel* won't do; it sounds like some sort of non-fiction novel or faction or something.

I'm going back to the bean curd and the organic hot dogs. Keep punching, tiger.

Larry

DATE: 9 September 1979
PLACE: New York City
TIME OF RUN: 8:30 a.m.
DISTANCE COVERED: 16 miles

Comments: Lord, everything hurts. It's good I don't write with my feet, critics' observations to the contrary, because I couldn't manage it today. The nice thing about running back and forth on the West Side Drive is you don't have to worry about forgetting the route. The bad thing is everything else. But I covered sixteen miles today, and at this rate I ought to be able to run the Jersey Shore Marathon in December. Imagine how horrible I'll feel after *that* . . .

Note in yesterday's mail from Brady, giving an unenthusiastic okay to the column idea. One thing that bothers him is that the column would only deal with novels, while a large proportion of *WD*'s readers are more interested in short fiction.

I spent maybe nine of this morning's sixteen miles trying to refute this argument. While the diary and epistolary forms may have been used more frequently in novels, there have certainly been short stories in these forms. Both *Pal Joey* and *You Know Me, Al* were published as magazine stories before being collected in book form. Back in the forties the *Saturday Evening Post* had a continuing series of stories about one Alexander Botts, a traveling salesman for Earthworm Tractors, the stories consisting of Botts's letters reporting on his progress. (Have to check author.)

Sue Kaufman liked novels in document form, and was particularly deft at writing them. Cf. *Diary of a Mad Housewife.* She did a piece for the *New York Times Sunday Magazine,* an article in the form of a fictional diary, on her reunion at Vassar or her memories of Vassar or something like that. What was the title—"Confessions of a Vassar Gel"? "Diary of a Vassar Gel"? Something like that.

There was another story called "Address Unknown" which I read at least twenty-five years ago. Published in *Reader's Digest,* I recall, and I believe there was some question as to whether it was fiction or not. (I read it years after its original publication, in some long-lost anthology.)

Premise of story: American Jew is corresponding with German business associate during Nazi period. The exchange of letters reveals that the German is acquiescing in the Nazi treatment of the Jews, and fails to aid a relative of the American letter-writer, who seeks revenge in an unusual manner. Knowing his letters are read by the Nazi censors, he writes in such a manner as to cast suspicion upon his German correspondent. His last letter concludes with the line, "May the God of Moses stand by your right hand," and it's returned stamped Address Unknown, and we infer that the intended recipient has been arrested as an enemy of the state.

Wish I could find that story. Be useful to cite it when writing column. *Goal for Tomorrow's Run:* Simple survival. Five easy miles is plenty.

New York City
12 September 79

Ms. Rose Adkins
Writer's Digest

Dear Rose,

I enclose herewith (1) the galleys of the December column and (2) "Documentary Evidence," the January offering. As you can see, it's itself masquerading as a collection of documents, and this letter to your estimable self is part of it. Wheels within wheels, Rose. If The Lord High Everything Else objects to the grammar and syntax and such, tell him it's all in the interests of verisimilitude. (You might want to check my spelling of verisimilitude, Rose.)

Keep those cards and letters coming, love. And try to keep Brady away from the prepubescent schoolgirls. One of these days he'll find himself in real trouble.

Larry

CHAPTER

Surprise!

IN THE past several chapters we've taken a good look at the towering importance of Story. The great majority of readers occupy themselves with fiction for any number of reasons—to identify with the characters, to learn about different backgrounds or epochs or ways of living, to deepen their understanding of their own lives, or to kill a few minutes between the soup and the salad course. But the one factor that keeps them turning pages is the overriding urge to learn what happens next.

The element of surprise is one way writers add excitement to the resolution of the question of what happens next. The surprise ending is a classic component of fiction, particularly in the short story. Indeed, that abbreviated form known as the short-short is rarely anything more than twelve or fifteen hundred words of build-up to a snapper of a surprise ending.

Endings don't have to surprise the reader in order to satisfy him. Whole categories of fiction are as predictable in their plot resolutions as the stars in their courses; while I would not go so far as to say, for example, that if you've read one gothic novel you've read them all, I doubt many of us could read too many of them and find ourselves bug-eyed with astonishment at their endings.

On a more exalted level, few works of great literature hold extraordinary surprises for the reader. They are rather more likely to have plots which move inexorably to conclusions which seem in retrospect to have been inevitable from the beginning. This does not render their hold on us any less compelling, any more than our attention wanders at a performance of *Macbeth* because we recall the ending from tenth-grade English. We're no less caught up in the question of What Happens Next for being able to recite the speeches along with the actors.

The surprise ending is very much with us, however, in both published and unpublished stories. Most mystery shorts, a good deal of science fiction, and a substantial number of general magazine short stories have surprise endings, and it shouldn't surprise anyone that the production of unestablished writers hews to this pattern. In one *WD* short-story contest, for example, it would seem in retrospect that perhaps a third of the entries had surprise endings. (Another third had come-to-realize endings, of the sort in which a woman on her way to commit suicide sees two sparrows courting in a birdbath and decides the world's not such a bad place after all. And another third of the entries had no discernible ending whatsoever—the woman sees the sparrows in the birdbath, say, so instead of committing suicide she goes to the hardware store and buys two pounds of nails and a shiny new hammer.)

Perhaps a look at some of the different kinds of surprise endings will give us an idea of what works and what doesn't—and why.

1. WITHHELD INFORMATION. Probably the most common amateur surprise ending is one in which the author, having deliberately concealed a central fact from the reader simply to make the story work, concludes by revealing that fact with a flourish. The narrator, say, whom we've made the silly mistake of assuming to be a human being, turns out at the end to have been all along an ear of Golden Bantam corn. Or the really odd planet that our space-traveling heroes have landed on turns out to be Good Ol' Terra Firma. Or—oh, never mind.

The reader's usual response to this sort of trickery is not awe at the author's imaginative powers and verbal legerdemain but cold fury at his unadulterated gall. The reader feels he's been unfairly gulled, and most of the time he's right. Most of time this kind of story falls so flat it might have been a soufflé and the ending the slamming of the oven door.

On the other hand, once in a while someone makes this kind of story work, and the result can be a masterpiece. The example that leaps to mind was a teleplay on an anthology show called *Danger*. I don't know when I saw it but it must have been twenty-five years ago. (I seem to recall peering at the set through the bars of my play pen.)

Here's the plot: A band of brave men are living under a dictatorship.

Their own country's been crushed by a neighboring country which has annexed them. We're with these guys as they risk everything on a plot to kill the dictator. In fact we're standing right beside him, cheering all the way, as their leader, a charismatic type named Johnny, sneaks up on the archfiend and shoots him dead.

And then Johnny leaps down from the balcony and shouts *"Sic semper tyrannis,"* and we catch our first glimpse of the slain dictator, and it's Abraham Lincoln.

I'll tell you. It's a quarter of a century since I saw that show, and just telling you about it leaves a chill at the bone.

That was withheld information, but it was artfully withheld, and there were clues all along the way, and there was, ultimately, a reason for the subterfuge. One did not feel cheated by the ending. One felt thunderstruck.

Here's another example. *Ellery Queen's Mystery Magazine* published an impressive tour de force in June of 1977, a first story by Kenneth Watts called "The Sounds of Summer." The viewpoint character is held hostage by a fugitive; we find out at the end, after the fugitive has been captured as a result of the lead's action, that the lead is a deaf man—*he never even knew the fugitive was there!* This is withheld information, all right, but it works brilliantly, and all in the space of perhaps a thousand words. I would urge you to find a copy of that issue and see for yourselves how and why the story works; I've ruined the ending for you because there was no other way to discuss the story, but I don't think that will altogether nullify your enjoyment of the story.

One writer who makes a habit of tricking the reader with withheld information is William Goldman; he likes to pull off surprises this way not just at the ending but throughout the course of a work. In *Father's Day,* for example, we keep getting emotionally involved in a line of action, thinking it's really happening and caring how it turns out, only to learn that it's the protagonist's fantasy. *Marathon Man* is one cute trick after another. Sometimes this works and sometimes it doesn't. Goldman's a master at this sort of thing, but sometimes reading him for me is like watching card tricks with a hangover.

2. TOO MUCH DOG, NOT ENOUGH TAIL. One of the reasons "The Sounds of Summer" works as well as it does is that it's short. When revelation constitutes the ending of a story, all that has preceded it has been build-up, important only as a means of achieving that ending. We wouldn't object to reading a thousand words to get to Mr. Watts's surprise, but the same story wouldn't be nearly so effective at triple the length, and it's hard to believe anyone would write a whole novel, say, leading up to that sort of surprise.

But it wouldn't be the first time. Consider this plot, for example. Guy wakes up in Central Park. His wallet's gone and so's his memory. Doesn't know who he is or how he got where he is. There's a scrap of paper in his pocket with the word *Buddwing* on it. This means nothing to him but he figures maybe it's his name. So he spends the day trying to work out the facts of his existence, and he has some adventures and meets some interesting people and engages in sprightly conversation, and finally he finds his way back to his actual apartment and opens the door and there by George is his wife's dead body hanging from the chandelier, and this sight sends him reeling in shock, so much so that he stumbles back to Central Park and right back into amnesia, and we're left with the impression that this cycle has been repeating on him like a bad cucumber for days now.

Not a bad notion at three or four thousand words tops, right? Evan Hunter's novel *Buddwing* runs about a hundred thousand words, and the ending positively ruins it. It's a short-short ending on a full-length novel and even a writer with Hunter's technical facility can't make it work.

3.   WHO'S SURPRISED? When the whole story's a build-up to the surprise at the end, you've got a real investment in that surprise. If the reader has seen it coming a mile away, the story's in serious trouble.

The example that comes quickest to mind is not a story but a film. A few years back Dustin Hoffman played the title role in *Who Is Harry Kellerman and Why Is He Saying All Those Terrible Things About Me?* Seems that one Harry Kellerman was phoning up everybody in Hoffman's life to spread dreadful rumors about him, and Hoffman spends the whole movie trying to find out the answer to the titular question, and have you guessed it yourself yet? Yeah, Dusty himself was Harry K., doing the dirty on himself in some sort of split-personality number, and nothing could have come as less of a surprise to the viewers. Most everybody tumbled to the secret ten minutes into the film, and some clever types guessed the ending without even entering the theater.

How do you know whether a surprise ending is going to work or not? Tricky point. I guess you just have to develop, from your own analysis of what works and what doesn't work in the things you read over the years, a sense of what is and what is not genuinely surprising.

Here again, the importance of a solid reading background is evident. Originality is an essential quality of a successful surprise ending, and how can you know whether your gimmick's original if you haven't read widely in your field?

4.   A SURPRISE—PLUS A NEW PERSPECTIVE. The best surprise endings don't merely surprise the reader. In addition, they force him to reevaluate

everything that has preceded them, so that he views the actions and the characters in a different light and has a new perspective on all that's he's read.

Consider Mark Hellinger's "The Window." Three bedridden women share a room at a sanitarium. One, by right of seniority, has her bed next to the window. Day after day she recounts to the others what she sees through the window—little daily dramas in the lives of children playing outside, lovers quarreling and making up, the changing seasons, birds flying south, and so on.

Then she dies. The woman who's been there the longest after her inherits her spot, and the other woman moves up one, and a new woman is moved into the room, and the woman who's got the window now is very excited to see what she's been hearing about for years, and she looks out the window, and—*surprise!*—it opens on a blank wall. And *surprise!* she looks at it for a couple of seconds and then proceeds to tell what she sees, the children playing, the woman sweeping her porch steps, the buds on the trees, making up stories for her roommates' entertainment just as her predecessor did.

Now that's a surprise ending. I could tell you some others, but—*surprise!*—I'm out of space. But read John Collier, read Gerald Kersh, read Saki, read the stories in the current magazines. See what works and what doesn't, and keep on reading and rereading until you see why and how. Write your own stories and make your own mistakes. Send out your stories if they turn out well. Send 'em out again when they come back.

And, when what you get back is a small white envelope instead of a big brown one, congratulations. That's the best surprise of all.

PART FOUR

One Damned Word After Another:

Fiction as a Craft

CHAPTER **36**

Never Apologize, Never Explain

ONE THING I've noticed in reading the work of new writers, published and unpublished, is a tendency to explain too much. It seems to me that this generally stems from one of two things—a desire to control the reader's interpretation of what one has written or a reluctance to trust the reader's ability to make sense out of what is going on.

It takes considerable self-confidence and monumental ego to write fiction in the first place. In order to put one word after another, we have to be able to believe that the plots and characters we invent, spun like spider webs out of our own innards, and couched in the particular words we arbitrarily select and arrange on the page, will be grippingly interesting and involving to some faceless reader whom we have never met and of whom we know nothing.

This same ego quite naturally makes us want to take charge utterly, to control and direct everything with the fervor of a kid playing traffic cop. This desire can manifest itself in any of a number of ways. Here's an example:

"Don't talk to me like that," Margo shouted. She was really angry. "You can't talk to me like that!"

"I'll talk to you any way I want," Roy flared. He couldn't stand the way she was acting.

"I mean it," she said, furious. "I've had enough."

"Oh?" He drew back, worried at the new quality he could detect in her voice. "What will you do about it, then?"

"I'll do something," she said. But even as she spoke she could feel the determination draining from her . . .

Do you see what the author's doing here? He's stepping right up onto the stage with his characters, leaning in over their shoulders and explaining why and how they're reading the lines he's given them. Instead of letting them reveal their feelings by what they say and do, he insists upon interpreting everything for us.

This particular example is one I've created for the occasion, to illustrate a point. But I'm paraphrasing a short story a friend of mine asked me to read, and I think it's interesting to note that he's a stage director of some reputation. I pointed out to him that he was doing in his fiction what it's his job to do in the theater, telling the characters their motivation and how to deliver their lines. But as a director he doesn't get up there with the actors on the night of the performance, and neither can he get on the page with his characters without blunting the effectiveness of his dialogue.

Dialogue is by no means the only area in which an author can get in the way with words of explanation. I ran across a rather clear example in one of the entries in last year's *WD* short-story contest. As I recall, one of the characters told a joke, whereupon the author wrote: *Paul forced a laugh at Hilliard's weak joke.*

The word *weak* came from the author; he's butting in, assuring us that Hilliard's joke was a stinker. But we already knew that, for heaven's sake. We just heard the joke, and it bombed, and obviously it was a weak joke or Paul wouldn't have had to force a laugh over it, so why on earth shove your way in and *tell* us it was weak?

Over-explanation can come not only through the intrusion of the author's presence. Sometimes the author uses his characters to tell us more than we need to know. One example of this is what has been called Soap-Opera Dialogue, because one of its functions is to render things crystal clear for those viewers who happened to miss the last couple of episodes. What happens is that the characters have a stilted conversation, explaining things to each other at unnecessary length, in order to convey information not to each other but to the reader.

Like this:

"Your brother-in-law Sidney called this afternoon."

"Sheila's husband? I haven't spoken to him since I heard he was scheduled for surgery. What did he want?"

"He's very worried about Rita. He would have called you, Charles, but Sheila told him how busy you've been with the Ackroyd case."

Well, you get the idea. There's no earthly reason for Charles to say "Sheila's husband?" other than to let the reader know who Sidney is, in case he's forgotten. The whole passage shows us two people talking through each other in order to pass information on, and in the process the conversation ceases to appear realistic.

Another form of over-explanation derives similarly from the writer's inability to trust the reader to keep up with what's happening. I've noted this tendency myself in my early suspense novels. Whenever my lead character began to figure something out, I had him think out loud so the reader would be able to follow what was going on in his mind. Whenever my lead set things in motion, I explained as I went along so the reader wouldn't be lost.

I learned, eventually, that the reader doesn't *have* to be kept that completely in the picture. Sometimes it's a good deal more fun to watch the lead character go through his paces without knowing exactly what he's getting at; that way you can do a little guesswork and try to figure out just what's going on, and why.

I first got the hang of this in a series of books I wrote about a private detective named Matthew Scudder. Scudder was a great character to work with, quirky and angst-ridden, and he did a lot of things without telling the reader why he was doing them. Some of the time he didn't know himself why he was doing certain things. When he began to dope things out, and set wheels in motion to work out whodunit, he didn't think out loud so that the reader would be with him every step of the way.

Gregory Mcdonald's novels about a reporter named Fletch are an even better example of how to keep the reader in the dark without explanation or apology. In *Fletch* and *Confess, Fletch* especially, the hero goes through a great deal of convoluted business, setting up elaborate bits of plot machinery. We know what he's doing but we don't know why he's doing it or what it's supposed to lead to—and that's one of the things that makes the books work so effectively. We keep reading to find out not only how things will work out but why Fletch has been doing thus and so right in front of our eyes.

Earlier I likened the writer to a theatrical director, moving his characters around the stage and telling them how to deliver their lines. In the theater, one important concept is that of the audience as constituting the fourth wall. In other words, the interpretive ability of the audience is part of the dynamic of the theatrical performance.

I think the same thing holds true for fiction. A short story or novel constitutes a subtly different experience for every person who reads it, simply because each reader brings a different perspective and background to bear upon what he reads. A fictional scene about a woman undergoing an abortion in a railroad car traveling across Kenya will differ in its effect upon the reader depending whether that reader is a man or a woman, has or has not had an abortion, is or is not familiar with railroad cars, and has or has not been to Kenya. Further, its effect will depend on the nature of the reader's particular experience—on the abortion table or in Kenya, or whatever.

To that extent, then, we cannot control how the reader will receive our fictional message, nor should we be able as writers to assert such control. The best we can do, I believe, is write as carefully and as honestly as we can and let the reader make of our work what he will. If we write well, enough people will get enough of the message.

The idea of fiction as a reader-participation medium is certainly not original with me. Here's a passage from Laurence Sterne's *Tristram Shandy*, published in 1760:

> Writing, when properly managed, (as you may be sure I think mine is) is but a different name for conversation: As no one, who knows what he is about in good company, would venture to talk all, so no author, who understands the just boundaries of decorum and good breeding, would presume to think all; The truest respect which you can pay to the reader's understanding is to halve this manner amicably, and leave him something to imagine, in his turn, as well as yourself.
>
> For my own part, I am eternally paying him compliments of this kind, and do all that lies in my power to keep his imagination as busy as my own.
>
> 'Tis his turn now. I have given an ample description of Dr. Slop's sad overthrow, and of his sad appearance in the back parlor—his imagination must now go on with it for awhile.

Isn't that lovely? I could explain at this point that the punctuation is Sterne's, and that they handled the odd comma and semicolon a bit differently in the eighteenth century. Or I could explain that I've never actually read *Tristram Shandy*, although I was once presumed to have done so for a course in the early English novel, but that I happened on this passage just last week in London. I was in the library of the British Museum, you see, and there was a case of first editions of important books, and while looking them over this passage leaped out and caught my eye, the copy of *Tristram Shandy* having been left open to this particular page. I promptly copied it down, and I might tell you as much and go on to talk about serendipity, and the manner in which that happenstance gave me the theme for this chapter. I might even go on to write yet another chapter on the manner in which serendipitous browsing can lead to ideas for fiction.

But I won't, because I've learned not to explain too much.

CHAPTER

He Said She Said

LAWSON CLEARED his throat. "Bollinger was in to see me this morning," he drawled laconically.

"Oh?" Jarvis mouthed. "What did he want?"

Lawson's eyebrows crawled skyward as his eyes took the measure of the man opposite him. "What do you think he wanted?" he wondered aloud, the sarcasm dripping from his tones. "He's upset about Myrna. Seems she told him where you went the other night."

Jarvis was alarmed. "That's crazy," he insisted gamely.

Lawson seemed unconvinced. "Is it?" he wanted to know.

Jarvis was adamant. "You know it is," he asserted, stressing his point by pounding the tabletop.

"Maybe," murmured Lawson. "But Bollinger doesn't think so."

We don't have to concern ourselves with the problems and identities of Myrna and Bollinger and Lawson and Jarvis in order to appreciate that something is very wrong with this passage. A quick reading would suggest that it's rotten dialogue, but that's not really the case. The dialogue itself is fine; it's just gummed up with a ton of unnecessary sludge.

The simplest way to write good dialogue is to let it stand by itself. When we let our example stand alone it looks like this:

"Bollinger was in to see me this morning."

"Oh? What did he want?"

"What do you think he wanted? He's upset about Myrna. Seems she told him where you went the other night."

"That's crazy."

"Is it?"

"You know it is."

"Maybe. But Bollinger doesn't think so."

The actual dialogue, then, works well enough when left alone. But the excesses in our first example are no worse than what lands on editors' desks every day, and (sad to say) not significantly worse than what occasionally finds its way into print. All of this asserting and mouthing and drawling just gets in the way, and the silly adverbs just make everything worse.

There is no more important component of fiction than dialogue. The words your characters speak to one another do more to convey their nuances to the reader than any words you can employ yourself to sketch them. Dialogue advances and defines a plot, renders complicated developments fathomable, and permits fiction to raise its voice, speaking not merely to the mind but to the ear as well. It's not an exaggeration to maintain that a novel's readability—not its worth or quality, but its sheer *readability*—is in direct proportion to the amount of conversation it contains. The more nearly a novel resembles a play in prose form, the simpler it is for the average reader to come to grips with it.

Which brings us to Rule 1: If your characters are good, and if the dialogue you hand them is natural, you should leave it alone as much as possible. Put them onstage and let them talk to each other. And stay the hell out of their way.

The first thing you must do is learn to pay attention to Rule 1.

The second thing you must learn is when to break it.

A chief reason for breaking Rule 1 is in order to make it clear to the reader who's saying what to whom. I recently read a novel (*American Made,* by Shylah Boyd, if you care) in which all dialogue, including sections which went on for several pages at a clip, was allowed to stand utterly alone. There was never a single indication as to who was speaking—and this was true too of scenes in which half a dozen people were shooting lines back and forth. That's damned confusing, and in this case readability would have been greatly increased by chucking in *he said* and *she said* where necessary for clarification.

Some exchanges don't need much of this. If one person is asking questions and the other is answering them, the reader will understand the question-

and-answer format and follow it effortlessly for pages on end. When *he said* and *she said* are indicated, there's no rule as to how often they should be sprinkled in. This depends upon the length of individual speeches, the general rhythm of the dialogue, and other factors impossible to reduce to a formula, not the least of which is the author's presumably individual style.

When else do you depart from the rule? Well, you might want to slow the pace deliberately and convey to the reader a sense of the scene and the interplay of the speakers; this may be as important as the actual information that passes between them in their conversation. Consider:

> "Bollinger was in to see me this morning."
>
> "Oh?" Jarvis lowered his eyes, set his coffee cup down. "What did he want?"
>
> "What do you think he wanted? He's upset about Myrna. Seems she told him where you went the other night."
>
> Jarvis searched the other man's face. Then his eyes went to the clock on the far wall. "That's crazy," he said.
>
> "Is it?"
>
> "You know it is."
>
> "Maybe," Lawson said levelly. "But Bollinger doesn't think so."

This passage clearly does not read as quickly as it would with the conversation standing alone. On the other hand, the extra material may help us visualize the two speakers, especially Jarvis, and may give us more of a feeling of the unspoken interplay between them.

Sometimes you'll want to use the *saids* as punctuation marks, popping them in to establish the rhythm, sometimes giving a string of them all to one character for emphasis:

> "Bollinger was in to see me this morning."
>
> "Oh?" Jarvis said. "What did he want?"
>
> "What do you think he wanted? He's upset about Myrna. Seems she told him where you went the other night."
>
> "That's crazy," Jarvis said.
>
> "Is it?"
>
> "You know it is," Jarvis said.
>
> "Maybe. But Bollinger doesn't think so."

Said, said, *said.* Dean Koontz told me once that he makes it an absolute rule never to use any verb but *said* in dialogue. I suppose you'll stay out of trouble this way, but I do feel that any number of alternate verbs have their uses from time to time. They can be good accent points in dialogue, and the less frequently you employ them the more effective they will be. And they serve a definite purpose when you've got a line which can be read any of several ways and you feel it's important the reader gets it the way you meant it.

Words like *state* and *aver* and *avow* and *affirm* and *declare*, words that newspaper reporters use frequently so that their stories will read like newspaper stories, have little or no place in fiction. But words like *drawl* and *murmur* and *whisper* indicate how a line is spoken. Prose fiction, after all, differs from drama in that one is not assisted by actors on stage or film. It is the writer's job to *shout* or *whisper*. I won't give an example of this—I'm sure you get the point—but you might find it an instructive exercise to knock out a few versions of your own of the imperishable conversation between Lawson and Jarvis. (While I've shown Jarvis as nervous in earlier examples, the dialogue itself is neutral, and, by giving the conversation's superstructure the right coloring, Lawson might emerge as timid while Jarvis could be bold, dominant, untouched, or whatever.)

In first-person narration, dialogue can never stand completely alone because the persona of the narrator exists to filter everything to the reader. The narrator's presence is a constant in first-person work, and if that particular voice drops out entirely in an extended dialogue sequence, the result is sort of jarring.

In first-person dialogue, the narrator may limit himself to *he said* and *I said.* Or he may report what he sees as well as what he hears. Or, additionally, he may toss in thoughts and observations for one purpose or another, as for example:

> I let him sit there for a minute or two. Then I said, "Bollinger was in to see me this morning."
>
> "Oh?" He started to take a cigarette from my pack, then remembered that he'd given up the habit. "What did he want?"
>
> I took the cigarette he'd rejected, thumbed my lighter and took a hit. What had Bollinger wanted? Hell, what did anyone want, I wondered. Why did anyone bother? Why did people get out of bed in the morning?
>
> But Jarvis didn't want to hear my Philosophy 101 lecture. So I looked at him through the smoke and said, "What do you think he wanted? He's upset about Myrna. . . ."

I'll tell you, I'm getting a little upset about Myrna myself.

This last example, you'll note, adds substantially to the word-count of our little scrap of dialogue. The words on the page still read rapidly enough; it's just that there are more of them.

Does this mean the material is padded? Maybe yes, maybe no—the question can't really be answered out of context. Padding is wordage without purpose. If a whole book or story were larded with introspection and cigarette-lighting and the observation of minutiae, then you'd be justified in calling it padding or simple bad writing. But when certain scenes are stretched this way for a purpose, when the information contained in the bare dialogue is secondary in importance to other elements you want to convey to the reader, then the extra words pay their way.

Sometimes a scene exists only to move a story along. At other times it's pivotal and possesses genuine dramatic value, and often in such instances the words your characters speak are of less moment than the changes they are going through while they speak. When you write such a scene, you *want* to slow the reader down a little—as we have seen—and make the scene take more of his time. You don't want to be a bore, of course, and you don't want padding to be identifiable to anyone as padding, so you make sure those extra unspoken words are interesting, either creating distinct sensory images, or delineating moods, or giving the reader something to think about.

So let's amend Rule #1 accordingly, rendering it in a form that will make it supremely useful to all writers of fiction.

To wit: *Dialogue should be allowed to stand alone, pure and simple. Except when it shouldn't.*

Is that clear?

CHAPTER **38**

Verbs for Vim and Vigor

I MARMALADED a slice of toast with something of a flourish, and I don't suppose I have ever come much closer to saying "Tra-la-la" as I did the lathering, for I was feeling in mid-season form this morning. God, as I once heard Jeeves put it, was in His heaven and all right with the world. (He added, I remember, some guff about larks and snails, but that is a side issue and need not detain us.)

The speaker is young Bertram Wooster, the work cited is *Stiff Upper Lip, Jeeves,* and the author is P. G. Wodehouse of blessed memory. Wodehouse lived to be ninety-three, and wrote about that many novels, fitting them in between plays, musical-comedy lyrics, screenplays, essays, articles, and, I have no doubt, blurbs for the backs of breakfast cereal boxes and screeds to be tucked into fortune cookies. He did all of this with consummate grace, dovetailing a plot like DiMaggio gathering in a fly ball, making it all look quite effortless.

I have lately discovered Wodehouse, and while I must have read a few of the books before I have never been as appreciative an audience for him as I find myself today. And what a treat it is to uncover a passion for an author who has written nearly a hundred books! Years of uncomplicated reading stretch out before me like an expanse of untrodden lawn. The only f. in the ointment, as the master might put it, is that one tends to go about talking like B. Wooster himself, to the extreme distress of one's companions.

But I digress. Return your attention, if you will, to the passage quoted above. The operative word is "marmaladed."

The meaning of the word is by no means elusive. Even the dimmest reader grasps quickly enough that the speaker has spread marmalade on his slice of toast. Yet no dictionary in my ken allows marmalade as a verb. It is a noun, derived via the French from the Portuguese word for quince, and it means a preserve made by boiling fruit with sugar. It may also mean the fruit of *Lucuma mammosa,* or that tree itself.

When he deploys marmalade as a verb, Wodehouse attracts our attention by using a familiar word in an unfamiliar fashion. We may read it in one of three ways. We can merely breeze along with the breeze, paying no particular attention to this unorthodox use of marmalade. Or we can note it, cock an eye at it, smile at the author's linguistic imagination, and keep going.

Or, finally, we can think about it. We can muse that the language itself affords precedent for what Wodehouse has done here. When one lubricates a slice of toast with butter, for example, the verb *to butter* is in widespread use. If one can butter a slice of bread, why shouldn't one be permitted to marmalade it? One oils various articles—an engine, a watch, whatever. Could one oil a bowl of salad, preparatory to vinegaring it?

This particular sort of verb play crops up often in Wodehouse. When Bertie picks up something or other and tucks it into his pants pocket, he's apt to describe himself as having trousered the article, whatever it might be. Now one does not as a general rule go about trousering things, but one does pocket them, so why shouldn't one be able to trouser them as well? Might a woman pick up a cigarette lighter and purse it? Or may one only purse one's lips?

This is fun, and I hope it will spark an appetite for Wodehouse while stimulating an interest in what words are and are not permitted to do. But I dug that passage out of *Stiff Upper Lip, Jeeves* for a reason. (Actually I had rather little digging to do; it's the first paragraph in the book.) It seems to me to illustrate, perhaps by way of exaggeration, the manner in which vigorous verbs strengthen a piece of prose.

Someone—it may have been Hemingway—is supposed to have instructed all tyro writers to go through their work and cross out all the adverbs and adjectives. While a piece of prose thus treated would be precious close to unreadable, the underlying point is well taken. The vitality of English prose—and very likely all prose—abides in its nouns and verbs. The nouns are what is and the verbs are what's happening.

Consider the following passage:

> Parker went through the window elbows first, the rotted wood and shards of glass falling out in front of him. He lowered his head, landed hard on his right shoulder, rolled over twice, and was moving before he was well on his feet. He heard shots behind him but didn't know if they were coming at him or not. He ran for a corner of the barn, and as he went around it a bullet dug into the wood beside his head, sending splinters toward his cheek.
>
> He fell, rolled some more, until he was against the side of the barn and out of sight of the house. He put his hand inside his coat and touched an empty holster.

That's not bad writing. It's very good writing, actually, with fast action vividly described. But it's not quite as good as the actual way Richard Stark wrote this passage in *The Sour Lemon Score*. Here's his version:

> Parker dove through the window elbows first, the rotted wood and shards of glass spraying out in front of him. He ducked his head, landed hard on his right shoulder, rolled over twice, and was running before he was well on his feet. He heard shots behind him but didn't know if they were coming at him or not. He ran for the corner of the barn, and as he went around it a bullet chunked into the wood beside his head, spitting splinters at his cheek.
>
> He hit the dirt, rolled some more, and wound up against the side of the barn and out of sight of the house. He reached inside his coat, and his hand closed on an empty holster.

See the difference? When he goes through the window he dives and we sense the movement. The wood and shards of glass don't just fall out, they spray out. The bullet chunks into the wood beside him and we don't simply know it's there, we hear it and feel it because the unusual verb supplies sound and feeling. The bullet spits splinters at him, and the verb is doubly evocative, not only giving us a picture of what happens but endowing the moment with the contemptuousness of one person's spitting at another.

He doesn't drop or fall. He hits the dirt—it's more active that way—and he rolls and winds up against the side of the barn. He reaches inside his coat. His hand closes on an empty holster.

Wodehouse rewrote intensively. In a letter he described how he pinned pages of his current manuscript around the walls of his study, singling out those that were insufficiently energetic, returning to them again and again and reworking them. He was a perfectionist, convinced that every line of a Jeeves story had to have entertainment value.

Richard Stark, on the other hand, rarely does much rewriting. The two paragraphs quoted above very likely took final form in first draft. I don't do too much rewriting, either, but I have found when editing my copy that one change I'm apt to make involves verbs. When something's wrong with a sentence, more often than not it can be improved by changing a verb or two, making one of those action words more active, or more specific, or less ordinary, or, well, just plain better.

Back when I was in the eighth grade, right around the time dad and other barons made King John sign the Magna Carta, my English teacher had us think of synonyms for *get*. I have a feeling she may have been somewhat obsessive on the subject. In any event, she had us compile a lengthy list of alternatives for this verb, which she decried as banal, nonspecific, and a blight upon the mother tongue.

Well, early learned is late forgotten, and it's a rare morning when I type something like

> I got dressed, got myself downstairs and out of the house, pausing to get the mail out of the mailbox. When I got to the corner I got a paper from the newsdealer, then got a good breakfast at the Red Flame. I got a headache when I got the day's first cigarette going, but I got the waitress to get me a couple of aspirins and that got rid of it. Then I got out of there. On the way out the cashier told me a joke, but I didn't get it.

For exercise, you might want to rewrite that deathless paragraph. Then again, you might not.

I don't want to leave you with the impression that the unusual and colorful is always more desirable than the flatter and more ordinary verbs. What words you use and how you use them depends on what you're trying to accomplish, and that's as true with verbs as anything else. Colorless verbs have their place. So does repetition. There might be a time when you would want to write:

> He walked to the corner, turned left, walked three blocks, waited for the light to turn, then walked two more blocks to Glenda's apartment.

You get a much different quality by having him walk than if you made the bleeder stroll or march or sashay or whatever. By using the same verb three times in a sentence, you underscore the neutral quality of the verb. Without a single adverb to tell you *how* he walked, we wind up with a sense of how he did it, depending of course on what we know already about the character and his situation.

> He legged it to the corner, made a sharp left, stared at the light until it went green, then quick-marched two more blocks to Glenda's apartment.

Is that better? Or worse? It depends, obviously, on what the sentence is supposed to do. It's unquestionably a whole lot different, though, and the difference is vested in the verbs.

For myself, prose style is largely intuitive. I don't often give it conscious thought while I'm actually writing. Nor would I suggest that you scrawl PUT VITAMINS IN YOUR VERBS on the wall above your typewriter. There's not much point in becoming self-conscious about your style.

I would suggest that you notice, in your reading, how other writers use verbs, and what you do or don't like about their techniques. See what changes you'd make, in their writing and in your own. And, if you're interested in watching a master put not only verbs but all the other parts of speech through their paces, you might make the acquaintance of Pelham Grenville Wodehouse.

CHAPTER **39**

Modifiers for Mood-Swing

FIRST YOU write the story, Hemingway is supposed to have said. Then you go back over what you have written and cross out all the adjectives and adverbs. The result is a clean, spare, honest prose, stripped to the bare essentials without the intrusion of the author's perceptions.

I don't suppose that was the worst advice ever, especially at the time it was given, when the American novel was being reborn in a freshet of clean, spare, honest prose. I have read stories whose authors could profit by taking Hemingway's advice literally; a blue pencil would greatly help passages that run something like this:

> The tall, ungainly woman walked haltingly up the winding tree-lined path that led to the large green-shuttered sprawling old white mansion. Her old arthritic vein-corded hands gripped her silver-topped cane, and its worn brass ferrule stabbed feebly at the unyielding earth with every faltering step she took. . . .

Cumbersome, isn't it? The modifiers pile up all over the place, and it takes us as long to read about it as it takes the lady to get to the house. What does the same passage look like stripped?

> The woman walked up the path that led to the mansion. Her hands gripped her cane, and its ferrule stabbed at the earth with every step she took.

That's better, certainly, if only because some of the clutter is gone and the prose has a better rhythm to it. But I don't think we can safely conclude that the quality of any prose passage is in inverse proportion to the number of adverbs and adjectives it contains, and that these parts of speech ought to be ruthlessly purged from our professional vocabularies. Because there is one significant fault which the second example bears in relation to the first. It's trimmer, unquestionably, and it reads faster, but it gives us a lot less of the picture than does the first example.

When we read the stripped-down version, we don't know if the woman in question is young or old, tall or short, sprightly or lethargic. We have no picture of the path she's walking or the house she's approaching. We get hints from some of the verbs and nouns; we'd know even less than we do, for example, if the path led not to a mansion but to a house, if her hand held her cane instead of gripping it, and if the tip of the cane didn't specifically stab the earth but simply touched it. Even so, there are details to this picture which can only be sketched in by means of adjectives and adverbs.

Thus there is a question of balance involved. If we use sufficient modifiers to describe everything in full detail, we'll produce clumsy prose and spend several pages just getting the old lady up the path to the house. If we cut out the modifiers, the reader won't know what's going on.

There's no single right way to write anything, this sample passage included. The writer has to make choices, and generally makes them quickly and intuitively at that. The writing of prose, you see, is rather more like painting than photography. We cannot point a camera and, with the click of the shutter, record instantly all that is visible to the lens. Instead we must wield words as a painter wields a brush, spotting a detail here and there while leaving another section purposely vague.

> The woman walked haltingly up the path to the green-shuttered mansion . . .

That's one way, focusing on the woman's walk and the house's green shutters. If this were a class, I might suggest that you try rewriting the passage yourself, producing three different versions of it. (And you might elect to do that on your own, class or no class.) Instead, let's have a look at some other examples.

> The body of the whale flashes like a marble sepulchre; though changed in hue, it has not lost anything in bulk. It floats away, the water round it torn and splashed by the sharks, and the air above vexed with flights of fowls, whose beaks are like so many poniards in the whale. The phantom floats further and further from the ship, and every rod that it so floats, what seem square roods of sharks and cubic roods of fowls, augment the din. For hours and hours from the ship that sight is seen. Beneath the sky, upon the face of the sea, wafted by breezes, the mass of death floats on and on, till lost in infinite perspectives.

That, of course, is from *Moby Dick,* by Herman Melville. It is, however, rather different from the way the author wrote it, and is more like what would have resulted had he gone back and crossed out the adjectives. Melville, as it happened, used a great many adjectives in this passage. Having read it once in an abridged version, please consider it in full:

> The peeled white body of the beheaded whale flashes like a marble sepulchre; though changed in hue, it has not perceptibly lost anything in bulk. It is still colossal. Slowly it floats more and more away, the water round it torn and splashed by the insatiate sharks, and the air above vexed with rapacious flights of screaming fowls, whose beaks are like so many insulting poniards in the whale. The vast white headless phantom floats further and further from the ship, and every rod that it so floats, what seem square roods of sharks and cubic roods of fowls, augment the murderous din. For hours and hours from the almost stationary ship that hideous sight is seen. Beneath the unclouded and mild azure sky, upon the fair face of the pleasant sea, wafted by the joyous breezes, the great mass of death floats on and on, till lost in infinite perspectives.

Adjectives certainly bring this scene to life—or to death, one might prefer to say. Some of Melville's phrases make the passage almost unbearably vivid—the *peeled white* body, the *rapacious* flights of *screaming* fowls, the *vast white headless* phantom floating in the *murderous* din.

But notice, if you please, what Melville does in the final sentence of the passage. All of a sudden the adjectives change altogether in tone. All at once the author is directing our attention to the *unclouded* and *mild* sky, the *fair* face of the *pleasant* sea, the *joyous* breezes. The effect is shocking, and Melville has heightened it by selecting—deliberately, I would assume—adjectives which are not merely gentle and positive and life-affirming, in contrast to those employed earlier, but adjectives which are definitely bland and unimaginative, even banal. The fair face of the pleasant sea? The joyous breezes? The unclouded sky? These would be clichés but for the context in which they appear.

We can decide for ourselves why Melville wrote that last sentence the way he did. Perhaps he wished to contrast the enormous energy of destruction with the banality of life. Perhaps he wanted to show life going on in the face of death. Perhaps, like so many writers, he didn't have anything consciously in mind but merely thought the paragraph would have a certain something going for it if he wrote it in that particular fashion.

The passage from *Moby Dick* is additionally instructive because the author uses several different kinds of modifiers. First we have these adjectives which simply describe, and do so in an uninflected fashion. The *peeled white* body of the *beheaded* whale—these adjectives fill in a picture for us without telling us how the author feels about it, or suggesting how we ought to feel. The ship, we are told, is *stationary*. The body floats *slowly*. The sky is *unclouded*.

A second class of adjectives includes those which, while still deliberately factual, are concerned as well with our response to what is going on. It is a fact that the sharks are *insatiate,* that the fowls are *rapacious* and *screaming,* that the bulk of the dead whale is *colossal,* but how we feel about the noise and appetite of the scavengers and the size of the whale is colored by the choice of modifiers.

Other adjectives are still more subjective. That the din is *murderous* is not a measure of its volume, nor does it have anything to do with what is actually going on—the whale is already dead, so the act performed by birds and sharks is only figuratively murderous. That the sight is *hideous* is similarly a conclusion of the author. Finally, *fair* and *pleasant* and *joyous* are wholly subjective, telling us nothing about the actual effect or appearance of the sea and the breezes but instructing us as to how they are to be perceived.

As a general rule, I believe we do best to stick to adverbs and adjectives which describe and limit our employment of those which attempt to control the reader's response. Modifiers of the latter sort don't add any detail to the picture we are painting. They add clutter, and they simultaneously interpose the author's perceptions between the writing and the reader.

Consider:

> She was a pretty girl, with a cheerful grin and a keen glint in her warm eyes. Her figure was well-proportioned, her clothing attractive.

There doesn't seem to be anything wrong with those two sentences, and they certainly don't glare at one. But they're quite empty, and if a writer were to go on in this vein for pages on end, the result would be deadening. Because we don't see the girl any better after she's been thus described than we did before. We know that the disembodied narrator likes the way she looks, but we don't know what she looks like, nor have we been given any reason why *we* should believe that she's pretty, that her clothing's attractive, that her grin is cheerful and her eyes warm.

The same two sentences, I might add, would be somewhat less objectionable in first-person narration, where everything is deliberately filtered through the perceptions of the narrator, whose reactions to phenomena are a legitimate part of the story. Even so, this isn't very good writing. The modifiers are not descriptive but judgmental.

These judgmental adjectives are handy. While they're a natural refuge for the lazy writer, who finds it much easier to dictate the reader's reaction than to take the trouble to sketch in a picture, they're useful as well when one doesn't want to waste space describing something of minor importance. If a bit player strides by carrying a blaring transistor radio, it may be simpler to call it harsh and obnoxious than to discuss the nature of the music played and its decibel count.

It all depends, of course, on what you're trying to do. I wouldn't care to propose any rules here. There are no good and bad adjectives—all have their place, even *good* and *bad.* Nor would I want you to think too much about what I've written here while you're doing your own writing. Afterward, though, when you reread what you've done, you might want to see whether your modifiers, your descriptive words, do the job you've given them. Should they be more or less specific? Should they be more descriptive? More judgmental? Are you trying to control the reader's reaction? Should you aim for more show and less tell? Have you overloaded your prose with adverbs and adjectives? Or have you gone overboard in the other direction, being rather too sparing in their use?

I'll wish you the best. I'm just breezing along with the joyous breeze, floating on and on, till lost in infinite perspectives.

CHAPTER 40

Writing With Your Eyes Closed

WRITING'S SO hard I can do it with my eyes shut.

Now that I've got your attention, let me explain. Some of my most productive time as a writer of fiction is spent seated at my typewriter with my fingers still and my eyes closed. In this fashion I'm able to see a picture within my mind. Once I've seen and experienced it, it's a much simpler matter to open my eyes, hit the typewriter keys, and convert what I've seen into prose and dialogue.

Suppose I'm about to write a scene that takes place in some minor character's furnished room, a setting I haven't previously described in my work-in-progress. I'll sit back, close my eyes, and let an image of that room come into my mind. The picture I create in my mind may indeed be that of a room I've visited sometime before in real life. It may be wholly imaginary. Most likely, it will be a combination of elements, containing aspects of rooms I've seen, rooms I've read about, images that linger in the back of the mind from plays and films and conversations.

When you think of an apple, what picture comes into your mind? No particular apple, I don't suppose. You've doubtless seen thousands, from Macintosh to Cezanne, and while they certainly don't all look alike neither do they hang around in the memory as individuals. But all of those apples you've seen and smelled and held in the hand and chomped into have merged in the mind to the point that you conjure up an image when you hear the word *apple*.

But let's get back into that imaginary room. I'll see it first from the doorway, say, if that's where my viewpoint character stands when he takes his first look at the place. I'll pay some attention to the furniture. There's a bed, of course. And a chest of drawers. Any chairs? What do they look like? A rug on the floor? Linoleum? What kind of shape is it in?

Pictures on the wall? A calendar, perhaps? Is the bed made? The room itself—is it neat or disorderly? Any windows? Curtained or shaded or what?

How big is the room? Does the bed take up most of it? Just how much room is there to move around?

Now the answers to these questions derive both from the demands of the story and the picture with which my mind has supplied me. In other words, certain things about the room are predetermined by what's already been established about the person who inhabits it, his character and his circumstances. The action which will take place in the room is another predeterminant; if somebody's going to find something in the closet, for example, the room has to have one. But other elements of the room—a floor lamp with a fringed shade, a fireplace that's been sealed off and painted over—may have nothing to do with the demands of plot and characterization. They're just part of the scenery.

Furthermore, I may never mention or describe them when I write the scene.

This is an important point. This process of visualization is not designed solely to enable the writer to describe what he has seen to the reader. That may not even be its primary purpose. Visualization is most valuable to me because it allows me to *experience* what I see in my mind—and then, having had the experience of the furnished room or the apple or whatever, I can write out of that experience in creating fiction for my own purpose.

What does this mean? Well, maybe I can give you an example. The passage which follows is an unremarkable one from a novel of mine and describes the fatal heart attack of one of the characters.

> He returned to his own house, ate dinner with his wife at the usual hour. He helped her load the dishwasher. While it ran they sat with newspapers in the front room. First he read the *Times* while she read the Buffalo *News.* Then they traded. She was reading Clive Barnes's review of a new English play when he said, "Syl?"
>
> She lowered the paper. His face looked drawn and his expression was one of puzzlement.
>
> "I don't feel well," he said.
>
> "What's the matter? Stay right there, I'll phone Irv Zucker."
>
> "Oh, it's probably nothing," he said, and then he sat back in his chair and died. Her eyes were on him as it happened and she knew instantly what had happened. He was there and then he was not, he was gone.

I've bothered to quote this passage because I remember the extent to which I visualized it before writing it. I had a very strong image of the room in which those two persons sat reading their newspapers. I saw their chairs and knew the distance between them. I felt the mood in the room, relaxing with newspapers after cleaning up the dinner dishes. I saw each character from the other's point of view. And, as the scene unfolded, I *felt* it.

I certainly didn't describe the room much. The scene is rendered briefly, almost sketchily. But because I visualized and experienced the entire scene before I wrote it, I intuitively selected certain words and rejected others, included certain observations and left others unvoiced. Because I had the experience of this scene, I was equipped to make it a real scene for the reader. No reader will be likely to picture the same room I pictured, but that hardly matters.

This may be a subtle point, as hard to convey as the principles of Zen archery. It has elements of commonality, I suspect, with the tricks actors use to prepare themselves for roles, calling on bits and pieces of their own past to center themselves and get into character.

Maybe it would be helpful if I gave you an exercise.

Let's give it a try. Sit comfortably with your eyes closed. Picture in your mind a piece of fruit—the apple we mentioned earlier or something else. See it. Experience it. Get a sense of its dimensions. Notice its color. Sense the amount of space it occupies. Imagine yourself holding it in your hand, weighing it. How much mass does it have? How heavy is it?

How does it feel in your hand? What's its temperature?

Is it moist or dry to the touch? Rough or smooth?

See yourself drawing it close to your face. Smell it. Can you imagine the aroma? Pierce the skin with your thumbnail and smell it again, its inner juices released to the open air.

Imagine yourself peeling or cutting into it. Taste the fruit. Go ahead—chew it up, swallow it. Taste it. Experience the act of eating it.

You may have noticed, while performing this exercise, that the fruit changed somewhat from one moment to the next. You may have realized such elements as color and weight and odor more vividly at one time than at another. That's fine. This process of visualization is a fluid one, and the images we conjure up are apt to keep redefining themselves for us.

This simple exercise becomes increasingly useful if you practice it on a more or less regular basis. The capacity for visualization seems to develop with this sort of training. You might prefer to conjure up other things than pieces of fruit. As a change of pace, now and then you might enjoy focusing on an actual past experience, recreating it in your mind as completely as possible. When you do this, you might find it helpful to concentrate less on linear memory and more on sensory memory—in other words, don't dwell on what actually took place as much as on how everything looked and sounded and felt and tasted and smelled, and how you felt about it and experienced it.

This is a good exercise for any time of the day. Another exercise is more specifically useful before undertaking the day's stint at the typewriter, and that involves seeing what you're going to write before you write it, as we discussed at the beginning of this piece.

Perhaps I should stress that I don't always see every scene fully and completely. Some of the stage sets I use are more real to me than others. Some are more completely furnished. Some change in certain unimportant aspects from time to time, just as that piece of fruit changed while you were imagining it. Sometimes my mental picture will be more painting than photograph, with details alternately stressed or blurred. I have found, though, that the more completely I realize scenes before writing them, the more at ease I am in recreating them for the reader and the more apt I am to be satisfied with my work.

There was once a school of thought in the theater that maintained that scenery should be as detailed as possible, even down to details which could never possibly be apparent to the audience. If there was a desk on stage, for example, there ought to be papers and pencils and such in its drawers, even if those drawers were destined to remain shut throughout the performance.

I don't suppose there are many set designers nowadays who devote much time to filling up unopened desk drawers, but I think the principle is a sound one. I know it works at the typewriter, and at root the reason is as basic a one as you can get.

Fiction, let us never forget, cannot work properly without the reader's voluntary suspension of disbelief. He *knows* it's just a story but he elects to discard this knowledge. While he reads its, he chooses to believe in it.

But first is it not essential that the writer suspend his own disbelief? He more than anyone knows it's just a story—after all, he's the one who's inventing it. To the extent that he visualizes it first, to the extent that he has the experience of his fiction himself before he puts it on paper for someone else, his work acquires an essential reality in his own eyes. He suspends his own disbelief and makes it easier for the reader to go and do likewise.

I hope I haven't succeeded only in taking a rather simple process and making it unbearably complicated. I can only suggest that you reread the exercise and give it a try. See it first, and then write it. It works.

CHAPTER **41**

Hum a Few Bars . . . and Fake It

IRATE NEIGHBOR: Do you know your bleeping piano is driving me crazy?
PIANIST: No, but hum a few bars and I'll fake it.

When I told a friend the theme of this chapter, she treated me to a look of moral reproach. "Telling writers how to fake," she said, "is like teaching children how to steal. You should be ashamed of yourself."

I should indeed be ashamed of myself, and I often am, but not this time. For fakery is the very heart and soul of fiction. All our novels and short stories are nothing but a pack of lies.

Unless your writing is pure autobiography in the guise of fiction, you will continually find yourself practicing the dark arts of the illusionist and the trade of the counterfeiter. In order to foster the voluntary suspension of disbelief which fiction demands, you must give the reader the clear impression that you know a great deal more about things than you in fact do. If your story is set in some exotic clime, you want the reader to think your passport has more stamps than the Post Office. If an important character is an auto mechanic, you've got to look as though you know a camshaft from a hood ornament. Otherwise the reader is forcibly made aware of the fact that he's reading something somebody made up, that it's all a story, that it didn't really happen—that there's no life in it, no reality.

One way to make your writing seem authentic is to write about the things you know. Sometimes, though, plots may suggest themselves which cannot be situated in your home town or peopled with your friends or neighbors. When this is the case, you create the illusion of reality through a combination of research and verbal sleight-of-hand.

Shall I hum a few bars?

1. FAKING LOCATIONS. I once wrote a con game novel set in Toronto

and Olean, New York. I was living in Buffalo at the time and spent two days in Toronto and one in Olean, jotting down the names of streets and restaurants and otherwise doing research. It was fun, in a way; I was young and felt professional as all hell doing what I assumed writers were supposed to do.

A couple years later, when I wrote a series of spy novels that hopped all over the globe, I discovered it wasn't necessary for me to go to Yugloslavia just because I was sending my lead character there. And if I didn't have to go to Belgrade, I certainly didn't have to go to Olean. The only place you really have to go is the library.

Travel guides are an obvious source. Telephone directories, usually accessible at the phone company, often contain rudimentary city maps. The Yellow Pages help you salt your work with references to hotels and restaurants and local landmarks in some unknown-to-you town.

I've found novels similarly useful. Before a spate of moves decimated my library, I kept every book I ever bought. If I wanted to drop a little local color into something I was writing, I could almost always put my hand on a book with the appropriate setting.

Sometimes it's easier and just as effective to avoid research altogether and bluff your way through. For example, I wrote a book a few years ago loosely based on the Starkweather murders in the midwest. I wanted a Nebraska locale, and decided against creating a town and making up a name for it. Instead I selected Grand Island, a city I have never visited and knew no more about than the *Encyclopaedia Britannica* could tell me, which was very little indeed.

I made up street names, neighborhoods, stores, everything. I didn't bother worrying what the real Grand Island was like because in the context of the novel it did not matter. Perhaps one reader in a thousand would know there's no Kleinhans Mens Wear in Grand Island, and the odds are good that he'd simply think I had described a specific store and changed the name to avoid a lawsuit.

2. FAKING EXPERTISE. Bernie Rhodenbarr is a gifted man; he could pick his way into Fort Knox with a hairpin. Since he made his appearance, any number of people have asked me somewhat apprehensively how I know so much about the ins and outs of burglary.

I've told them, honestly enough, that I studied up on the subject a couple years ago when it looked as though I'd need a second career. (It's a natural for writers—you work alone and set your own hours.) What I didn't add is that Bernie knows more about the business than I do. For example, he talks very knowledgeably about the merits of the Rabson lock. Now there's no such brand; I used the name because Archie Goodwin always used to praise Rabson locks in the Nero Wolfe books.

3. EASY DOES IT. When you try too hard to look as though you know what you're talking about, the reader may be able to tell that you're protesting too much.

I have a tendency to overcompensate when I'm setting a scene in unfamiliar territory. In an effort to prove I know what I'm writing about, I take all my guidebook research and hurl it in the reader's face. On such occasions, I can't send my hero across a bridge without quoting the cornerstone inscription, all the way down to reporting who was mayor when the span was completed. If somebody drives crosstown through streets unfamiliar to me, I'll chart the route on a map and report every left and right turn to the reader.

What I have to keep reminding myself is that the purpose of my fiction is not to convince the reader that I've been a lifelong resident of Wall, South Dakota—or whatever setting I've chosen. The test, of course, is a simple one: Would I put in all this crap if I were more sure of myself? Would I include as much information if the scene were set in my own neighborhood? If not, I'm probably overdoing it.

4. WATCH OUT FOR SHARP MULETAS. Ages ago I wrote a short story in which a wise old ex-bullfighter kills a neophyte by stabbing him in the throat with his *muleta*. Now this would have been a neat trick because the *muleta* is the cloth, not the sword, and that's the sort of thing I really ought to have known. The story would have been unpublishably bad regardless, but that certainly didn't help my cause.

5. TAKE CARE OF THE PENCE. Just as a misbegotten *muleta* can utterly destroy credibility, so can a well-chosen detail endow a whole book with an air of authenticity.

In *Tanner's Twelve Swingers*, the hero at one point teaches some Latvian to a Lithuanian child, and we have the following passage:

> "*Runatsi latviski*," I said. "You will speak Lettish." I took her hand. "You see how the words change? *Zale ir zalja*—the grass is green. *Te ir tēvs*—here is father. *Tēvs ir virs*—father is a man. *Mate ir plavā*—mother is in the meadow."
>
> "*Mate ir plavā zalja*," said Minna. Which meant that mother was in the green meadow, and which also meant that Minna was getting the hang of it. . . .

All that was painstakingly faked with the aid of a book called *Teach Yourself Latvian*, a volume I may have been the only person ever to buy and peruse. The response I got from various Latvian-Americans more than justified the time I spent on research. A couple of years later, when I was keeping company with a young lady born in Riga, *Tanner's Twelve Swingers* was a great help in establishing good relations with her parents.

One never knows, does one? Get a few little details right and people begin to think you know what you're doing.

Sometimes phony details work just as well. Another of Tanner's adventures took him to Bangkok. When I read galleys I was startled to learn that a CIA agent pointed out "drops and meeting places and fronts—a travel agency, a tobbo shop, a cocktail lounge, a restaurant. . . ."

What on earth was a tobbo shop?

I checked my manuscript. I'd written a "tobacco shop" and a creative linotypist had vastly improved on it. I decided a tobbo shop would be the best possible CIA front, adding a crackerjack bit of local color. Yeah, a tobbo shop. Why not?

So I left it like that.

And now I look forward to the day when I spot in someone else's fiction a reference to the notorious tobbo shops of Siam.

And who's to say? If enough of us write about tobbo shops, sooner or later some enterprising Thai will open one. Life does imitate art, after all.

CHAPTER **42**

Character Building

I JUST finished reading an English mystery set in turn-of-the-century Paris. The author knows a lot about French history and conveyed a good deal of his knowledge in his novel. The plot, while not remarkable, was adequate. The writing, if occasionally clumsy, was no great drawback. What kept me from getting caught up in the book was my inability to respond greatly to the characters. They lacked the spark of life, and the detective, an inspector of police, never came alive for me.

I've commented before, in this space and elsewhere, on the importance of characterization. In order for a piece of fiction to work, its characters must fulfill three requirements. They must be plausible, they must be sympathetic, and they must be original.

When characters are implausible, the reader cannot manage that trick of voluntary suspension of disbelief without which fiction never becomes involving. "No policeman would react that way," he says. "No character in this position and supplied with these attributes would do thus and so. Therefore I cannot escape the fact that I am reading a book, that someone sat at a desk and painstakingly invented all of this, and if I am forever aware of all this, how can I possibly gull myself into giving a damn what happens next?"

When characters are unsympathetic, the reader loses interest for a different reason. To believe in them and to get caught up in their fate is to spend time in their company, and if they are unsympathetic the prospect is unpleasant. A character need not be a saint to be sympathetic. Indeed, flawless characters tend to be curiously unsympathetic because they come across as lacking in humanity. A character can in fact be more than a bit of a villain, as long as there is something about him to which a reader can comfortably respond and with which he can identify. "If I were that type of person," he ought to be able to say, "then I'd be like that, too. If I were that kind of guy, that's the kind of guy I'd be."

When a character is lacking in originality, the reader's capacities for both believing and identifying are strained. If the hero walks through the pages like an empty suit of clothes, how can we regard him as more than a mechanical device of the author's invention? His features, metaphorically speaking, remain fuzzy around the edges. Nothing sets him off and makes him a living, breathing individual, so why are we to care what happens to him?

It's not uncommon for writers to do a lot of labeling and mistake it for originality of characterization. "I'm starting a detective series," a hopeful writer said to me not long ago, "and I think I've got something really original. My character never gets out of bed before noon, and he makes it a rule always to wear one piece of red clothing, and the only thing he ever drinks is white crème de menthe on the rocks. He has a pet rhesus monkey named Bitsy and a parrot named Sam. What do you think?"

What I think is that the speaker has not a character but a collection of character tags. It might work to have a character with any or all of these labels in his garments. Matter of fact, I wrote the above paragraph thinking of a detective character of the late David Alexander's who lived upstairs of a

42nd Street flea circus, always wore a loud vest, drank only Irish whiskey and never took a drink before four o'clock or refused one after that hour. That character, however, was not the mere sum of these attributes. It is not the quirks that make an enduring character but the essential personality which the quirks highlight. How that character views the world, how he acts and reacts, is of much greater importance than what he had for breakfast.

In my own writing, I have found that my most effective viewpoint characters are aspects of myself. This is not to say that they are based on me, or that I share their views or attitudes or patterns of behavior. Perhaps the best way I can put it is to say that they act as I would act if I happened to be them. In addition, some aspects of their nature and circumstances can often be seen to derive from my own nature and circumstances.

Perhaps I can best show how this works in the case of a character named Matthew Scudder. I wrote three novels and two novelettes about Scudder in the mid-seventies, and have just finished a fourth novel about him after having left him in cold storage for several years. I was more than a little apprehensive at the prospect of taking him up again. I have changed, certainly, in the intervening years, and I was unsure of my ability to resume seeing the world through Scudder's eyes and reporting in his voice.

Happily, getting back into character turned out to be virtually effortless, no harder to relearn than swimming or riding a bike. Now this does not prove that the book I've just written is any good, or even that Scudder, now or half a dozen years ago, is any great shakes as a character. What it does demonstrate, however, is the extent to which Scudder was and is a vital character *for me*. Clearly I find him plausible, sympathetic, and original. Clearly I know just who he is in a way that goes beyond his wardrobe and his mannerisms. I can believe in him, and I can care about him—and I can write about him.

Scudder provides a better example than most of the process of character construction because I knew a great deal about him before I started chronicling his adventures. Often my characters develop on the page as I write. Scudder did, to an extent, and still does evolve while I'm at the typewriter, but he was largely conceived and developed before any words went onto paper.

I had talked with Bill Grose, then at Dell, about developing a character for a detective series. A reading of Leonard Shecter's *On the Pad* gave me the idea of using a corrupt policeman who happened to solve homicide cases while actively seeking opportunities for graft. I liked the notion, but it became quickly evident to me that I could not comfortably write about a member of a bureaucracy like the police force. My detective had to be operating on his own hook.

So Scudder would be an ex-cop, working as a private detective. But what would his life be like? And why would he have left the force?

Quite naturally, I borrowed elements of my own life and gave them to Scudder. I had recently separated from my wife and children and moved from rural New Jersey to midtown Manhattan. I decided that, after Scudder had left the police force, his marriage had fallen apart and he'd moved from Long Island to the city. Because I liked the neighborhood I lived in and wanted to use it as a backdrop for fiction, I placed Scudder right on my block, West 57th between Eighth and Ninth Avenues. I had an apartment, but I felt a hotel room was more Scudder's style, and I put him in one.

Why had he left the force? Because of a scandal, I thought, and then I rejected the thought. I wanted to give him a more personal kind of a scar, wanted him to bear more guilt in his own eyes than in the eyes of others. I decided he'd been drinking in a tavern while off-duty, had foiled a holdup attempt, but that one of the shots he fired had ricocheted and killed a child. While he was exonerated of any wrongdoing, he'd been unable to exonerate himself.

Where did this come from? I couldn't have told you this at the time, but it strikes me now that it constituted a pretty clear projection of self into character. I had abruptly quit a marriage of over a dozen years' standing. I believed, and professed to feel, that I had been correct in so doing. But, if I had not killed a child, I had abandoned three of them, and on some level I could not exonerate myself.

One of the quirks with which I furnished Scudder was a propensity for hanging out in churches. He didn't attend services and had no formal belief in God, but after moving to Manhattan he found himself frequently entering churches and using them as a source of peace and quiet. In this instance, I was simply supplying Scudder with a behavior pattern I had lately adopted myself. New York is noisy, and churches do provide a quiet place to sit and think. There was very likely an element of unconscious spiritual quest in my visits to churches, and no doubt this was true of Scudder as well. I did make his behavior pattern rather more rigid, though, and I had him make a thing of lighting candles for people who had died, invariably including the little girl his ricocheting bullet had killed.

In addition, I had him tithe in a compulsive fashion, giving a tenth of whatever income his detection brought him to whatever church he next visited. He did this not because he felt they would do something worthwhile with the money, or for any reason that made sense to him, but because it had come to be something he simply did. In explaining this in the character sheet I wrote about him, I noted, "He does a lot of things without knowing why." While I certainly have never tithed, and seriously doubt that I ever shall, I certainly did things without knowing why. And still do.

Since Scudder was already a denizen of my neighborhood, I let him hang out at the same saloon where I spent a great deal of my own time. I was drinking pretty heavily around that time, and I made him a pretty heavy drinker, too. I drank whiskey, sometimes mixing it with coffee. So did Scudder.

He and I were different in innumerable ways. He'd been a cop for all those years, and he still looked and thought and reacted like one. His attitudes and responses were not mine. But there was enough of me in him so that I knew him, and his organic evolution made him plausible, sympathetic and original.

It was good to renew that acquaintance. It was good to spend two-hundred-plus pages in his company, good to be able to report that Matthew Scudder is alive and well and living on West 57th Street.

CHAPTER

Casting

THE WAITRESS watched him with wary hostility, as if she were afraid he might be putting her on. She was middle-aged and hard-faced, with a beehive of champagne-colored hair that she kept patting and touching to reassure herself it was still there in all its glory. But she was not a bit out of place in the steakhouse, with its linoleum-covered floor and tube-steel furniture and blaring, country-rock jukebox.

That's from *Cutter and Bone,* by Newton Thornburg. It's good writing, but then if there's a bad sentence anywhere in the novel I didn't notice it. I picked this particular passage to quote because the writer has given us such a perfect description of a bit player. That's all we're ever told about this waitress. She doesn't have a line of dialogue, never turns up in another scene. But we already know everything we have to know about her. For some readers, her moment on stage will be memorable—as it evidently was for me, as I thought of her when I sat down to write this piece. For others she's part of the scenery, serving to evoke the ambience of the restaurant in which the protagonists are about to have a conversation and thus to lend atmosphere to that conversation. It doesn't really matter whether she's memorable or not. She's a bit player, a spear carrier.

The way you delineate such minor characters is one of the things that separates . . . hmmmm. Not "the men from the boys." That's sexist. "The adults from the children?" "The sheep from the goats?" "The fool from his money?"

Enough. Out in Hollywood, where they know how to delegate responsibility, it's the job of the casting director to select actors for minor roles. The casting director studies the script, conceptualizes the characters for their roles as written, and combines intuition, experience, and familiarity with available talent to pick the right people.

The poor prose writer, hack of all trades, has to be his own casting director. He uses his intuition and experience, adds his powers of imagination and observation, and does his best.

Where do you find your minor characters? A good many writers do their casting from the world they live in, patterning characters after friends, acquaintances, or passers-by. This is perfectly legitimate, and is quite different from the *roman à clef,* where a real story about real people is told in the guise of fiction. Instead your real-life model serves to give you a handle on the character you're creating—a conversational mechanism, a physical trait, an attitude of one sort or another.

Wherever your minor characters come from, one thing you ought to train yourself to do is visualize them in your mind before rendering them on paper. Perhaps "visualization" is the wrong word here; it implies sight, and for some characters your process of realization may not be specifically visual at all. Sometimes I will get a strong visual impression of a character. I'll be able to picture him as graphically in my mind as I would a close friend. Other times I'll know instead how his voice sounds, or that he shifts his weight from foot to foot as he talks, or that there is something noteworthy about his eyes or hands.

He stood five-ten, weighed around 155 pounds. His hair was dark brown verging on black, slicked down and combed straight back. He had a broad forehead and a strong, hawklike nose. His eyes were a medium brown. His mouth was wide, full-lipped, and when he drew back those lips to smile he showed large even teeth. His suit was a gray sharkskin, a three-button model with padding in the shoulders. He wore a buff-colored shirt with a tab collar, a navy silk tie with a restrained below-the-knot design. He—

There's nothing horribly wrong with the description above but neither is there anything terribly right with it. It's photographic. It tells us how tall and how heavy the character is, what his features are like, what he's wearing. It's exactly the sort of description a cop would want to get from an eye-witness. As a quick study of a minor character in a work of fiction, it tells us more than we need to know and less than we'd like to know.

In contrast, look again at the description of the waitress from *Cutter and Bone.* Thornburg doesn't tell us if the lady's tall or short, heavy or thin. He doesn't tell us much about her physical appearance, just a few words about her hairstyle and the hardness of her face. But *I* know what she looks like. And so do you. And while my picture of the woman may differ from yours, and while each of ours will differ from Thornburg's, that's irrelevant. We have a sense of the person, and we can fill in the rest ourselves to reflect our own intuition and experience and imagination. Reading, after all, is an audience-participation venture, and every story is a slightly different experience for every reader.

What's important, then, is to furnish the reader with those details which impress themselves upon you when you visualize the character. Here's an example from "Out the Window," a detective novelette of mine which appeared in *Alfred Hitchcock's Mystery Magazine:*

> The door opened. He was tall and thin, with hollow cheeks and prominent eyebrows and a worn, wasted look to him. He must have been in his early thirties and he didn't really look much older than that but you sensed that in another ten years he'd look twenty years older. If he lived that long. He wore patched jeans and a tee-shirt with THE SPIDER'S WEB silkscreened on it. Beneath the legend there was a sketch of a web. A macho spider stood at one end of it, grinning, extending two of his eight arms to welcome a hesitant girlish fly.

I chose this paragraph partly out of vanity (it *is* a nice paragraph, isn't it?) but also because I remember how it evolved. When I started writing it I didn't know what the guy looked like. I knew who he was—a bartender who'd been living with the girl whose death the lead character is investigating. I had a vague impression of his face, my idea amounting to a sort of composite of the faces of a slew of footloose predatory males I've met in life and on celluloid. More important, I had a sense of who he was. The paragraph all grew out of this knowledge and did so spontaneously and quickly. I'd already selected The Spider's Web as the name of his place of employment, and the idea of the tee-shirt came to mind of its own accord.

By concentrating on details and not attempting to describe photographically, you greatly increase your chances of writing something the reader will happen to remember. By relating those aspects of the character worth mentioning, and by omitting pedestrian physical description, you make an impression upon the reader. I won't quickly forget that waitress touching her hair "to reassure herself it was still there."

There's a thin line between this sort of impressionism and out-and-out caricature. The art of a caricaturist consists of ignoring the ordinary and exaggerating the remarkable. Sometimes, to convey a minor character rapidly and indelibly, caricature is tempting.

Ian Fleming did this all the time, and not without knowing what he was about. James Bond's supporting players were all caricatures, deliberately twisted to comic-book grotesquery. They had improbable names and unlikely physical attributes and mannerisms. This made the Bond books vivid and memorable and had a great deal to do with their success. It also made them utterly unrealistic and ruined them for those readers for whom the illusion of reality is a requirement for the enjoyment of fiction.

If you are trying to write realistic fiction and you people it extensively with overdrawn characters, you're working against yourself. You can occasionally get away with filling books and stories with grotesques, but unless your name's Carson McCullers it gets tricky.

A less obvious form of caricature consists of giving an otherwise ordinary character a trait or attribute or mannerism on which the reader may focus his attention. The waitress with her beehive hairdo is an example. If she figured more prominently in the book than she does, and if we had that hair-patting reported constantly, it could get to be a bit much. As a quick snapshot it's fine.

In *Time to Murder and Create,* I've got a character in the first chapter named Spinner Jablon. He got his sobriquet because of his habit of spinning a silver dollar on the table as he talks. Well, by the end of the chapter old Spinner's dead as a lox, and it's a damn good thing, because I couldn't have endured his spinning his way through the next sixty thousand words. As it stands, I'm afraid Spinner verges on caricature.

Sometimes the work you do on casting pays off in the plotting area. As I write this column I'm at work on a novel about a burglar who's recruited by a friend to filch something from the apartment of the friend's ex-wife. (While he's doing this the woman gets killed, the friend gets jugged for the killing, and the heroic burglar comes to his aid and investigates the murder.)

I tried to figure out who this friend should be. I decided he could be a poker buddy of the burglar's, but I wanted them to have some other connection as well. I decided that the friend ought to be the burglar's dentist, and I imagined a scene where Bernie the Burglar is in the chair getting a tooth drilled, all those things hanging out of his mouth and all, and the dentist is laying this whole riff on him.

And I decided the dentist wanted the something-or-other filched because he wants to remarry, and the girl he wants to marry is his dental hygienist, who'd be introduced cleaning Bernie's teeth, and later in the book the two of them could get involved, and the murder weapon, hell, the murder weapon could be one of those fiendish dental implements that all dentists have a whole arsenal of, and the actual murderer could be—

Sorry. You'll have to read *The Burglar in the Closet* to find that out. But all that plot business evolved from a casting decision.

On the basis of that, I suppose I could say something about there being more than one use for the old casting couch. Or I could work up some sort of wordplay on casting pearls before swine, or bread upon the waters. Or aspersions.

But *I* wouldn't do anything like that. Trust me.

CHAPTER

Name Calling

HOW CAN you pick names for your characters? If there are tricks to every trade, what are the tricks in this one?

Let's grant, first of all, that the success or failure of a piece of fiction rarely hinges upon the names of the characters. I've never heard of an editor buying or rejecting a story on this basis. Not consciously, at any rate; on another level, character names can certainly influence how he *feels* about what you've written, and thus can weigh in the eventual decision to accept or reject.

What names to use is a decision you have to make every time you sit down to write a piece of fiction. And your decisions in this regard frequently have to be made spontaneously—no matter how thoroughly I may work things out in advance, any session at the typewriter will see the emergence of some unanticipated minor character, some bit player or spear carrier who needs to be named. One might as well learn how to do this sort of thing effectively.

Here then, in no particular order, are some observations on the name game:

1. AVOID CONFUSION. This might be too obvious to mention but for the fact that even published writers slip up from time to time, hurling Carl and Cal and Carol and Carolyn all into the same chapter, peopling a crowd scene with Smathers and Smithers and Dithers and Mather. Be conscious of this sort of thing and avoid it. The fact that such duplication occurs in real life makes no difference. True, you will often find yourself in the presence of four or five Johns at the same time. Well, that's one of the differences between life and fiction, after all. Fiction is supposed to make sense.

Some writers try not to give any two characters the same first or last initials. Common sense should help you decide where this particular line ought to be drawn. Most readers probably won't confuse Al and Adrian, or Gooch and Gulbrandsen; many might be confused, or at least annoyed, by duplications like Hal and Mal, Gerry and Gary, Janet and Janice, etc.

2. WATCH OUT FOR FALLING STARS. Sometimes a name will pop into your mind. It has such a nice feel to it and fits your concept of your character so perfectly that you don't realize you've heard the name before.

Or even seen it in lights. When I worked for an illiterary agent some years back, a manuscript came in featuring a female character named Irene Dunne. A fine name, that, but *I* remembered mama, even if our client did not. When I pointed out that Irene Dunne was indeed the name of a rather prominent actress, he nodded thoughtfully. "It had a nice ring to it," he said. "But I couldn't quite think why."

Even if you don't fill your stories with people named Clark Gable and Norma Shearer, it's very easy to use the names of prominent people with whom you yourself may be unfamiliar. This is not something you need agonize over. If you're in any doubt about a particular name, if it sounds as though it might be too good not to be true, check an encyclopedia and a copy of *Who's Who*. (And, when you've done that, use your own judgment. The lead in *After the First Death*, a mystery of mine, was named Alexander

Penn. Before the book saw print, I discovered there was a poet in the Soviet Union by that name. I thought about it for a while, and I realized how many changes I'd have to make, all the puns on the last name and everything, and I decided to let *him* change it.)

3. PICK INTERESTING NAMES. I know there are a lot of John Smiths in the world, and I wish them well, but I certainly don't want to encounter any more of their number in fiction. And if I were an editor I would certainly not be much impressed by an author with so impoverished an imagination as to fasten such a name on a character of his. Names like Smith and Jones and Thompson and Miller and Williams and Johnson are so common in real life as to be colorless in fiction. You might ring one in now and then for a minor character, but tend to avoid them altogether. They're just not interesting enough.

In this regard, let me furnish you with a piece of incidental intelligence. People who are rank amateurs at this business of inventing names, people picking an alias for a motel register or making up a false name on the spur of the moment, have a marked propensity to select as a last name an adapted first name. Richards, Peters, Johnson, Edwards—these are all common last names in their own right, but they're especially common as aliases.

What constitutes an interesting name and how do you pick it? Interesting question. I've become increasingly fascinated by names over the past few years and have devoted more attention to the problem of naming characters than I once did. Personally, I've come to favor lengthy last names rather than short ones, and uncommon names rather than common ones.

Some of the names I like best for characters are ones I've invented (which is not to say that they may not exist somewhere in real life). I've been doing a series of stories for *Ellery Queen's Mystery Magazine* featuring a criminous lawyer named Martin Ehrengraf, whose presumably unique surname is composed of two reasonably ordinary German words. My burglar, who's starred in two novels so far, is Bernie Rhodenbarr, and my friend Bill Pronzini wrote to ask if I'd created his name by combining those of two major-league pitchers, Rhoden and Barr. I hadn't; while trying to think of a name I recalled a relative of mine named Rodenberg, and I changed the ending, and I put the *h* in because it looked better that way, and a star was born.

If you keep a notebook—and you really should—you can stockpile interesting names for future use. A few years back writer and bridge expert Patricia Fox Sheinwold was boasting about her dog Honey Bear, whom she hoped to star in some dogfood commercials. "If Bear turns out not to be photogenic," Pat said, "they can always use her to do the bark-overs."

I laughed politely—what, after all, are friends for?—and I scribbled

Barkover in my notebook. In due course one Simon Barckover appeared as a talent representative in a book called *The Topless Tulip Caper,* by Chip Harrison.

Once I spent a night in a motel room in Grenada, Mississippi, with nothing to read but the phone book. Someone must have swiped the Gideon Bible. So I read the phone book and discovered that there was a local family named Palmertree. I think that's a wonderful name, but I haven't yet found a place to use it. It's in my notebook, waiting.

4.   FIRST NAMES CAN BE INTERESTING, TOO. Of late I've taken to using surnames as first names, and I like the effect of it. Nothing endows a character with the trappings of wealth and status like a proper British surname for his first name. Remember, a substantial number of first names started out as surnames—Milton, Seymour, Irving, etc. And the practice of giving a child a family name as a first name is a long-established one. In recent months I've named characters Wilson Colliard, Grantham Beale, Walker Gladstone Murchison, and so on.

Grantham Beale, by the by, started out as Graham Beale. But that began to sound too much like Graham Bell to me, as in Alexander Graham Bell, so he became Grantham instead.

5.   DON'T GET TOO CUTE. If too many of your character names are *too* interesting, plausibility is sacrificed. You don't want the reader to be drawn into constant awareness of the unusual and original names you've fastened on your characters; that kind of awareness just gets in the way.

Ross Thomas likes interesting names for his characters, and I sometimes think he goes overboard. The police chief in *The Fools in Town Are on Our Side* is Homer Necessary, for instance. Now parents do name their sons Homer now and again, and Necessary is a perfectly legitimate surname, not an invention of the author's, but I just have a lot of trouble believing in Chief Homer Necessary, especially in the same book with Lucifer Dye.

Of course, if your fiction isn't supposed to be taken seriously, then your characters' names can be as outlandish as you can make them. Think of Ian Fleming's Pussy Galore, for example, or my own personal favorite—Trevanian's Urassis Dragon. (Hint—say it aloud.)

6.   DON'T TWIST THE READER'S TONGUE. Even though your story or novel may not be designed to be read aloud, and even though you are not aiming your fiction at an audience of lip-movers, you should avoid throwing a jawbreaker of a name at your reader. He ought to be able to pronounce everything he reads. He may not say it out loud but he'll certainly be hearing it in his head, and it can throw him off-stride if he's unsure how it ought to sound.

This doesn't mean names have to be of the sort that every reader will pronounce identically. What's important is that the reader can assume he knows how to pronounce them.

Kerr, for instance, is sometimes pronounced to rhyme with fur, other times to rhyme with bar. The reader can't know for certain which you intend, but neither will he very likely lose much sleep over the question. He'll make up his own mind, probably without hesitation, and will forever after think of your character as Car or Cur, as the case may be. But if your character's named Przyjbmnshkvich, it's going to rub the reader the wrong way every time he encounters it.

7. RESEARCH YOUR ETHNIC NAMES. If one of your characters is a Latvian or Montenegrin or whatever, it's easy to add an authentic note to your work by picking a suitable name for him. A good encyclopedia comes in handy. If you want a Latvian character, look up *Latvia* and *Latvian Language and Literature.* Those articles will contain the names of any number of historical personages and writers. You take the first name of one and the last name of another, you put them together, and you've come up with an authentic and original Latvian name. It takes very little time and the result is quite impressive.

What's in a name? Plenty—and don't think Shakespeare didn't know it, considering the apt tags he fastened on so many of his characters. A rose by any name might smell as sweet, but would you send anybody a dozen American Beauty Skunkweeds?

CHAPTER 45

Repeat Performances and Return Engagements

EVAN TANNER had the sleep center of his brain destroyed by a piece of North Korean shrapnel, and he hasn't had a wink of sleep since. He lives in New York, on 105th Street west of Broadway, where he shares a fifth-floor walkup apartment with Minna, the sole surviving descendant of Mindaugas, ninth-century king of independent Lithuania. Tanner speaks dozens of languages, belongs to political nut groups and supports lost causes, and earns a living writing masters and doctoral theses for irresolute students. Intermittently he leaves the country as a sort of free-lance secret agent, nominally attached to a super-secret Washington agency but bending methods to serve his own ends.

Bernie Rhodenbarr also lives on New York's Upper West Side, at 71st Street and West End Avenue. He operates Barnegat Books, a marginal second-hand bookstore on East 11th Street, and hangs out a lot with Carolyn Kaiser, who operates the Poodle Factory, a dog-grooming salon a couple doors down from Barnegat Books. For a living, Bernie steals things. He's a burglar, and no Raffles-style amateur cracksman either. He's a pro, and he does it for the money plus the undeniable thrill he gets out of it. He knows all this is morally reprehensible but there's nothing he can do about it.

Matthew Scudder's an ex-cop. Once a moderately corrupt New York police detective, Scudder went through changes when a bullet of his ricocheted and killed a young girl. He left his wife and sons, moved to West 57th Street, took a room in a seedy hotel, and began drinking alcoholically. He earns his bread and booze as an unlicensed private eye. Although he has no faith, he hangs out in churches and unobtrusively slips a tenth of his earnings into poor boxes. He's a brooder, hip-deep in existential angst, working as an outsider with an insider's understanding of the system.

Chip Harrison's an eighteen-year-old kid who lives about a block away from his employer, private detective Leo Haig. Haig's a lifelong mystery fan who has always wanted to be Nero Wolfe. An uncle's legacy permitted Haig to set up shop upstairs of a Puerto Rican bordello in the top half of a carriage house in Chelsea, where he breeds tropical fish and tries to emulate his hero's eccentricity and acuteness. Chip runs around in a state of perpetual lecherous innocence, helping Haig solve such classic crimes as present themselves.

Martin H. Ehrengraf is a diminutive criminal lawyer with a passion for poetry and a dandy's attention to the niceties of dress. He keeps himself immaculate, although his office is generally in disarray. Ehrengraf is unique in that he handles criminal cases on a contingency basis, collecting fees only when his clients are acquitted or otherwise released. He rarely appears in court, operating behind the scenes to get his clients off the hook—and doing so by fabricating evidence, framing other persons, committing murders of his own, and otherwise launching end runs around the long arm of the law. Ehrengraf's home base is unspecified, but an astute reader might identify the city as Buffalo.

You won't find him in the Buffalo telephone directory, however, nor will you be able to locate any of the other four chaps in the New York phone book. They are all series characters of mine. Tanner has appeared in seven novels, Bernie Rhodenbarr in three, Chip Harrison in four. There have been three novels and two novelettes about Scudder, while Ehrengraf has been the subject of half a dozen short stories.

All five of them are exceedingly real to me. Some of them are less active than others, to be sure. It's been more than a decade since I wrote a word about Tanner, and several years since the most recent appearance of Chip Harrison. This hasn't diminished their reality in my eyes. I may not know precisely what they look like, and certain aspects of their backgrounds may be somewhat unclear. I may or may not write about any or all of them again. That's all beside the point. These gentlemen have played a predominant role, not only in my literary career but in the continuing evolution of my consciousness. They have been, and continue to be, a part of my life. They have evolved and grown and changed and defined themselves upon the printed page even as I have done likewise in what we presumptuously call the real world. If they are aspects of me, so too have they become parts of me.

The creation of a series character was an early ambition of mine. Once I passed the stage of merely wanting to write some indefinable great book and developed specific auctorial aims, I recognized the desire to create an enduring character and write voluminously about him.

Part of this urge stemmed from the amateur's conviction that there's an easy way to literary success. A great many non-writers tend to make this assumption. "Once you've got a formula, I suppose you've got it made," no end of people have said to me, the envy unmistakable in their tone. It strikes me that they've made two false assumptions—(1) that I've got a formula and (2) that I've got it made. Wrong and wrong. (As we'll see later, once I *do* have a formula I'm likely to be in Deep Trouble.)

Akin to the nonsense about formula, these same non-writers assume that the development of a series character is a major step toward success, financial security, and a final solution to the heartbreak of psoriasis. "Once you've got a character," they say, "all you have to do is write about him for the rest of your life."

Terrific. Once you've got a pair of running shoes, all you have to do is leg it from Hopkinton to Boston. Once you've learned the Australian crawl, all you have to do is swim the Channel. Once you've hit puberty—oh, never mind.

More to the point, I wanted to write about a series character because I enjoyed reading about other people's series characters. Once I had made the acquaintance of an attractive and compelling lead character, I wanted to meet him again and learn more about him. If his world view was one I found interesting and illuminating, I wanted to see more of the world through his eyes.

This ambition notwithstanding, it wasn't until I'd been writing professionally for seven or eight years that I first created a series character. I did attempt to carry over one Ed London, the detective narrator of *Death Pulls a Doublecross,* and I faintly recall writing one or perhaps two magazine novelettes about him. But I never did get the handle on a second Ed London novel, and I think that's just as well. London wasn't much of a character, and in many respects I wasn't much of a writer. I could keep stories moving and my prose and dialogue were adequate, but my people had relatively little to them.

With Tanner, my first series character, I had a handle on his personality and lifestyle years before I had a book to put him in. By the time I came up with the plot of *The Thief Who Couldn't Sleep,* I already knew a great deal about Evan Tanner. I was to find out a great deal more in the course of writing the book, as Tanner's character and narrative style defined itself on the page, and before I finished the book I knew beyond doubt that I wanted to learn—and to write—a great deal more about the man.

Other volumes followed in due course, and Tanner books established a pattern, if not a formula. Chronicling Tanner's adventures became very nearly a fulltime occupation, until after having written seven books I stopped abruptly and went on to other things.

Why the sudden halt? Well, while the books were not drugs on the market, neither did they set any sales records, and I'm sure this influenced me. If the series had ever really taken off commercially I might have sustained enthusiasm for a longer run. Then too, changing times made Tanner's world rather less amusing. All the lost causes he'd embraced were suddenly blossoming in the real world, with wars breaking out and bombs going off. What had been quaint had turned suddenly nasty, and I felt it was time my sleepless knight lay down for a nap.

But far more important a reason was that there was a sameness about the books that made them increasingly tedious for me to write. Tanner's fans—a small but ardent band—were never put off by this sameness. Nor, to be sure, am I as a reader ever angry at a series writer for mining the same vein repeatedly. Richard Stark's Parker novels are all of a piece; I not only take comfort in this but am delighted when a remembered character returns from an earlier volume. Rex Stout's books about Nero Wolfe have a sameness to which I have never objected, and those atypical volumes in which Stout takes his hero away from the 35th Street brownstone and onto *terra incognita* have always seemed the weaker for it. Similarly, I want to meet Agatha Christie's Jane Marple on her own turf, in the stifling little village of St. Mary's Mead. When Christie broke the pattern by transplanting Marple to London or the Caribbean, I felt cheated.

Series fans, then, want each book to be the same only different. But Tanner's fans were spending six or eight or ten hours a year reading about their hero while I was devoting that many months a year to writing about him, and I was accordingly more affected by what I perceived as repetition.

I suppose, too, that I was ready to outgrow Tanner as a vehicle for self-expression. I had not yet finished developing as a writer and needed other books, other sorts of stories, in order to facilitate this growth.

Some writers handle this by allowing the character to grow. The most striking example that comes to mind is Ross Macdonald's Lew Archer, who was not a whole lot more than a wisecracking carbon copy of Raymond Chandler's Philip Marlowe in his earliest appearances. As Macdonald grew, so did Archer, and by the time *The Galton Case* was published in the late fifties, Archer had undergone a radical change. This evolution has continued over the years, and I reach for each new volume as it is published, wondering what Archer's up to now.

I don't think I could have done anything like this with Tanner. To change him would have been to lose him utterly. Better to lay him to rest, or put him out to pasture, or let him go his own way while I went mine.

Chip Harrison, on the other hand, *did* change dramatically so that I might continue writing about him. He made his debut in *No Score* as a seventeen-year-old virgin with a desperate yearning to change his status. The book was episodic, with Chip traveling around and getting into various scrapes and never managing to get it together with an acquiescent young woman until the final chapter, when his efforts were crowned with success.

I never expected to write more about Chip. But *No Score* did exceptionally well on the newsstands, and it occurred to me that I would enjoy spending a month or so seeing the world through Chip's innocent eyes. I sent him roaming in *Chip Harrison Scores Again,* which was essentially the mixture as before, and it worked fairly well.

That made two books but it didn't make a series, and I found I wanted to do more with the character. So I thought up Leo Haig and put Chip to work for him, retaining his character pretty much intact as a sort of lecher in the rye but making an apprentice detective out of him.

I'm certainly not the first person to turn an unintentional series character into a detective. In *The Name of the Game Is Death,* Dan Marlowe created as his lead a hardened professional criminal named Earl Drake. The book worked well and was well received, and in the course of writing further about Drake, Marlowe gradually turned him from a criminal into a problem-solver, working (as I recall) at the behest of some national security agency. I stopped reading the books when Drake stopped pulling heists and became just another secret agent, feeling the essence of the character had been lost.

Still, I can understand what prompted Marlowe to make the change. It's difficult to sustain the criminality of a series character. Over a period of time, such characters tend to mellow, to work increasingly on the side of the law. It is as if their creators are uncomfortable with them as criminals and yearn to reform them. Perhaps, at the risk of plumbing psychoanalytical depths, we might suggest that they're uncomfortable with themselves writing repeatedly from a criminal perspective.

Voltaire, it is said, made a visit to a highly specialized bordello and enjoyed himself. He declined an opportunity to return for a second visit. "Once, a philosopher," he said. "Twice, a pervert."

So it is, perhaps, with writers. To explore the mind of the criminal by writing from his viewpoint is one thing. To establish him in an extended series of books as one's literary alter ego is something else.

Harrumph. Bernie Rhodenbarr is unquestionably a criminal, and very much a professional at that. He, too, is unquestionably an unintentional series character. Bernie's prototype was born in a never-finished Scudder novel as a burglar who found himself framed for murder and enlisted Scudder's help. When I scuttled that particular book I held over the basic situation while remaking the character entirely, making Bernie flip and urbane and making him solve the murder himself.

He became a series character because I found I liked writing about him. I wrote a second book and a third, and by the time you read this I hope and pray I shall have written a fourth. I don't know that I can go on writing about Bernie indefinitely, given my propensity for outlasting my series characters, but he certainly would seem to have another book or two in him, and as long as I feel that way I suppose I'll carry on. I sincerely hope, though, that I don't let the clown turn respectable. The image of a Bernie-turned-straight using his talents for illegal entry on behalf of the forces of law and order is one I find more than a little sick-making.

Same thing goes for Martin Ehrengraf, of whom I suspect I may already have finished writing. Ehrengraf was another unintentional series character; one story led to another, and each time it became a little more difficult to hatch a new plot that would lend itself to his particular character. Fred Dannay has pointed out that Randolph Mason, a similarly corrupt fictional attorney, ultimately reformed and used his talents to uphold the law. I have no intention of allowing Ehrengraf to come to such a bad end.

Matt Scudder was my one series character who was so conceived before a word was written about him. I had an opportunity to develop a series for Dell and went into a huddle with myself to dream up a character. Leonard Shecter's book *On the Pad* got my mind working, and as we observed in the chapter on "Character Building," I shaped and molded my impression to fit my own perspective. I have long felt that every series character is very much a projection of self, and in Scudder's case the parallels were clear enough.

Before I began work on *The Sins of the Fathers,* the first Scudder novel, I had written a handful of pages about Scudder's character and lifestyle, first as a sort of letter to myself to clarify my grasp of the character, then as a series proposal for Bill Grose at Dell. By the time I began writing the book, I accordingly knew a great deal about my lead. But I didn't really know him until he began to develop on the page, speaking in his own voice and showing me how he was inclined to act and react, how he perceived the world and related to it. Writing, however well I prepare for it, is never a simple matter of filling in the blanks. The magic that happens at the actual moment of creation is an indispensable part of the whole.

For all my prior planning, Scudder grew and ripened from one book to the next. Infuriatingly, one reviewer groused that the third book seemed a bit weaker than the second; as it happened, Dell reversed the second and third books when publishing them.

For several years it looked as though Scudder and I were through with one another. Then, as I've mentioned earlier, I wrote a fourth book about the character, and it was like embracing an old friend. Perhaps an actor feels something similar when he plays a role with which he had a success years earlier. I was particularly pleased to find that Scudder was a better character for his time at leisure; the book, *A Stab in the Dark,* is to my mind the best to date.

While I would hardly set myself up as an expert on series novels, I do seem to have fulfilled my youthful dream with a vengeance. Perhaps some thoughts on series in general might be of value to those of you out there dreaming a similar dream.

1. CONCENTRATE ON THE BOOK AT HAND. I've occasionally had letters from neophyte writers who describe themselves as working on the first volume of a series, and I know that first novels thus described frequently turn up in the hands of agents and publishers. The agents and publishers are not much impressed. Their interest in a manuscript is in its own merits or lack thereof, not in what may or may not follow it in the course of time.

It's hard enough to write a novel and make it work. Projecting an entire series merely dilutes your efforts. Stay in the now, work on the book you're working on, and leave the question of future books open until you've finished the job.

2. SOME BOOKS USE UP THEIR LEAD CHARACTERS. The strength and appeal of a character is not in and of itself reason to hang a series on him. *Such Men Are Dangerous* (written under the pen name Paul Kavanagh) is arguably my best book, and had as strong a lead character as I've created. But the book used him up, not in the sense of killing him off but in that he completed his business by its end. Hollywood of late has been making sequels of everything that does well at the box office, and the lamentable quality of most of these sequels shows the fallacy of this principle. If your lead character is sufficiently altered by what he has experienced, you can't put him in another book and make him do the same thing over again without losing something. In my own experience, I had to jam Chip Harrison into a detective series so that he would *not* be used up.

3. DON'T PRESUME THE READER HAS READ THE PREVIOUS VOLUMES. The sixth book you write about Private Eye Studd Boring will be some reader's introduction to your hero. You can't take prior knowledge for granted. On the other hand, you don't have to reiterate every single fact you've established about your hero in the course of all of the earlier books. There's a delicate balance here. You want to make things fully comprehensible for the new reader without boring the jaw teeth out of your longtime fans. For my own part, I've grown tired of hearing again how Meyer Meyer got his name and lost all his hair; every Ed McBain 87th Precinct novel tells me the story over again. My own readers may be every bit as tired reading about how a bullet of Scudder's ricocheted to kill Estrellita Rivera and plunge my hero into the Slough of Despond. A delicate balance indeed.

4. REMEMBER WHAT YOU WROTE. The maddening thing about writing a series over a period of years is keeping track of what you established about your characters and their friends and relations in earlier books. What floor does Tanner live on? What's the name of Carolyn Kaiser's lover's aunt in Bath Beach? Or did we establish that the aunt lived in Bensonhurst? What's the name of the bar where Chip likes to watch the Mets game? That hooker Elaine whom Scudder pals around with—what's her last name? And that tie Ehrengraf always wears at triumphal moments—it's the official cravat of the Caedmon Society, but what's the color combination?

Some writers let the chips fall where they may. Rex Stout furnished any number of street numbers over the years for Nero Wolfe's 35th Street brownstone, and sprinkled the books with a multitude of other minor inconsistencies. I myself am sufficiently obsessive-compulsive to make every effort to avoid that sort of thing, and the only way I've found is to stop writing and start paging through my collected works. Arthur Maling has a chart with all the characters and their interrelationships in his Price, Potter and Petacque series. If I had such a chart, I'd doubtless fail to keep it up to date—or I'd always find myself needing to know some minor point I hadn't bothered entering in the first place.

5. THE FIRST-PERSON/THIRD-PERSON CHOICE. Of my series characters, all but Ehrengraf speak in the first person. That doesn't mean this is the right way to do it. As a rule of thumb, I would suggest that larger-than-life characters like James Bond, Sherlock Holmes, and Nero Wolfe are more effectively handled either via third-person narration or with the aid of a Watson—i.e., a first-person narrator other than the lead character. Direct first-person narration is more likely to work when the writer identifies strongly with the lead character and wants to write from the inside out, showing the

world through his character's eyes. But whatever comes most naturally to you as a writer is probably the best choice.

Much of my most enjoyable hours at the typewriter have been spent in the company of one or another of my series characters. And, when a series seems to have run its natural course, I'm not without a pang of regret, as though I've abandoned an old friend by ceasing to write about him. I'm grateful that my writing career has not been so rigid, glad I've not spent the past fifteen years writing nothing but Tanner books—and yet I sometimes feel guilty for having cast him aside like a tattered shirt.

Is the series for you? You'll find out—a book at a time, over the years. Enjoy it.

CHAPTER

We Can Always Change the Title

ONCE UPON a time, many long years ago, a woman wrote a novel of the Civil War and called it *Tomorrow Is Another Day.* By the time the book saw print its title had been changed at the publisher's suggestion. The new title was *Gone With the Wind.*

The clarity of hindsight is never more vivid than when dealing with titles. It's a simple matter now to argue that Margaret Mitchell's novel owed a measure of its enormous popular success to its title change, and to maintain that *Tomorrow Is Another Day* wouldn't have sold ten thousand copies.

I'm not so sure that's true. When a book has enough going for it, it seems capable of finding its audience with or without a strong title. When it doesn't, the most intriguing title in the world won't add up to impressive sales figures.

But I do think it's safe to say that *Gone With the Wind* is a better title than

Tomorrow Is Another Day, and that the superior title contributed to the effectiveness of the book's advertising and promotion campaign and enabled it to find its audience faster and with more immediate impact.

Fair enough.

Now the tricky question. *Why* is *Gone With the Wind* a better title than *Tomorrow Is Another Day?*

One is tempted to reply as any number of musicians are said to have done when pressed for a definition of jazz. "If you have to ask," they said, "you'll never know." In other words, one ought to be able to grasp intuitively the intrinsic superiority of *GWTW* to *TIAD.* The one is lively, provocative, compelling. The other is tired, humdrum, prosaic.

On the other hand, the publishing industry has known for years the only honest definition of a good title. A good title, you see, is the name of a best-selling book.

Peyton Place, for instance, is a terrific title. It's even managed to become a part of the language. Without Grace Metalious's novel, however, it's nothing much more than three syllables' worth of alliteration and meter. Because the book happened to sell like Geiger counters in Harrisburg, the title promptly became a household word. A bandwagon effect helped this process along; for several years every faintly steamy book set in a small town was ballyhooed as "another *Peyton Place,*" and this did the original novel immeasurable good.

Is *The Exorcist* a good title? I certainly wouldn't have thought so in advance of the book's publication. I doubt most of the public knew what the word meant. But if it was a bad title, it doesn't seem to have harmed sales much.

How about *The Other?* If there's any merit whatsoever to that title I'd be pleased to have it explained to me. It's absolutely flat. It doesn't linger in the mind. You get no sense from it of what the book's about, or even of what type of book you're dealing with. Nor is there a mystery in the title intriguing enough to make you pick up the book and find out what the title means. Yet the book certainly sold well.

Is *Twins* a good title? Or *The Thorn Birds?* Or *The Shining?* How about *Coma,* perhaps the first novel ever named for what it induces? What makes a good title, anyway? And how do you go about picking one for your own story or novel?

First let's place the whole question in perspective. The title you give your manuscript is very likely the least important factor in determining whether or not it sells. A really sensational title may well predispose an editor in favor of your script, but it won't do a thing for you if your work doesn't live up to its promise. Similarly, while a weak title may lessen the enthusiasm with which an editor approaches your material, it won't keep him from being receptive to a good piece of writing; he certainly knows that the title can always be changed.

That said, here are some random thoughts on this whole business of titles.

1. A TITLE SHOULD BE MEMORABLE. I've been reading entries in the *WD* short-story contest. While no title has yet made a bad story good or a good story bad, I've been struck again this year by the high proportion of singularly dull "label" titles. Entry after entry passes across my desk with titles like "The Dog" or "The Pen" or "The Teacher" or "An Autumn Afternoon" or "Marilyn" or "The Affair" or—but that's enough, isn't it? These titles are flat and not terribly interesting. They don't promise much. They don't whet the appetite, and they should.

2. A TITLE SHOULD FIT THE BOOK OR STORY THAT FOLLOWS IT. When you've written a certain type of material, the title should indicate as much. If you call your book *Gunfight at Rio Lobo,* most people are going to leap to the conclusion that it's a western. If it's not a western, that's probably not the best possible title for it—even if there is a central incident in the book involving a shootout at a place called Rio Lobo.

A couple of years ago Charles McGarry wrote a novel of suspense and intrigue called *The Secret Lovers.* The title was supposed to mean that the principal characters—spies and bureaucrats—had a love of secrets. That's fine if you've got a little miniature salesman attached to each copy of the book to explain what the title means. In the absence thereof, a lot of folks assumed McGarry had written a Harlequin Romance.

3. WATCH OUT FOR UNPRONOUNCEABLE WORDS. Robert Ludlum's titles are always carefully chosen and invariably combine a distinctive proper name and a noun—*The Scarlatti Inheritance, The Osterman Weekend, The Matlock Paper, The Matarese Circle.* One book was very nearly entitled *The Wolfsschanze Covenant,* until an informal survey revealed that a lot of people were by no means confident of their ability to pronounce *Wolfsschanze* correctly. As *The Holcroft Covenant,* the book made its way to the top of the bestseller list. Would it have done so regardless? Perhaps. Perhaps enough readers would have picked up the book wordlessly and carried it to the cash register. Perhaps others would have asked for "the latest Ludlum novel" if intimidated by its title.

But why take chances?

4. DON'T MAKE THE TITLE DO THE STORY'S JOB. Years ago, when I spent

a year reading slush at a literary agency, it sometimes seemed to me as though a full forty percent of the stories I read were entitled "As the Twig Is Bent." Another thirty-five percent were called "So Grows the Tree."

Doubtless I exaggerate. But I've noted in this year's contest entries that a lot of new writers still fashion titles from tired proverbs. The problem is twofold. First of all, the titles thus formed have a trite quality to them; more to the point, they pull the punch of the story by telling the reader in advance what conclusion he is meant to draw from it. It's tiresome enough to have a story's moral spelled out, but when it's spelled out ahead of time, why bother reading the story at all?

Other stories get defused when too much information is given in the title, often in the name of quaintness. "The Day Jimmie Jeff Rayburn Drove Clear to Harrisonville for the Papers" might be an example of this sort of thing.

When I first started publishing short stories, my titles tended to be pedestrian and unmemorable. In recent years I've been happier with my ability to come up with something striking. Sometimes I can see the title I would have used, had I approached it with a little less imagination. I did a story about a gas station holdup, for instance, that I once would have been pleased to call "Highway Robbery." Instead the title I used was "Nothing Short of Highway Robbery"; it's more arresting and memorable, and it fits the story better.

My favorite title is *Burglars Can't Be Choosers,* and I've never doubted that it contributed to the sale of the first Bernie Rhodenbarr mystery. It was a neat enough play on a familiar phrase, and it managed to convey a sense of the book, that it would offer a lighthearted look at criminous matters. Once I hit on that title it seemed to have been the inevitable choice from the beginning.

But I almost missed it. I didn't have a title when I was readying the first fifty or sixty pages for submission to Random House. While proofreading, I happened on the phrase in one of Bernie's interior monologues. I didn't even remember having written it, but fortunately I was able to recognize a good title when it bit me, so I quick-typed out a title page.

Series titles, incidentally, constitute a special problem. On the one hand, they provide an opportunity for you to let the reader know that the books are indeed volumes in a series. A certain amount of uniformity it thus desirable. Too much uniformity, though, and it can become very difficult for a reader to remember if he's read a particular book or not. Consider the Matt Helm titles—*The Betrayers, The Ambushers, The Ravagers,* etc. How does the mind keep them separated?

John D. MacDonald found an answer in the Travis McGee books, using a different color in each title but otherwise making no effort at uniformity.

Nightmare in Pink, A Tan and Sandy Silence, The Scarlet Ruse—the titles fit the individual books, with only the memorable color word providing series continuity.

After my second novel about Evan Tanner was published with the title *The Canceled Czech,* I decided to try for similar word-play in future volumes. Tanner #3, dealing with romance in Latvia, was submitted as *Letts Fall in Love,* with an alternative title of *The Lettish Tomatoes.* It was published as *Tanner's Twelve Swingers.* Tanner #4, concerning a sexually unsuccessful Siamese, was proudly handed in as *The Scoreless Thai.* Fawcett published it as *Two for Tanner,* and I decided the hell with it.

All of which suggests that perhaps we shouldn't attach too much importance to titles. Publishers not only change bad ones, but they're sometimes just as quick to change good ones. On several occasions Hollywood studios have (a) bought a book for its title, (b) scrapped the story and written a wholly original screenplay, and (c) then changed the title. Publishers rarely go that far, but they're capable of bizarre behavior.

Back in the late fifties, science-fiction writer Randall P. Garrett had a standing assignment to deliver ten thousand words a month to *Amazing Stories.* Each month he submitted three or four pieces of fiction, each with a title and with one of his regular pen names. Each month, sure as death and taxes, *Amazing*'s editor would change all Randy's titles and all of his pen names.

Randy decided he shouldn't bother being creative if his titles weren't going to be used anyway, and that he might as well enjoy himself. His agent's files can testify that, over the next year or so, he wrote and submitted and sold the following works of fiction: *Great Expectations,* by Charles Dickens, *The Mill on the Floss,* by George Eliot, *Tom Jones,* by Henry Fielding, *Moby Dick,* by Herman Melville, and so on. Nobody at *Amazing Stories* ever cracked a smile. The checks came in, invoiced accordingly, and the stories—titles and pen names changed—appeared in due course.

Which reminds me—I'm not sure why—of the perhaps apocryphal story of the reporter who cornered a Hollywood studio boss for an interview. "Pardon me, sir, but my name is Henry Gorgenplatz, and I—"

"Don't worry about a thing," said the studio head. "We can always change it."

PART FIVE

Isn't That the Truth:

Fiction as a Spiritual Exercise

A Writer's Prayer

LORD, I hope You've got a few minutes. I've got a whole lot of favors to ask You.

Basically, Lord, I guess I want to ask You to help me be the best writer I possibly can, to get the most out of whatever talent I've been given. I could probably leave it at that, but I think it might help me to get a little more specific.

For starters, help me to avoid comparing myself to other writers. I can make a lot of trouble for myself when I do that, sliding into a routine that might go something like this:

"I'm a better writer than Alan, so why don't I have the success he has? Why don't I get book-club sales? Why wasn't my last book optioned for a TV mini-series? How come Barry gets so much more advertising support from his publisher than I do? What's so great about Carol that she deserves a two-page review in *The New Yorker?* Every time I turn on the TV, there's Dan running his mouth on another talk show. What makes him so special? And how come Ellen's in *Redbook* four or five times a year? I write the same kind of story and mine keep coming back with form rejection slips.

"On the other hand, I'll never be the writer Frank is. He can use his own experience with a degree of rigorous self-honesty that's beyond me. And Gloria has a real artist's eye. Her descriptive passages are so vivid they make me aware of my own limitations. Howard's a real pro—he can knock off more work in a day than I can in a month, and do it without working up a sweat. Irene spends twice as much time at the typewriter as I do. Maybe she has the right idea, and I'm so lazy I don't deserve to get anyplace at this game. And as for Jeremy—"

Lord, let me remember that I'm not in competition with other writers. Whether they have more or less success has nothing to do with me. They have their stories to write and I have mine. They have their way of writing them and I have mine. They have their careers and I have mine. The more I focus on comparing myself with them, the less energy I am able to concentrate on making the best of myself and my own work. I wind up despairing of my ability and bitter about its fruits, and all I manage to do is sabotage myself.

Help me, Lord, to write my own stories and novels. At the beginning I may have to spend a certain amount of time doing unwitting imitations of other people's work. That's because it may take me a while to find out what my own stories are and how to tap into them. But I'm sure they exist, and I'm sure it will ultimately be possible for me to find them.

Flannery O'Connor said somewhere that anybody who manages to survive childhood has enough material to write fiction for a lifetime. I believe this, Lord. I believe every human being with the impulse to write fiction has, somewhere within him or her, innumerable stories to write. They may not bear any obvious resemblance to my own experiences. They may be set in a land I never visited or at a time I never lived. But if they're the stories I am meant to write they will derive from my observations and experience in a significant way. I'll know the feelings, the perceptions, the reactions, for having lived them in some important way.

Of the traits likely to help me get in touch with these stories, perhaps the most important is honesty. Help me, Lord, to be as honest as I'm capable of being every time I sit down at the typewriter. I don't mean by this that I feel I ought to be writing non-fiction in fiction's clothing, that I think honesty entails telling stories as they actually happened in real life. Fiction, after all, is a pack of lies. But let my fiction have its own inner truth.

When a character of mine is talking, let me listen to him and write down what I hear. Let me describe him, not with phrases dimly recalled from other books, but as I perceive him.

It seems to me that a major element of writing honestly lies in respecting the reader. Please, Lord, don't ever allow me to hold my audience in contempt. Sometimes I find this a temptation, because by diminishing the reader I am less intimidated by the task of trying to engage his interest and hold his attention. But in the long run I cannot be disrespectful of my reader without my work's suffering for it.

If I cannot write for a particular market without contemning that market's readers, perhaps I'm banging my head against the wrong wall. If I can't write juveniles without being patronizing to young readers, I'm not going to be proud of my work, nor am I going to perform it well. If I can't write confessions or gothics or mysteries or westerns because I think the product is categorically garbage or the people who read it are congenital idiots, I am not going to be good at it and I am not going to gain satisfaction from it. Let me write what I'm able to respect, and let me respect those people I hope will read it.

Lord, let me keep a dictionary within arm's length. When I'm not sure of the spelling of a word, let me look it up—not so much because a misspelled word is disastrous as because of a propensity of mine for substituting another word out of simple laziness. By the same token, let me use the dictionary when I'm uncertain of the precise meaning of a word I want to use.

But don't let me keep a really good dictionary on my desk, Lord. Let me reserve my *Oxford Universal Dictionary* for important matters. If I grabbed it up every time I wanted to check the spelling of *exaggerate,* only to spend twenty minutes in the happy company of word derivations and obsolete usages and other lexicographical debris, I'd never get any work done. A small dull pedestrian dictionary close at hand is sufficient.

Checking spelling and definitions requires a certain degree of humility, Lord, and that's a characteristic I could use more of. It's easy for me to run short of humility—which seems curious, given how much I've got to be humble about. But it strikes me that writing demands such colossal (I just looked up "colossal"—thanks) arrogance that humility gets lost in the shuffle. It takes arrogance, doesn't it, to sit down at a typewriter making up stories out of the whole cloth and expecting total strangers to be caught up in them? I can think of little more arrogant than every artist's implicit assumption that his private fantasies and perceptions are worth another person's rapt attention.

Humility helps me keep myself in perspective. When my humility is in good order, both success and failure become easier to take. I'm able to recognize that the fate of empires does not hinge upon my work. I can see then that my writing will never be perfect, and that perfection is not a goal to which I can legitimately aspire. All I ever have to do is the best I can.

Please let me learn, Lord, to let it go at that. My capacity for arrogance and self-indulgence is balanced by an equally limitless capacity for self-deprecation. I can be awfully hard on myself, Lord, and it serves no purpose. If I turn out five pages a day I tell myself that with a little extra effort I could have produced six or eight or ten. If I write a scene without researching a key element of it, I accuse myself of being slipshod; if I do the research, I beat up on myself for wasting time that could have been spent turning out finished copy. If I rewrite I call it a waste of time, a process of washing garbage. If I don't rewrite I call it laziness.

This self-abuse is counter-productive. Give me, Lord, the courage to get through life without it.

Help me, Lord, to grow as a writer. There are so many opportunities to do so, to gain in skills and knowledge just by practicing my craft and keeping my eyes open. Every book I read ought to teach me something I can use in my own writing, if I approach it with a willingness to learn. When I read a writer who does things better than I do, enable me to learn from him. When I read another writer who has serious weaknesses, allow me to learn from his mistakes.

Give me the courage to take chances. There was a point early in my career when I spent far too long writing inferior work, work that did not challenge me, that I could no longer respect, and that I no longer was able to grow from. I did this out of fear. I was afraid to take chances, either economically or artistically, afraid I might produce something unpublishable.

I have only grown when I have been willing to extend myself, to run risks. Sometimes I have failed, certainly, but help me to remember that I have always been able to learn from this sort of failure, that it has invariably redounded to my benefit in the long run. And, when I do take chances and do fail again, let me remember that so that the memory may soften the pain of failure.

Let me be open to experience, Lord, in life as well as at the typewriter. And give me the courage to take my experience undiluted, and to get through it all without chemical assistance. There was a time, Lord, when a little green pill in the morning seemed to concentrate my energies and improve my writing. It turned out that I was merely borrowing tomorrow's energy today, and the interest turned out to be extortionate in the extreme. There was a time, too, when other chemicals in pill or liquid form brought me what passed for relaxation. All of those props limited my capacity for experience and narrowed my vision like blinders on a horse. I thought I needed those things to write, Lord, and have since found out how much better I can write without them. They kept me from growing, from learning, from improving. Please help me keep away from them a day at a time. Let me know, too, where my responsibilities as a writer begin and end. Help me to concentrate my efforts on those aspects of my career I can personally affect and let go of those over which I can have no control. Once I've put a manuscript in the mail, let me forget about it until it either comes back or finds a home. Let me take the appropriate action, Lord, without diluting my energies worrying over the result of that action. My primary job is writing. My secondary job is offering what I've written for sale. What happens after that is somebody else's job.

Don't let me forget, Lord, that acceptance and rejection aren't all that important anyway. The chief reward of any artistic effort (and perhaps of every other effort as well) is the work itself. Success lies in the accomplishment, not in its fruits. If I write well, I'm a success. Wealth and fame might be fun (or they might not) but they're largely beside the point.

Let me accept rejection, when it comes, as part of the process of gaining acceptance. Let me accept dry spells as part of the creative process. All across the board, Lord, let me accept the things I can't do anything about, deal with the things I can, and tell which is which.

And let me always be grateful, Lord, that I am a writer, that I am actually doing the only work I've ever really wanted to do, and that I don't need anyone's permission to do it. Just something to write with and something to write on.

Thanks for all that. And thanks for listening.

INDEX